Careers in Environment & Conservation

Careers in Environment & Conservation

Editor
Michael Shally-Jensen, Ph.D.

SALEM PRESS
A Division of EBSCO Information Services, Inc.
Ipswich, Massachusetts

GREY HOUSE PUBLISHING

∞ The paper used in these volumes conforms to the American National Standard for Permanence of Paper for Printed Library Materials, Z39.48-1992 (R1997).

Library of Congress Cataloging-in-Publication Data

Careers in environment & conservation / editor, Michael Shally-Jensen, Ph.D. -- [First edition].

pages : illustrations ; cm. -- (Careers in--)

Includes bibliographical references and index.
ISBN: 978-1-61925-535-7

1. Environmental sciences--Vocational guidance--United States. 2. Environmental protection--Vocational guidance--United States. 3. Environmental engineering--Vocational guidance--United States. 4. Nature conservation--Vocational guidance--United States. 5. Conservation of natural resources--Vocational guidance--United States. I. Shally-Jensen, Michael. II. Title: Careers in environment and conservation

GE60 .C375 2014
363.70023/73

First Printing

PRINTED IN THE UNITED STATES OF AMERICA

CONTENTS

PUBLISHER'S NOTE

Careers in Environment & Conservation contains twenty-five alphabetically arranged chapters describing specific fields of interest in these industries. Merging scholarship with occupational development, this single comprehensive guidebook provides environment and conservation students and readers alike with the necessary insight into potential careers, and provides instruction on what job seekers can expect in terms of training, advancement, earnings, job prospects, working conditions, relevant associations, and more. *Careers in Environment & Conservation* is specifically designed for a high school and undergraduate audience and is edited to align with secondary or high school curriculum standards.

Scope of Coverage

Understanding the interconnected nature of the different and varied branches of these fields is important for anyone preparing for a career within them. *Careers in Environment & Conservation* comprises twenty-five lengthy chapters on a broad range of branches and divisions within these industries, including traditional and long-established fields such as Forestry Worker, Geologist, and Farmer, as well as in-demand and cutting-edge fields such as Energy Auditor, Hazardous Materials Technician, and Landscape Architect. This excellent reference also presents possible career paths and occupations within high-growth and emerging fields in these industries.

Careers in Environment & Conservation is enhanced with numerous charts and tables, including projections from the US Bureau of Labor Statistics, and median annual salaries or wages for those occupations profiled. Each chapter also notes those skills that can be applied across broad occupation categories. Interesting enhancements, like **Fun Facts**, **Famous Firsts**, and dozens of photos, add depth to the discussion. A highlight of each chapter is **Conversation With** – a two-page interview with a professional working in a related job. The respondents share their personal career paths, detail potential for career advancement, offer advice for students, and include a "try this" for those interested in embarking on a career in their profession.

Essay Length and Format

Each chapter ranges in length from 3,500 to 4,500 words and begins with a Snapshot of the occupation that includes career clusters, interests, earnings and employment outlook. This is followed by these major categories:

- **Overview** includes detailed discussions on: Sphere of Work; Work Environment; Occupation Interest; A Day in the Life. Also included here is a Profile that outlines working conditions, educational needs, and physical abilities. You will also find the occupation's Holland Interest Score, which matches up character and personality traits with specific jobs.

- **Occupational Specialties** lists specific jobs that are related in some way, like Animal Trainers and Kennel Attendants, and Range Managers and Soil Conservationists, all with detailed comparisons. This section also includes a list of Duties and Responsibilities.
- **Work Environment** details the physical, human, and technological environment of the occupation profiled.
- **Education, Training, and Advancement** outlines how to prepare for this occupation while in high school, and what college courses to take, including licenses and certifications needed. A section is devoted to the Adult Job Seeker, and there is a list of skills and abilities needed to succeed in the job profiled.
- **Earnings and Advancements** offers specific salary ranges, and includes a chart of metropolitan areas that have the highest concentration of the profession.
- **Employment and Outlook** discusses employment trends, and projects growth to 2020. This section also lists related occupations.
- **Selected Schools** list those prominent learning institutions that offer specific courses in the profiled occupations.
- **More Information** includes associations and other groups that the reader can contact.

Special Features

Several features continue to distinguish this reference series from other career-oriented reference works. The back matter includes:

- Appendix A: Guide to Holland Code. This discusses John Holland's theory that people and work environments can be classified into six different groups: Realistic; Investigative; Artistic; Social; Enterprising; and Conventional. See if the job you want is right for you!
- Appendix B: General Bibliography. This is a collection of suggested readings, organized into several major categories.
- Subject Index: Includes people, concepts, technologies, terms, principles, and all specific occupations discussed in the occupational profile chapters.

Acknowledgments

Special mention is made of editor Michael Shally-Jensen, who played a principal role in shaping this work with current, comprehensive, and valuable material. Thanks are due to the many academicians and professionals who worked to communicate their expert understanding of the environment and conservation to the general reader. Thanks are also due to Alllison Blake, who took the lead in researching and writing "Conversations With" with help from Catherine Pritchard and Vanessa Parks, and to the professionals who communicated their work experience through our interview questionnaires. Their frank and honest responses provide immeasurable value to *Careers in Environment & Conservation*. The contributions of all are gratefully acknowledged.

EDITOR'S INTRODUCTION

An Occupational Overview

Protecting the environment, which has long been of vital interest to many people, has become an important goal for many organizations and individuals alike. A way to achieve this goal is to pursue sustainability, which is using resources available today to meet one's needs without compromising future resources. Although sustainability most often is associated with environmental protection and conservation, it also has social and economic impacts. In fact, many companies operating today have adopted sustainability strategies to increase profits, and the environmental benefits are an added bonus. Government organizations, too, are increasingly expected to follow environmentally sound practices.

Sustainability is a diverse field that includes a wide variety of professionals and workers. Sustainability specialists can be business managers, scientists, or engineers—or they can come from other backgrounds. Although their specific career paths might differ, sustainability workers and professionals promote environmental protection, social responsibility, and profitability. Sustainability specialists help organizations achieve their goals by ensuring that their practices are economically, socially, and environmentally sound—in both the short term and the long term.

Here are some of the major areas in which sustainability practices are commonly pursued and in which workers and professionals have the opportunity to apply their skills.

Water Conservation and Treatment

Fresh water is, of course, one of the world's most important resources. Without it, life would be impossible. Because fresh water resources are limited, water conservation is an important aspect of the green economy. Water conservation and treatment workers ensure that our fresh water supplies remain adequate for human consumption and wildlife use, and that wastewater is properly treated and discharged. Careers in water conservation and treatment include those in science, engineering, planning and outreach, construction, agriculture, plant operations, and grounds maintenance.

Many different types of workers are involved in water conservation and treatment. Scientists may find new methods of treating water for human consumption or find ways to use water more efficiently. Engineers design and develop new products and procedures for saving water and treating waste. Planning and outreach workers ensure that communities and businesses use water efficiently, and they educate people about water conservation. Construction and water operations workers implement water-saving devices and procedures. Agriculture and grounds maintenance workers help reduce the use of water for farming and landscaping. These careers span several education levels, ranging from little formal education to various levels of postsecondary education.

Sustainable Land Use and Natural Environments

Forests, rangeland, inland waterways, oceans, and other natural environments provide a variety of resources, habitats for wildlife, and recreation opportunities. Conservation workers strive to ensure that our nation's natural areas will continue to be used in an environmentally responsible way while at the same time supplying numerous commercial and industrial products. Careers in conservation include those in the basic sciences, natural resources development, and environmental protection.

Many different types of workers preserve and maintain healthy natural environments. Scientists study and monitor ecosystems. Environmental protection workers manage pollution control and prevention measures. Forest conservation and logging workers cultivate and harvest trees for wood and paper products. Land-use professionals monitor the extraction of minerals and other natural resources. Farmers and agricultural workers seek to make the most use of the land they cultivate. Each of these groups is responsible for certain aspects of maintaining a healthy environment and ensuring that natural resources are used effectively. The educational requirements for these careers span from the high school level to postsecondary education.

Green Energy

Sunlight is the most abundant source of potential energy on the planet. If harnessed properly, sunlight could likely exceed current and future electricity demand. As solar power becomes more cost-effective, it has the potential to make up a larger share of growing US energy needs. Another renewable form of energy, wind power, has been used for centuries but is a relatively new source of electricity generation. As the wind energy industry continues to grow, it will provide many opportunities for workers in search of new careers. In the search for new energy resources, scientists have also discovered ways to use the earth itself as a valuable source of power. Thus, geothermal power plants use the earth's natural underground heat to provide clean, renewable energy. Finally, alternative fuels such as biofuels—i.e., fuels composed of or produced from biological raw materials—can reduce the use of fossil fuels and be more environmentally friendly.

A wide variety of workers and professionals are employed in the green energy sector. Scientists study the basis of energy production and ways in which to exploit new sources of energy. Engineers develop and implement systems for acquiring and distributing energy resources, moving power from the source to the user. Construction and engineering crews build the systems at the site or inside the communities and businesses that make use of renewable energy resources. Planners and administrators work to ensure that sustainable practices are followed and that customers receive the energy they need. These careers span several education levels, ranging from high school education to various levels of postsecondary education.

Green Construction

Buildings erected today are quite different from those built a hundred years ago. As interest in protecting the environment grows, "green," or sustainable buildings have become more commonplace. At first glance, these buildings might not appear to differ much from their predecessors, but they feature specialized designs and materials that act to limit their environmental impact. Green buildings conserve as much energy and water as possible and are constructed of recycled or renewable materials in order to achieve maximum resource efficiency. Creating these new buildings requires skilled workers and professionals with knowledge of new design and construction techniques.

Architects design buildings and other structures. They are responsible for the overall look of buildings as well as their functionality, safety, and suitability for the people who use them. Landscape architects analyze the natural elements of a site, such as the climate, soil, drainage, vegetation, and slope of the land and plan the location of roads, walkways, and other landscaping elements. Construction managers plan, direct, coordinate, and budget a wide variety of construction projects, including roads, schools, hospitals, and other residential, commercial, and industrial structures, while construction laborers perform a wide range of tasks on construction sites.

As green construction becomes more widespread, new opportunities to participate in the field will arise. A market increasingly focused on sustainable construction techniques should build job prospects for many workers in the near future. Green construction is able to provide jobs to people with a broad range of education and experience levels.

Environmental Remediation and Recycling

Cleaning up the environment, or remediation, is an important focus of the green economy. Sites that are polluted because of industrial activity, the use of fertilizer or pesticides, or the release of other pollutants must be cleaned up in order to redevelop them or return them to their natural state. Prior to the enactment of modern environmental regulation, many companies simply released hazardous materials into the environment. They would dump chemicals and other pollutants onto unused land or into lakes, rivers, and streams. Sites also would become polluted through accidents or improperly functioning equipment. Polluted sites that can be cleaned and redeveloped are known as brownfield sites.

Several types of workers are involved in each step of a remediation project. Managers oversee the project at each stage. Business specialists who work in environmental remediation are experts in regulation issues, cost estimation, or public relations. Cartographers and imaging specialists create maps and images of the contaminated areas. Scientists and engineers determine the most effective methods of cleaning up a site and perform tests to determine the extent of the contamination and to monitor the progress of the remediation project. Construction workers and operators of various types of heavy equipment carry out the day-to-day work on the project. As with other jobs in the environment and conservation, a wide range of educational backgrounds is present in this field.

Recycling

Recyciling is the practice of reusing materials in existing products to create new ones. This can be accomplished in expected ways—such as using recycled paper as packaging material—or unexpected ways—such as using recycled glass to make artificial turf. Recycling helps to conserve limited resources, and, its supporters argue, it has other environmental benefits as well. For example, reusing existing materials means that fewer new ones have to be produced, which can lower factory emissions, reduce the need for new natural resources, and lower dependence on landfills.

As recycling continues to grow, more workers will be needed to collect, sort, and process recyclables. Recycling jobs require people with a broad range of skill levels. For example, becoming a sorter has few specific skill requirements; but mechanics and technicians in the recycling industry are highly skilled. Materials recovery facility (MRF) managers usually have at least a bachelor's degree. But whether driving large vehicles or operating an MRF, prior work experience—particularly in other areas of waste management—is helpful for those seeking to make a career in the recycling industry.

In short, as conservation and sustainability practices become more widespread, new opportunities to contribute to the green economy almost certainly will arise.

—M. Shally-Jensen, Ph.D.

Sources

Bureau of Labor Statistics. "Green Career Information." Washington, DC: BLS, 2010-13. Available at: http://www.bls.gov/green/greencareers.htm

---"Green Technologies and Practices." Washington, DC: BLS, 2011. Available at: http://www.bls.gov/news.release/gtp.nr0.htm

Hendricks, Bracken, et al. "Seven Questions about Green Jobs: Why the Most Productive Jobs in the Future Will Be Green Jobs." Washington, DC: Center for American Progress, 2009. Available at: http://www.americanprogress.org/issues/green/news/2009/04/22/5873/seven-questions-about-green-jobs/

Ringo, Jerome. "Green Jobs Are Putting America to Work." *US News and World Report*, Feb. 22, 2010. Available at: http://www.usnews.com/opinion/articles/2010/02/22/green-jobs-are-putting-america-to-work

US Department of Labor. *Why Green Is Your Color: A Woman's Guide to a Sustainable Career.* Washington, DC: Dept. of Labor, 2012. Available at: http://www.dol.gov/wb/Green_Jobs_Guide/

Animal Caretaker

Snapshot

Career Cluster: Animal Science; Environment & Conservation; Hospitality & Tourism
Interests: Animals and Animal Maintenance and Training
Earnings (Yearly Average): $22,510
Employment & Outlook: Faster Than Average Growth Expected

OVERVIEW

Sphere of Work

Animal caretakers tend to the needs of mammals, birds, fish, amphibians, and reptiles for various nonprofit organizations, research facilities, and private businesses, as well as for individuals. Animal caretaking encompasses many job titles and occupational specialties, including trainers, groomers, pet sitters, aquarists, zookeepers or animal keepers, veterinary assistants, and attendants in animal shelters, pet shops, and kennels.

Work Environment

Animal caretakers work in zoos, kennels, pet stores, shelters, animal hospitals, wildlife sanctuaries, horse stables, grooming salons, and animal laboratories. Pet sitters usually attend to animals in private residences. Some caretakers travel between client homes or with their animals to special shows. Although some caretakers are limited to working either outside or inside, most divide their time between indoor and outdoor locations. Flexible schedules are common and hours might include nights, evenings, weekends, and/or holiday shifts.

Profile

Working Conditions: Work both Indoors and Outdoors
Physical Strength: Medium to Heavy Work
Education Needs: On-the-Job Training, High School Diploma or G.E.D., Technical Education, Apprenticeship
Licensure/Certification: Usually Not Required
Physical Abilities Not Required: N/A
Opportunities For Experience: Apprenticeship, Volunteer Work, Part Time Work
Holland Interest Score*: RCS

* See Appendix A

Occupation Interest

Animal caretaker positions attract people who respect animals and understand their particular needs and abilities. In exchange for performing hard physical labor and sometimes unpleasant tasks, animal caretakers gain insight into the unique behavior of animals. They need to be patient and kind yet firm in their treatment of animals. Prospective animal caretakers should be good at following schedules and directions, reading animal behavior, solving problems, and communicating with people.

A Day in the Life—Duties and Responsibilities

The two most common responsibilities of animal caregivers are feeding animals and cleaning their living environments. They feed animals according to guidelines set by veterinarians or other professionals, or the animals' owners. Most animals are given pre-packaged, formulated food, although some may be fed live prey such as rodents, insects, or other small animals. Some baby mammals must be fed by a bottle or dropper. Before cleaning a cage, stall, aquarium, or other enclosure, the animal caretaker typically removes the animal and places it in another safe location. The habitat is then emptied of debris and sprayed, wiped, mopped, or scrubbed with a strong disinfectant and/or detergent. After rinsing and drying, the caretaker applies a fresh layer of bedding and/or replaces heat lamps, lights, toys, water bottles, and other equipment. In addition to cages, animal caretakers must clean carriers, dog runs, quarantine areas, medical treatment areas, and other supplies and rooms that may become contaminated. Bathing, grooming, exercising, and socializing are also typical components of animal care. Caretakers may walk dogs, ride horses, or observe mice scurrying through special mazes, which are often among the greatest rewards of the work.

Some animal caretakers assist professional trainers or train animals themselves for educational, entertainment, security, and medical purposes. They also transport animals to shows, animal hospitals, and other locations. Depending on training and work setting, animal caretakers may perform health-care tasks, such as dressing wounds and administering medications. They are also sometimes involved with the death of animals or assist with euthanasia.
When not working directly with animals, animal caretakers often keep records, maintain inventories of food and supplies, and greet customers or give educational presentations.

Duties and Responsibilities

- **Watering and feeding animals**
- **Washing and grooming animals**
- **Leading animals between living areas and other locations**
- **Exercising animals**
- **Administering prescribed medications/vitamins**
- **Assisting in the transport of animals**
- **Maintaining cleanliness of animal living spaces**

OCCUPATION SPECIALTIES

Animal Keepers

Animal Keepers feed, water, and clean the quarters of the birds and animals in zoos, circuses, and menageries. They prepare the food to be given to the animals and add vitamins and medication to the food.

Animal Trainers

Animal Trainers train animals for riding, security, performance, obedience, or assisting people with disabilities. They familiarize animals with human voices and contact, and they teach animals to respond to commands.

Animal-Nursery Workers

Animal-Nursery Workers care for newborn and young animals in a zoo nursery and exhibit area. They prepare the liquid formula and other foods for the animals and standard diets for mothers and newborns according to the requirements of the species.

Kennel Attendants

Kennel Attendants maintain dog kennels and assist trainers in teaching dogs to be obedient, guide the blind, hunt, track, or work as police dogs.

Pet Shop Attendants

Pet Shop Attendants show pets to customers, order and sell supplies, and keep sales records.

Pet Sitters

Pet Sitters work with clients' pets in their homes, feeding, walking, and otherwise tending to them as requested by the client.

Stable Attendants

Stable Attendants exercise animals regularly, polish saddles and bridles, and assist with horseshoeing. They may also harness, saddle, and unsaddle horses as well as rub them down after exercise periods.

Aquarists

Aquarists attend fish and other aquatic life in aquarium exhibits. They also take water samples for laboratory analysis and maintain records of numbers and kinds of fish.

WORK ENVIRONMENT

Physical Environment

Animals and their environments often come with strong odors or noises. Animal caretakers are at some risk for diseases, bites, scratches, or kicks from animals, and they can be exposed to harsh cleaning chemicals, germicides, and insecticides. The work may be physically demanding, requiring heavy lifting, standing for long periods, and regular bending and kneeling. Some caretakers might also find the work emotionally difficult at times.

Relevant Skills and Abilities

Interpersonal/Social Skills

- Being able to work independently
- Communicating with others

Organization & Management Skills

- Being reliable
- Following instructions
- Performing routine work

Work Environment Skills

- Working with animals

Human Environment

Many animal caretakers spend as much time working with humans as they do animals. Most report to a supervisor, director, or manager, and interact with volunteers and various staff members, such as veterinarians, research scientists, and professional groomers or trainers. Self-employed pet sitters interact with their clients and household staff. Caretakers who work in animal shelters and commercial settings also interact with the public. Animal trainers and attendants in zoos, public aquariums, and marine parks may stage live demonstrations for audiences.

Technological Environment

The level of technological sophistication varies with the type of facility. Some caretakers work in fully equipped offices with computerized feeding schedules and high-tech security systems. Many caretakers also use hand and power tools to maintain cages or other animal environments. Some animal caretakers drive wagons, trucks, vans, or cars to transport animals.

EDUCATION, TRAINING, AND ADVANCEMENT

High School/Secondary

A high school diploma or its equivalent is required for most jobs. A vocational course in animal science, usually offered through agricultural education programs, will provide a suitable foundation for some animal caretaker jobs; however, students interested in becoming a zookeeper, aquarist, or veterinary technician must follow a college-preparatory program. Important courses include biology, health, English, and speech communication. Volunteer or part-time work in an animal shelter, veterinary office, pet store, kennel, or farm, or pet sitting for friends and neighbors will provide the experience desired by many employers. Students should also consider 4-H and similar extracurricular opportunities that build familiarity with animals and their care.

Suggested High School Subjects

- Agricultural Education
- Biology
- English

Famous First

The first animal humane society in the United States was the American Society for the Prevention of Cruelty to Animals (ASPCA), founded in New York City in 1866. Its founder, Henry Bergh, had been a member of a U.S. diplomatic mission in St. Petersburg, Russia, where he witnessed carriage drivers beating their horses. Upon his return to America he organized the ASPCA, patterned after the Royal SPCA in London.

OUR FRIEND IN RED KEEPS HIS HORN GOING

College/Postsecondary

Most animal caretakers are trained on the job. Continuing education courses in animal care, offered through community colleges, vocational schools, and various animal and veterinary organizations, provide additional skills and knowledge and might be necessary to attain certification for more advanced positions. Business courses will help those who intend to open a kennel or operate a professional pet-sitting business. A bachelor's degree in zoology or biology is usually the minimum requirement for professional zookeepers and public aquarium specialists, while an associate's degree is sometimes the minimum requirement for animal laboratory caretakers and veterinary technicians.

Related College Majors

- Agricultural Production & Management
- Animal Science
- Biology
- Environmental Science
- Fisheries Sciences & Management
- Zoology

Adult Job Seekers

Adults with the appropriate educational background and firsthand experience as pet owners, animal foster caretakers, or volunteers in pet shelters or rehabilitation centers may be qualified for many animal caretaker jobs. Pet sitting and grooming may offer the most flexible schedules. Interested landowners might be in a good position to establish a kennel or boarding stables. The necessary skills and knowledge for animal care can be learned from online courses, as well as evening or weekend continuing education courses. Qualified animal caretakers should apply directly to companies and organizations that have posted open positions.

New animal caretakers are often limited to cleaning cages and feeding animals but are given additional responsibilities after gaining experience. Animal caretakers can move into supervisory or management positions with additional experience or education.

Professional Certification and Licensure

There are no licenses required for animal caretakers, although the owners of kennels, laboratories, and rescue shelters are regulated. Professional certification is available from the National Association of Professional Pet Sitters (NAPPS), American Association for Laboratory Animal Science (AALAS), and other professional associations. Most certifications require completion of an exam, which in some cases includes a practical section.

Additional Requirements

A driver's license is required for many jobs. Animal caretakers also need to be in good health, with good eyesight and hearing. Familiarity with the Animal Welfare Act (AWA) is also beneficial.

Fun Fact

Veterinary technicians have a higher-than-average rate of injury on the job, and it's not hard to imagine why. Sick or injured animals can get a bit snippy during treatment, most often when be-ing held, restrained, or cleaned. Vet techs are trained to identify aggressive behavior, which can help prevent injury.

Source: veterinary-technician-colleges.com and they cite bureau of labor statistics.

EARNINGS AND ADVANCEMENT

Earnings depend on the employer, size and geographic location of the facility, and the individual's education and experience. Animal caretakers earned a mean annual salary of $22,510 in 2013. The lowest ten percent earned less than $16,580, and the highest ten percent earned more than $32,660.

Animal caretakers may receive paid vacations, holidays, and sick days; life and health insurance; and retirement benefits. These are usually paid by the employer.

Metropolitan Areas with the Highest Employment Level in This Occupation

Metropolitan area	Employment*	Employment per thousand jobs	Hourly mean wage
Chicago-Joliet-Naperville, IL	5,390	1.46	$11.05
Los Angeles-Long Beach-Glendale, CA	3,930	0.99	$11.72
Dallas-Plano-Irving, TX	3,400	1.58	$10.15
Washington-Arlington-Alexandria, DC-VA-MD-WV	3,350	1.42	$11.65
Houston-Sugar Land-Baytown, TX	3,040	1.10	$9.84
Nassau-Suffolk, NY	2,920	2.36	$11.60
Atlanta-Sandy Springs-Marietta, GA	2,910	1.26	$10.15
New York-White Plains-Wayne, NY-NJ	2,820	0.54	$12.52
Phoenix-Mesa-Glendale, AZ	2,590	1.45	$10.83
St. Louis, MO-IL	2,150	1.67	$10.36

* Does not include self-employed.

EMPLOYMENT AND OUTLOOK

There were approximately 150,000 animal caretakers employed nationally in 2013. Most animal caretakers were employed by boarding kennels, animal shelters, stables, grooming shops, animal hospitals and veterinary offices.

Employment of animal caretakers is expected to grow faster than the average for all occupations through the year 2022, which means employment is projected to increase about 15 percent. This is owing to the continual growth of the pet population, as more people take on pets.

Employment Trend, Projected 2012–22

Nonfarm animal caretakers: 15%

Animal trainers: 15%

Animal care and service workers: 15%

Total, all occupations: 11%

Note: "All Occupations" includes all occupations in the U.S. Economy. Source: U.S. Bureau of Labor Statistics, Employment Projections Program.

Related Occupations

- Farmer/Farm Manager
- Marine Biologist
- Wildlife Biologist

Conversation With . . .
LEXA ELWELL

Veterinary Assistant, 8 years
Tidewater Veterinary Hospital
Charlotte Hall, MD

1. **What was your individual career path in terms of education/training, entry-level job, or other significant opportunity?**

   I didn't go to college but had jobs like waiting tables or being a receptionist. I stumbled across my vet hospital's ad eight years ago. I wasn't looking for a job in the animal field but I love dogs and cats and am the type who always wants to be around animals. Like everyone, I wanted to be a veterinarian when I was little. But I didn't have an interest in doing more school; I'm more of a hands-on person. I think this is what I'm meant to do in life. I wake up every day wondering what's going to happen. A veterinary assistant is someone who did not go to school to get a degree in the veterinary field and has to work under a doctor.

2. **What are the most important skills and/or qualities for someone in your profession?**

   I work for six doctors and that gets demanding. You need to think fast, remember routine things, be organized, and be ready for what the day brings. We often have to work fast, especially in a crisis. Say a dog is not breathing. There's no time to prepare. You have to be on top of things.

3. **What do you wish you had known going into this profession?**

   Since I'm not a licensed or certified veterinary technician, I have to do things like injections under the supervision of a doctor. Still, I wish I could do mathematics off the top of my head to figure out injection doses and those types of needs like the veterinarians can do.

4. **Are there many job opportunities in your profession? In what specific areas?**

   TIt's hard for me to say, but from what I've seen people seem to stay in their veterinary assistant jobs for awhile. It really does take a special kind of person; you don't get paid a lot and you need to have a heart for the animals. If you have a love of animals, I would suggest checking with vet hospitals in your area to explore the possible opportunities.

5. How do you see your profession changing in the next five years, what role will technology play in those changes, and what skills will be required?

There might be some new machines for diagnostic testing and they are always coming up with new ways to handle patient records. But this is a job where human care for the animals is not going to be replaced.

6. What do you like most about your job? What do you like least about your job?

Part of the job is that every day is different, and I like the adrenaline rush of an emergency. For example, we recently did a C-section for a dog, which is a pretty quick thing because you don't want the mom under anesthesia very long. The doctor does the surgery and usually a couple of us are assisting; the doctor hands each veterinary assistant a puppy and we get the placenta off, make sure it's breathing, and get the doctor involved if it's not. Another vet is around in case something additional needs to be done. We did one the other night. Unfortunately the dog had one puppy on its own that died but we ended up doing the C-section and she successfully birthed five more puppies.

My least favorite part of the job is when that dog, cat, or horse has been under our care for a long time — animals I have a relationship with — and we have to put them down. I also don't like being the person watching an animal as the owner drags his feet while the animal suffers, even though I know it's difficult to decide to let your animal go.

7. Can you suggest a valuable "try this" for students considering a career in your profession?

We have people come in and out of our clinic to shadow the doctors and staff. The biggest problem I notice they have — and not just the shadowers, but anyone new to the situation — is the first time they see an animal cut open. That's the test. If you can handle it, this job might be for you.

SELECTED SCHOOLS

Many agricultural, technical, and community colleges offer programs in animal science. Interested students are advised to consult with their school guidance counselor or to research area postsecondary schools and training programs. For those interested in pursuing a bachelor's degree, refer to the list of schools in the "Wildlife Biologist" chapter in the present volume.

MORE INFORMATION

American Association for Laboratory Animal Science (AALAS)
9190 Crestwyn Hills Drive
Memphis, TN 38125
901.754.8620
www.aalas.org

American Humane Association
63 Inverness Drive East
Englewood, CO 80112
800.227.4645
www.americanhumane.org

American Society for the Prevention of Cruelty to Animals (ASPCA)
424 East 92nd Street
New York, NY 10128-6804
212.876.7700
www.aspca.org

Association of Zoos and Aquariums
8403 Colesville Road, Suite 710
Silver Spring, MD 20910-3314
301.562.0777
www.aza.org

Humane Society of the United States
Companion Animals Division
2100 L Street, NW
Washington, DC 20037
202.452.1100
www.hsus.org

International Marine Animal Trainer's Association
1200 S. Lake Shore Drive
Chicago, IL 60605
312-692-3193
www.imata.org

National Association of Professional Pet Sitters (NAPPS)
15000 Commerce Parkway
Suite C
Mount Laurel, NJ 08054
856.439.0324
www.petsitters.org

Sally Driscoll/Editor

Botanist

Snapshot

Career Cluster: Agriculture; Environment & Conservation; Food & Natural Resources; Science
Interests: Plant life, plant biology, environmental studies, nature, working outdoors
Earnings (Yearly Average): $62,610
Employment & Outlook: Slower Than Average Growth Expected

OVERVIEW

Sphere of Work

Botanists are scientists who study and conduct basic and applied research on plants and plant characteristics, such as physiology and reproduction, as well as the environments in which plants grow, including soil, climate, and elevation. Some botanists specialize in the study of plant life processes or cultivate useful plants for food, while others focus on the structure of plants, species hierarchy, or how different plants react to adverse environmental conditions. Botanists are employed by universities, government agencies, and private organizations. In addition to their research and study of plant life, botanists frequently share their knowledge with the general public at botanical gardens and other venues.

Work Environment

Botanists study plant life and the environment in which they grow. Much of the work that is performed is conducted in the field, over time, and often in remote locations. Field botanists are accustomed to taking long walks, hikes, or drives in order to view research specimens. Botanists also spend time in the laboratory, conducting experiments and analyzing data. Many botanists are university and college professors, working in offices at institutions of higher learning. Additionally, a large number of botanists work in public settings, such as botanical gardens, zoos, and museums.

Profile

Working Conditions: Work both Indoors and Outdoors
Physical Strength: Light Work
Education Needs: Bachelor's Degree, Master's Degree, Doctoral Degree
Licensure/Certification: Usually Not Required
Physical Abilities Not Required: No Heavy Labor
Opportunities For Experience: Internship
Holland Interest Score*: IRS

* See Appendix A

Occupation Interest

ABotanists enjoy the study of plant species and how plants interact with their environments. Because of their knowledge of trees, algae, and many other forms of plant life, botanists are often consulted in the study of how pollution and other elements affect the air, ground, and water. Economic botanists research the effectiveness of certain plant species in fighting human hunger and disease, as well as supplementing a healthy diet. Botanists contribute to the understanding and stewardship of a wide range of important industries, such as agriculture, conservation, and forestry. First and foremost, botanists are individuals who love nature and the outdoors, and as such, they spend a great deal of time during their careers working outdoors, usually away from urban settings.

A Day in the Life—Duties and Responsibilities

Botanists conduct basic or applied research on trees, mosses, flowering plants, fungi, algae, and other types of plants. In basic research, inquiry is driven by curiosity; in applied research, study is geared toward testing a specific theory or advancing the development of a product. Applied research has a specific purpose.

In order to conduct their research, whether it is basic or applied, many botanists live in remote locations for long periods of time. During this time, they will take samples, study growth and distribution patterns, and take environmental readings. When they return to the laboratory or their base of operations, botanists will carefully study samples and data and write reports and scholarly papers to share their findings with the scientific community. Many botanists work for non-profit institutions such as universities and scientific foundations. To fund their research, they must spend time applying for grants, fellowships, and other private and public funding programs.

Many botanists are also employed by government agencies, such as the US Department of Agriculture and the US Department of the Interior. In these settings, botanists help the government gain a better understanding of current trends in environmental degradation, the impact of droughts and crop disease outbreaks, and other environmental incidents and trends.

A large number of botanists work in museums, botanical gardens, and zoological institutions. These botanists present scientific information about plant life to daily visitors, helping the general public to better understand the natural world. Botanists who are members of university faculties present this type of information to undergraduate and graduate students, conduct classes and seminars, and perform independent research.

Duties and Responsibilities

- **Conducting research in the field and in laboratories and greenhouses**
- **Observing and analyzing plant specimens**
- **Examining environmental conditions, including soil, water, and air quality**
- **Understanding plant habitats and potential threats to those habitats**
- **Being knowledgeable about plant diseases and methods for managing them**
- **Publishing research papers and teaching students**

OCCUPATION SPECIALTIES

Plant Pathologists

Plant Pathologists conduct research into the nature and control of plant diseases and the decay of plant products.

Plant Scientists

Plant scientists work to improve crop yields and give advice to food and crop developers about techniques that could enhance production efforts. They develop ways to control pests and weeds safely and effectively.

Paleobotanists

Paleobotanists study fossilized remains of plants and animals found in geological formations to trace evolution and development of past life.

Mycologists

Mycologists study all types of fungi to discover those that are useful to medicine, agriculture, and industry.

WORK ENVIRONMENT

Physical Environment

Botanists conduct frequent research, examining species in forests, in farm country, and other locations. A great deal of time is also spent in the laboratory, studying samples and analyzing data. Additionally, botanists often work in classroom settings, museums, botanical gardens, and similar venues, where they present to students and the general public.

Relevant Skills and Abilities

Analytical Skills
- Analyzing specimens and data

Communication Skills
- Speaking and writing effectively

Interpersonal/Social Skills
- Being able to work independently and as a member of a team

Organization & Management Skills
- Organizing information or materials
- Paying attention to and handling details

Technical Skills
- Working with tools and equipment
- Working with your hands

Work Environment Skills
- Working outdoors

Human Environment

In the field, botanists work in teams with other scientists and students. In the laboratory, botanists interact with equipment technicians and other scientists. Government officials, farmers, and foresters, and the general public sometimes contact botanists with questions about local plant and environmental issues.

Technological Environment

Botanists use laboratory analytical equipment such as microscopes, spectrometers, and photometers. They use cameras and similar surveillance equipment to monitor plant life remotely and to document research. Computers and research-related software, such as word processing, spreadsheet, and presentation programs, are typically used to share research results and theories with other scientists.

EDUCATION, TRAINING, AND ADVANCEMENT

High School/Secondary

High school students interested in careers in botany should take classes in biology, chemistry, physics, and geography. Math skills are useful as well, including algebra, calculus, and geometry. Basic writing classes help future scientists learn how to write research papers, a skill they will need throughout their careers.

Suggested High School Subjects

- Algebra
- Biology
- Calculus
- Chemistry
- Earth Science
- English
- Geometry
- Physics
- Science
- Social Studies
- Trigonometry

Famous First

The first DNA bank for plant species was the Tropical Plant DNA Bank, started in 1999 as a joint project between the Fairchild Tropical Botanical Gardens of Coral Gables, Florida, and Florida International University. The bank collects, stores, analyzes, and shares DNA samples from tropical plants worldwide, including more than one thousand species of palm.

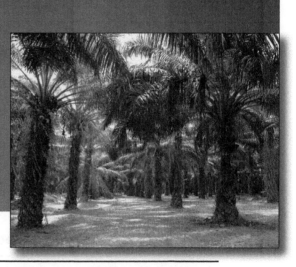

College/Postsecondary

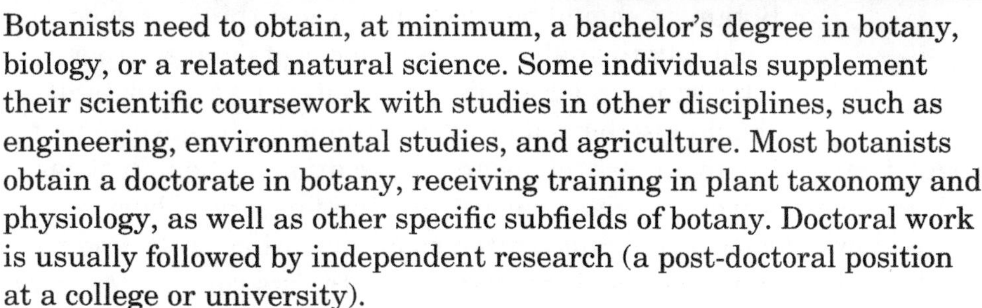

Botanists need to obtain, at minimum, a bachelor's degree in botany, biology, or a related natural science. Some individuals supplement their scientific coursework with studies in other disciplines, such as engineering, environmental studies, and agriculture. Most botanists obtain a doctorate in botany, receiving training in plant taxonomy and physiology, as well as other specific subfields of botany. Doctoral work is usually followed by independent research (a post-doctoral position at a college or university).

Related College Majors

- Biology
- Botany

- Ecology/Environmental Science
- Forestry
- Wildlife & Wildlands Science & Management
- Zoology

Adult Job Seekers

No matter the phase of life an individual decides to pursue a career in botany, all botanists must follow the same academic path. For those with the appropriate academic credentials, they may apply directly to universities with open faculty positions. They may also apply to government agency openings, such as the Department of the Interior, or to private organizations posting openings. Furthermore, botanists may join professional botany organizations, such as the Botanical Society of America, where they network with peers and other scientific professionals. They may also find employment by connecting with fellow botany enthusiasts through related associations such as the Torrey Botanical Society.

Professional Certification and Licensure

Botanists seeking positions with government agencies may be required to obtain professional licenses and certification, such as a professional engineer's license or a certificate to operate specific research equipment. Consult credible professional associations within the field, and follow professional debate as to the relevancy and value of any certification program.

Additional Requirements

Botanists should be excellent critical thinkers, with an ability to analyze complex concepts and a strong interest in understanding the natural world. Botanists should also have an understanding of the government regulatory environment, as well as an appreciation of the industries affected by their work (such as agriculture and forestry). They should have strong verbal and written communication skills, and be comfortable with public speaking. Because botanists conduct frequent field research, they should be physically fit, as they may need to hike great distances in challenging weather and terrain to study certain species.

Fun Fact

Plants are amazing! The mature seed pods of impatiens, a shade-tolerant staple of many subur-ban gardens, can explode in your hand. (source: http://www.life123.com/parenting/education/botany/terrifying-freaks-of-botany.shtml). Also, some types of bamboo can grow one meter per day.

Source: wonderweirded.com.

EARNINGS AND ADVANCEMENT

Advancement opportunities and greater earnings come with additional education and experience. Those with a doctoral degree will advance to the highest levels of research and faculty positions. According to a salary survey by the National Association of Colleges and Employers, average annual starting salaries for graduates with a bachelor's degree in biology were $36,338 in 2012.

Botanists had median annual earnings of $62,610 in 2013. The lowest ten percent earned less than $37,000, and the highest ten percent earned more than $95,000.

Botanists may receive paid vacations, holidays, and sick days; life and health insurance; and retirement benefits. These are usually paid by the employer.

Metropolitan Areas with the Highest Employment Level in This Occupation[1]

Metropolitan area	Employment	Employment per thousand jobs	Hourly mean wage
Seattle-Bellevue-Everett, WA	750	0.52	$38.59
San Diego-Carlsbad-San Marcos, CA	610	0.47	$30.21
Portland-Vancouver-Hillsboro, OR-WA	520	0.50	$35.14
Los Angeles-Long Beach-Glendale, CA	430	0.11	$36.33
Sacramento--Arden-Arcade--Roseville, CA	350	0.42	$44.24
Anchorage, AK	290	1.65	$31.56
Tampa-St. Petersburg-Clearwater, FL	290	0.25	$22.09
Minneapolis-St. Paul-Bloomington, MN-WI	280	0.16	$26.57
Boise City-Nampa, ID	240	0.89	$28.27
Olympia, WA	220	2.24	$30.04

[1] Includes Botanists, Wildlife Biologists, and Zoologists. Source: Bureau of Labor Statistics

EMPLOYMENT AND OUTLOOK

Botanists held about 36,000 jobs nationally in 2013. Employment of botanists is expected to grow slower than the average for all occupations through the year 2022, which means employment is projected to increase 3 percent to 9 percent. Jobs will be created by the need for research to discover new sources of medicine from plants and the protection of plants. Specialized fields like plant genetics will be in greater demand

Employment Trend, Projected 2012–22

Total, All Occupations: 11%

Scientific Occupations: 10%

Botanists, Zoologists and Wildlife Biologists: 5%

Note: "All Occupations" includes all occupations in the U.S. Economy. Source: U.S. Bureau of Labor Statistics, Employment Projections Program.

Related Occupations

- Agricultural Scientist
- Biological Scientist
- Forester & Conservation Scientist
- Marine Biologist
- Oceanographer
- Range Manager
- Soil Scientist
- Wildlife Biologist

Conversation With . . .
CHRISTOPHER T. MARTINE

David Burpee Professor of Plant Genetics and Research, 9 years, Bucknell University
Botanist, 18 years

1. What was your individual career path in terms of education/training, entry-level job, or other significant opportunity?

As a child I spent a lot of time outdoors but I didn't really understand that was something I could do as a career until a couple of years into college. I went to Rutgers University and took two courses that really inspired me: dendrology, where we'd identify trees and shrubs, and field ecology, where we went into a different habitat each week. After college I worked for the New Jersey Forest Service and the Mercer County Soil Conservation District and most of what I did was teach kids outside. That really helped me to figure out I loved teaching about plants. Then I did my Master's, then my PhD, and that's when I went from being a person who appreciated nature to a person who wanted to discover new things about it, and that plants were the group of things I really wanted to spend my time working on. I realized how much of the world was right there, right beyond my understanding.

2. What are the most important skills and/or qualities for someone in your profession?

You need to possess a patience and a willingness to unplug and carefully watch things because that's what biological research requires. Also, having a passion and enthusiasm for your work is important.

3. What do you wish you had known going into this profession?

I wish I had realized there are many paths to the same career goal. It's OK to not follow the exact steps you think everybody else has had to follow. Eventually, I learned this lesson by living it.

4. Are there many job opportunities in your profession? In what specific areas?

Botanists, who understand crop development and agriculture, are in the lead in terms of figuring out how to feed more people worldwide. The planet is also facing a major biodiversity crisis and there is a need to figure out what species are out there, how they all help to maintain the global ecosystem, and how we can best conserve their habitats. The fact that plants are the backbone of most biological systems means there are lots of opportunities for botanists to make a contribution. This takes a certain level of training and a certain ability to see things, but that's perfectly within reach of most people – and then the options open up. There are botanists, like me, who choose to become professors and academic researchers, but there are many other options. Across the U.S., many agencies at the county, state and federal level are doing on-the ground-management of natural habitat, have a mission to protect landscapes, and employ lots of people with botany backgrounds. Non-governmental organizations like The Nature Conservancy are great starting points for internships and seasonal jobs that can help someone get their feet wet; they also permanently employ scores of botanists.

5. How do you see your profession changing in the next five years, what role will technology play in those changes, and what skills will be required?

My work involves genetics and DNA; that area of study is only going to become more important. Having a background in biochemistry and in lab science will help anyone develop a career in botany. That ability to do high tech lab research in addition to being a natural historian who understands how real organisms work, is a perfect combination for folks hoping to make a career as a botanist.

6. What do you enjoy most about your job? What do you enjoy least about your job?

I love what I do. That's good because as a botanist, I'm at work every day — even if I'm working in the garden, or going to the grocery store — and I am seeing plants and observing nature. As a professor of botany, I love teaching and I really like to work with young people. There's a certain level of enthusiasm young people bring to my job every day. I also really appreciate that I get to do biological and botanical research. In the last five or six years, I've been part of teams that discovered six new species. It never gets stale.

On the difficult side, academic research can be a high pressure environment, particularly early in your career. It takes five to eight years to get your PhD and one to three years to get a post-doc before you can become a professor. Then you're trying to get a professorship in a tight job market. You have to be willing to put in the time and work on your skill set. It's totally worth it if you get there but it's not easy and it can be high stakes once you do arrive because of a grueling tenure process and continuous pressure to write grants to attract research money. And you won't become filthy rich. Being a professor and being a botanist is not for somebody who wants to acquire great wealth. You make a good living and enjoy a wonderful lifestyle, but it's a job you do because it's what you want to do.

7. Can you suggest a valuable "try this" for students considering a career in your profession?

Start a garden. Put seeds in the ground, grow some plants, watch them, and see if you can gather a harvest from them. If you're not hooked by this, perhaps botany isn't for you.

I do a lot of field work in the Australian Outback. So when I go out to find the plants I'm looking for, I am in a tent, sometimes for weeks at a time. Have outside experiences and see if that's the sort of thing you would enjoy doing for your career.

I also do a lot of lab work, and for that, it makes sense to work in a lab. Attempt to do an independent study with your high school teacher. Generate a hypothesis, develop a good experiment, collect data, and then synthesize the data. You need to be able to do that in any science field.

SELECTED SCHOOLS

Most colleges and universities have bachelor's degree programs in biology, often with a specialization in plant biology. The student may also gain an initial grounding in the field at an agricultural, technical, or community college. For advanced positions, a doctoral degree is commonly obtained. Below are listed some of the more prominent graduate schools in this field.

Cornell University
Graduate School
Caldwell Hall
Ithaca, NY 14853
607.255.5820
www.gradschool.cornell.edu

Iowa State University
Enrollment Services Center
Ames, IA 50011
800.262.3810
admissions.iastate.edu

Michigan State University
479 W. Circle Drive, Room 110
East Lansing, MI 48824
517.353.3220
www.msu.edu

Penn State University
Plant Biology Program
101 Life Sciences Building
University Park, PA 16802
814.865.8165
bio.psu.edu/graduate-portal

Purdue University
Botany and Plant Biology
915 W. State Street
West Lafayette, IN 47907
765.494.4614
ag.purdue.edu/btny

University of Arizona
Graduate College
Administration 322, PO Box 2106
Tucson, AZ 85721
520.621.3471
grad.arizona.edu

University of California, Berkeley
Graduate Division
Sproul Hall, 3rd Floor
Berkeley, CA 94704
510.642.7405
grad.berkeley.edu

University of California, Davis
250 Mrak Hall
One Shields Avenue
Davis, CA 95616
530.752.0650
gradstudies.ucdavis.edu

University of Missouri
Office of Research and Graduate Studies
210 Jesse Hall
Columbia, MO 65211
gradstudies.missouri.edu

University of Wisconsin
Graduate School
217 Bascom Hall
500 Lincoln Drive
Madison, WI 53706
608.262.2433
grad.wisc.edu

MORE INFORMATION

American Bryological and Lichenological Society
P.O. Box 7065
Lawrence, KS 66044-8897
785.843.1234
www.abls.org

American Phytopathological Society
3340 Pilot Knob Road
St. Paul, MN 55121-2097
651.454.7250
www.apsnet.org

American Society of Plant Biologists
15501 Monona Drive
Rockville, MD 20855-2768
301.251.0560
www.aspb.org

American Society of Plant Taxonomists
University of Wyoming
Department of Botany
1000 E. University Avenue
Laramie, WY 82071
307.766.2556
www.aspt.org

Botanical Society of America
P.O. Box 299
St. Louis, MO 63166-0299
314.577.9566
www.botany.org

Ecological Society of America
1990 M Street, NW, Suite 700
Washington, DC 20006-3915
202.833.8773
www.esa.org

Torrey Botanical Society
P.O. Box 7065
Lawrence, KS 66044-8897
800.627.0326
www.torreybotanical.org

U.S. Botanic Garden
245 First Street SW
Washington, DC 20024
202.225.8333
www.usbg.gov

U.S. Department of Agriculture
1400 Independence Avenue SW
Washington, DC 20250
202.720.2791
www.usda.gov

Michael Auerbach/Editor

Energy Auditor

Snapshot

Career Cluster: Architecture & Construction; Engineering; Environment & Conservation; Science& Technology
Interests: Science, mathematics, environmental and conservation issues
Earnings (Yearly Average): $46,110
Employment & Outlook: Faster Than Average Growth Expected

OVERVIEW

Sphere of Work

Energy auditors inspect energy usage in residential and commercial properties. They determine the amount of electricity, heating, and cooling a property uses and chart the related costs. Based on the information gleaned in the audit, energy auditors run tests of each system to assess whether it is operating in the most efficient manner. They then work with property owners to isolate areas where energy is wasted and to avoid future wastes in energy costs.

Work Environment

Energy auditors are based in office environments, where they meet with clients, analyze data, and write reports. Their offices are located in consulting firms, government agencies, utility companies, and environmental organizations. Outside the office, energy auditors work on-site at private residences, commercial offices, and larger buildings. There they inspect ventilation systems, wiring, furnaces, and other systems, which are typically located in basements, physical plants, or exterior locations. Energy auditors typically work structured schedules, conducting prescheduled audit appointments during standard business hours.

Profile

Working Conditions: Work both Indoors and Outdoors
Physical Strength: Light Work
Education Needs: Junior/Technical/Community College, Bachelor's Degree
Licensure/Certification: Recommended
Physical Abilities Not Required: No Heavy Labor
Opportunities For Experience: Internship
Holland Interest Score*: RIE

* See Appendix A

Occupation Interest

Energy auditors are part of a growing field of "green jobs" that focus on seeking ways to reduce energy expenditure without negatively impacting production or function. Their expertise not only helps individuals and businesses save money but also helps conserve natural resources. Those drawn to energy auditing usually have a science background and are passionate about the environment. There are a wide range of employment options available, and prospective energy auditors can easily transition to the field from related industries. Furthermore, the demand for energy auditors is high and salaries are competitive.

A Day in the Life—Duties and Responsibilities

Energy auditors meet with clients to review their energy and utility costs, learn the building's history, understand the types of utilities that are involved, and record any additional information useful to conducting a comprehensive audit. They then inspect the building's mechanical, electric, and heating, ventilation, and air conditioning (HVAC) systems to determine the current and optimal levels of energy consumption. Such inspections may include analyzing insulation, air vents, fans and blowers, and windows and doors.

Once energy auditors have reviewed all of the systems in question, they collate the information and prepare their audit reports for the client. These reports include a comparison between the way systems should function and how they are actually performing. Audits also identify faulty systems, potentials health hazards such as mold or asbestos, and other elements that can contribute to poor system performance. Once the information is compiled, energy auditors meet with clients to identify areas in which energy use is inefficient or unnecessarily expensive and offer advice on cost-cutting practices regarding energy usage. They recommend alternative technologies, such as new insulation, window retrofits, and new HVAC system installations. Energy auditors also use this information to project the cost savings involved with making such repairs.

Energy auditors may also maintain long-term relationships with clients. In this arena, they frequently communicate with clients, answering any questions about new energy systems and energy-efficient appliances and machines.

Duties and Responsibilities

- **Auditing the energy use of buildings and heating-and-cooling systems**
- **Performing tests and measurements on system performance**
- **Developing techniques for preventing energy loss**
- **Recommending energy efficiency and alternative energy solutions**

WORK ENVIRONMENT

Immediate Physical Environment

Energy auditors work in office settings found in government agencies, environmental consultancies, corporations, and other industries. At a client's building or home, auditors operate in boiler rooms, power plants, and similar areas. Some physical activity may be required,

Relevant Skills and Abilities

Communication Skills
- Speaking effectively
- Reporting information

Interpersonal/Social Skills
- Being able to work independently and as a member of a team
- Being honest and helpful

Organization & Management Skills
- Initiating new ideas
- Paying attention to and handling details Managing Time
- Promoting change
- Making decisions
- Organizing information or materials
- Meeting goals and deadlines

Research & Planning Skills
- Creating ideas
- Identifying problems
- Determining alternatives
- Identifying resources
- Gathering information
- Solving problems
- Analyzing information
- Developing evaluation strategies
- Using logical reasoning

Technical Skills
- Performing scientific, mathematical or technical work
- Working with machines, tools or other objects
- Working with data or numbers

Unclassified Skills
- Using set methods and standards in your work

such as bending down for extended periods and performing heavy lifting. They are also at some risk for electrical shock from aging wires and for exposure to mold, asbestos, or other dangerous substances.

Human Environment

Energy auditors interact with a wide range of individuals, including business executives, government officials, engineers, environmental technicians, construction personnel, and manufacturing employees. Although they may call upon others to assist in editing audit reports, experienced energy auditors typically work alone. Depending on the organization, beginning energy auditors may assist their more experienced colleagues.

Technological Environment

Energy auditors work with many HVAC, electrical, and other technologies. These systems include circuit boards, furnaces, fans and blowers, and automated equipment such as hand dryers and motion-sensing lights. During audits, they use gas monitors, air current testers, draft gauges, leak-testing equipment, and pressure-measuring manometers, among other tools. Furthermore, they use databases, the Internet, and photo-imaging, word processing, and analytical and scientific software.

EDUCATION, TRAINING, AND ADVANCEMENT

High School/Secondary

High school students interested in energy auditing should study industrial arts, including electronic and mechanical systems. Trigonometry, geometry, algebra, basic accounting, physics, and computer science are also essential courses for the aspiring energy auditor. Finally, high school students should hone their communication skills through English classes.

Suggested High School Subjects

- Accounting
- Algebra
- Applied Communication
- Applied Math
- Applied Physics
- Blueprint Reading
- Bookkeeping
- Business
- Calculus
- Chemistry
- College Preparatory
- Computer Science
- English
- Geometry
- Mathematics
- Physics
- Science
- Statistics
- Trigonometry

Famous First

The first heating system to heat buildings from a central heating station was installed by Birdsall Holly, Jr., in Lockport, New York, in 1877. Holly was an engineer and inventor who sought to heat a nearby structure by using the steam heating system in his own house. He ran an insulated steam line to the structure and discovered that there was no major loss of heat. Holly went on to found a company based on his successful application.

College/Postsecondary

Energy auditor positions are relatively new and therefore do not have standardized postsecondary education requirements. Energy auditors typically have an associate's degree in energy management or applied science or a bachelor's degree in engineering, architecture, environmental science, or a related field. As the market for energy auditors is growing and becoming more competitive, a master's degree in engineering or a related field is recommended.

Related College Majors

- Architectural Engineering
- Architecture
- Civil Engineering
- Electrical, Electronics & Communications Engineering
- Engineering
- Environmental/Environmental Health Engineering
- Mechanical Engineering

Adult Job Seekers

Energy auditors come from a wide range of backgrounds, including construction, HVAC service and repair, consulting, and manufacturing. Aspiring energy auditors should check the education, experience, and certification requirements of their prospective employers. Qualified individuals may apply directly to any government agency, corporation, or consulting firm that posts energy auditor openings. Many job websites are dedicated solely to green jobs and feature up-to-date postings.

Professional Certification and Licensure

Although there are no established requirements for certification or licensure in the field of energy auditing, energy management and engineering certifications are widely available and may help improve a job candidate's credentials in an increasingly competitive job market. The Association of Energy Engineers (AEE) and the Residential Energy Services Network (RESNET) are among the several professional organizations that offer voluntary energy management certifications. Education or training, work experience, and satisfactorily completion of an examination are typically required for certification. Ongoing certification requires continuing education.

Energy auditors may also specialize in a particular type of building or system. The Building Performance Institute (BPI) offers specialty certification in building analysis, envelope improvement, residential buildings, manufactured housing, heating, air conditioning and heat pump systems, and multifamily buildings. As with any voluntary certification process, it is beneficial to consult credible professional associations within the field and follow professional debate as to the relevancy and value of any certification program.

Additional Requirements

Energy auditors must be detail oriented and analytical, able to carefully review expenses and costs as well as read energy consumption data. They must also have strong communication skills, as working with customers is central to the position. Furthermore, energy auditors should be careful students of the business world, taking into account the costs borne by different types of business organizations. To that end, formal training in business management may be helpful.

Advancement opportunities and greater earnings come with additional education and experience. Those with a doctoral degree will advance to the highest levels of research and faculty positions. According to a salary survey by the National Association of Colleges and Employers, average annual starting salaries for graduates with a bachelor's degree in biology were $36,338 in 2012.

Fun Facts

Compact fluorescent light bulbs use about 80 percent less electricty than conventional bulbs and last up to 12 times as long.

Source: Royston, Angela. 2009. Sustainable Energy. Mankato, MN: Arcturus Publishing Limited.

Also, cooling and heating comprise about half of an average home's total energy bill in the U.S.

Source: Sherwin, Elton B. 2010. Addiction to Energy: A Venture Capitalist's Perspective on How to Save Our Economy and Our Climate. Knoxville, TN: Energy House Publishing. Both facts via http://facts.randomhistory.com/energy-facts.html

EARNINGS AND ADVANCEMENT

Earnings of energy auditors depend on formal training and experience. Mean annual earnings of energy auditors were $46,110 in 2013. The lowest ten percent earned less than $28,000, and the highest ten percent earned more than $69,000. Energy auditors may receive paid vacations, holidays and sick days; life and health insurance; and retirement benefits. These are usually paid by the employer.

Metropolitan Areas with the Highest Employment Level in This Occupation

Metropolitan area	Employment[1]	Employment per thousand jobs	Hourly mean wage
New York-White Plains-Wayne, NY-NJ	7,330	1.40	$27.35
Chicago-Joliet-Naperville, IL	5,460	1.48	$28.40
Houston-Sugar Land-Baytown, TX	5,380	1.95	$20.91
Dallas-Plano-Irving, TX	4,690	2.18	$22.49
Atlanta-Sandy Springs-Marietta, GA	4,660	2.02	$20.68
Washington-Arlington-Alexandria, DC-VA-MD-WV	4,520	1.91	$25.67
Phoenix-Mesa-Glendale, AZ	4,130	2.32	$23.12
Philadelphia, PA	4,050	2.20	$23.33
Los Angeles-Long Beach-Glendale, CA	4,040	1.02	$26.29
Boston-Cambridge-Quincy, MA	3,440	1.97	$28.49

(1) Includes heating and cooling technicians and energy auditors; does not include self-employed.
Source: Bureau of Labor Statistics

EMPLOYMENT AND OUTLOOK

Heating and cooling technicians, of which energy auditors are a part, held about 268,000 jobs in 2012. Employment of energy auditors is expected to grow faster than the average for all occupations through the year 2022, which means employment is projected to increase 20 percent or more. Increasing concern for energy conservation will continue the development of energy-saving heating and air-conditioning systems. An emphasis on better energy management should lead to the replacement of older systems and the installation of newer, more efficient systems in existing homes and buildings.

Employment Trend, Projected 2012–22

Energy Auditors and Other Heating and Cooling Technicians: 21%

Total, All Occupations: 11%

Installation, Maintenance, and Repair Occupations (All): 10%

Note: "All Occupations" includes all occupations in the U.S. Economy. Source: U.S. Bureau of Labor Statistics, Employment Projections Program.

Related Occupations

- Energy Engineer
- Heating & Cooling Technician
- Renewable Energy Technician
- Solar Energy System Installer
- Wind Energy Engineer

Conversation With . . .
ZACHARY MAULE

Energy Auditor, 3 years
Conservation Services Group,Westborough, MA

1. What was your individual career path in terms of education/training, entry-level job, or other significant opportunity?

At the University of Massachusetts in Amherst, I got an undergraduate degree in hospitality, tourism and management. I moved to Hawaii and managed a restaurant on Oahu. I realized how the island had to be self-sufficient; being out there I became more interested in energy conservation. It's a great climate, for example, for solar energy. I started thinking about what I ultimately wanted to do — I knew I didn't want to manage a restaurant forever — and gravitated towards energy efficiency. In researching jobs, I quickly learned that CSG is supposed to have a great training program. I had a friend who was working there and he said I should apply. So I came back home to Massachusetts and interviewed for a job. While I was in the training program, I liked it so much that I convinced my brother to move back from Portland, Oregon to join the company. I found the classroom experience was really fascinating and really enjoyed learning how a house works and how it's constructed. I was sold on the fact that my values were in line with what the company wants to do. This company offers incentives and rebates from utilities for energy efficient work or improvements. So, for example, when I go into a home I may be offering no-cost lighting, low-flow shower heads and sink heads, air sealing in attics and basement, or other energy-efficiency incentives offered through the Massachusetts Green Communities Act and other energy-conservation programs. .

2. What are the most important skills and/or qualities for someone in your profession?

I don't think this is a job for somebody who is not truly interested in the goals of a company like this. Being proud of what you do is a powerful motivator. Also, I think you have to be comfortable talking to people — strangers — in their own home. I like to think I'm introducing people to their homes in a completely new way. To do that, you have to be extroverted to some degree.

3. What do you wish you had known going into this profession?

I wish I had known about it sooner, because I would have gotten into it sooner.

4. **Are there many job opportunities in your profession? In what specific areas?**

   In energy auditing/advising, there are a lot of different companies that are popping up now. It's a really fast-growing profession. Solar's on the rise, geothermal, HVAC, plumbing, energy-efficient lighting and appliances...the web of energy efficiency is expanding and becoming more exciting. I see the need for energy efficiency programs growing.

5. **How do you see your profession changing in the next five years, what role will technology play in those changes, and what skills will be required?**

   People are going to be more connected to their environment from their smart phones. Recently, smart thermostat apps have come out; you can turn on the heat and air conditioning on your way home from your smart phone. Over the next five years,

   I see the need for energy efficiency growing as our natural resources deplete.

6. **What do you enjoy most about your job? What do you enjoy least about your job?**

   I really like educating people about their homes. I leave knowing the person has the ability to decrease his bills, the environment is less polluted, and fewer natural resources are being used. Also, the economy is being stimulated; our program has 80 licensed contractors for insulation alone that are affiliated with it who can come out and do the work we recommend. Others contractors install HVAC or companies produce energy efficient lights we install...the list goes on and on.

   This is a really good problem to have, but staying current in this fast-growing industry is a challenge. There are new programs all the time.

7. **Can you suggest a valuable "try this" for students considering a career in your profession?**

   Get a no-cost energy assessment. You can have somebody come out to your house and see the process yourself.

SELECTED SCHOOLS

Many agricultural, technical, and community colleges offer programs in constructions systems and technologies, including heating and cooling systems. Interested students are advised to consult with their school guidance counselor or to research area postsecondary schools and training programs. For those interested in pursuing a bachelor's degree, a state land-grant college or technical institute is probably the best place to start.

MORE INFORMATION

American Council for an Energy-Efficient Economy
529 14th Street NW, Suite 600
Washington, DC 20045-1000
202.507.4000
www.aceee.org

Association of Energy Engineers
4025 Pleasantdale Road
Suite 420
Atlanta, GA 30340
770.447.5083
www.aeecenter.org

Building Owners and Managers Association International
1101 15th Street NW, Suite 800
Washington, DC 20005
202.408.2662
www.boma.org

Building Performance Institute
107 Hermes Road, Suite 110
Malta, NY 12020
877.274.1274
www.bpi.org

Green Mechanical Council
1701 Pennsylvania Avenue NW
Suite 300
Washington, DC 20006
877.347.3360
www.greenmech.org

Office of Energy Efficiency & Renewable Energy
Department of Energy
1000 Independence Avenue, SW
Washington, DC 20585
800.342.5363
www.eere.energy.gov

Residential Energy Services Network
760.806.3448
www.resnet.us/professional

Michael Auerbach/Editor

Energy Engineer

Snapshot

Career Cluster: Architecture & Construction; Engineering; Environment and Conservation
Interests: Mechanical systems, environment, green energy
Earnings (Yearly Average): $80,100
Employment & Outlook: Faster Than Average Growth Expected

OVERVIEW

Sphere of Work

Energy engineers work in the construction industry to aid in the design, implementation, and maintenance of systems dedicated to energy efficiency. Energy engineers are commonly active in new construction, particularly as firms continually embrace ways to make structures that are more energy efficient. However, a large portion of energy engineering is solely focused on the renovation of antiquated structures and the specialized adaptation of modern energy-efficient systems to outdated infrastructure. Energy engineers span a variety of concentrations, from heating and cooling systems to water

filtration, solar energy dispersal, lighting, air quality, and long-term energy storage.

Work Environment

Energy engineers work in a variety of systems design, architectural, and construction environments depending on their particular expertise or discipline. Engineers dedicated to the creation of new energy-efficient and environmentally conscious systems often work in laboratory and machine-testing settings where they design and develop new technologies. Other energy engineers work in and around building construction and renovation sites, gauging which particular efficiency technologies would be best suited and most effective to a project's individual needs and constraints.

Profile

Working Conditions: Work both Indoors and Outdoors
Physical Strength: Light Work
Education Needs: Bachelor's Degree Master's Degree
Licensure/Certification: Required
Physical Abilities Not Required: No Heavy Labor
Opportunities For Experience: Internship
Holland Interest Score*: RIE

* See Appendix A

Occupation Interest

The field of energy engineering attracts students and professionals with a keen interest in technical and mechanical systems coupled with a strong desire and interest in practices such as environmentalism, conservatism, efficiency, reuse and reallocation, and green energy. The burgeoning field marries an emerging social consciousness toward energy efficiency with equally fast-moving technological developments focused on conservation, responsible waste management, and environmentally conscious design.

A Day in the Life—Duties and Responsibilities

The everyday duties and responsibilities of energy engineers are dependent on two factors: their area of specialty and the nature of particular projects. While the specific responsibilities of energy engineers differ given their particular industry—as in residential, commercial, or industrial—the field as a whole can safely be divided into two facets: engineering related to new construction and engineering related to renovations to existing structures or systems.

Engineers specializing in renovations or changes to existing structures are responsible for identifying, documenting, and presenting potential energy-saving opportunities. This is done by monitoring existing energy consumption and energy production methods and by reviewing the architectural, mechanical, and electrical layouts of existing systems in order to identify potential upgrade areas. The evaluation of existing heating, ventilation, and cooling systems is also paramount.

Energy engineers who focus primarily on new construction must be well-versed in the latest technologies related to energy efficiency. They review architectural, structural, and systematic design schemes and make recommendations as to which efficient systems would best suit a particular building or system, based on a diverse range of criteria. This criteria includes specific building uses, occupancy, surrounding seasonal climate, and, as with any major construction project, budgetary and time constraints.

Energy engineers in both facets of the industry must also dedicate a large portion of their professional calendar to certification acquisition and training programs in order to stay abreast of new technologies and laws regarding the implementation of energy-efficient systems and building materials.

Duties and Responsibilities

- **Designing and developing systems to improve energy efficiency during all stages of residential and commercial construction**
- **Preparing project plans and specifications**
- **Estimating the costs and requirements of projects**
- **Overseeing project construction and maintenance**
- **Inspecting newly constructed and existing systems**

WORK ENVIRONMENT

Relevant Skills and Abilities

Communication Skills
- Speaking and writing effectively

Interpersonal/Social Skills
- Being able to work independently
- Working as a member of a team
- Having good judgmentl

Organization & Management Skills
- Initiating new ideas
- Paying attention to and handling details
- Managing time
- Promoting change
- Making decisions
- Organizing information or materials
- Meeting goals and deadlines
- Performing duties that change frequently

Research & Planning Skills
- Creating ideas
- Identifying problems
- Determining alternatives
- Identifying resources
- Gathering information
- Solving problems
- Analyzing information
- Developing evaluation strategies
- Using logical reasoning

Technical Skills
- Performing scientific, mathematical or technical work
- Working with data or numbers

Unclassified Skills
- Using set methods and standards in your work

Physical Environment

Office settings predominate, with occasional on-site work.

Plant Environment

Energy engineers work in construction, heavy industry, transportation, government organizations, engineering firms, energy conservation firms, and materials manufacturing.

Human Environment

Energy engineers often work collaboratively with large groups of people across a wide variety of specific specialties.

Technological Environment

Advanced knowledge of construction engineering, heating, ventilation, and air conditioning systems, as well as knowledge related to energy conservation tactics, consumption habits, and emerging technologies is paramount. Familiarity with analytical and scientific software as well as computer-assisted design programs is also beneficial.

EDUCATION, TRAINING, AND ADVANCEMENT

High School/Secondary

Students can best prepare for a career in energy engineering with the successful completion of coursework in advanced mathematics, geometry, physics, chemistry, and industrial arts. Drafting, introductory computer design, and biology coursework can also lay important groundwork for students aspiring to a career in engineering. Participation in any and all extracurricular projects and clubs related to science, engineering, or environmentalism—notably science fairs—is also encouraged.

Suggested High School Subjects

- Algebra
- Applied Communication
- Applied Math
- Applied Physics
- Blueprint Reading
- Calculus
- Chemistry
- College Preparatory
- Computer Science
- Drafting
- English
- Geometry
- Humanities
- Mathematics
- Physics
- Science
- Social Studies
- Trigonometry

Famous First

The first patent for an air-conditioning system was obtained in 1906 by Willis Carrier, an engineer employed by the Buffalo Forge Company in Buffalo, New York. Carrier went on to develop patents for a humidity control system (1908) and the first home air-conditioning unit (1927). Today, the Carrier Corporation is a $12.5-billion company.

College/Postsecondary

Energy engineering is a relatively new but swiftly growing field of undergraduate study that is offered at several colleges and universities throughout the United States. Many undergraduate degree programs in energy engineering draw from the fundamentals of old curricula that concentrated on fuel sciences. Such programs have been updated to include coursework on renewables, green energy, and efficient energy waste disposal. Energy engineering degree programs are often complemented with an array of elective coursework related to the basics of business, risk management, and finance. Undergraduate students of energy engineering participate in courses related to thermodynamics, cellular fuels, fuel chemistry, and energy design.

Master's-level degree programs in energy engineering and related fields are also offered throughout the United States. Students seeking master's degrees in the field tailor specific energy-related coursework with their own specialized thesis projects in sustainable energy engineering; they may often complete such research in partnership with an energy engineering firm.

Related College Majors

- Architectural Engineering
- Civil Engineering
- Electrical, Electronics & Communications Engineering

- Engineering, General
- Environmental/Environmental Health Engineering
- Mechanical Engineering

Adult Job Seekers

Energy engineers traditionally work conventional business hours. Adults with previous educational or professional experience in energy resources or a related field may find transition to energy engineering to be a plausible career path. However, as renewable energy systems quickly replace the antiquated systems and logic that preceded them, such experience may begin to lose viability.

Professional Certification and Licensure

Numerous licensure and certification programs are available for energy engineering professionals. The most prominent program is professional certification to become a certified energy manager (CEM), a credential awarded by the Association of Energy Engineers. While CEM certification is normally a prerequisite for advanced roles in the field, firms may offer employees the chance to train and test for CEM certification as part of an internal professional development program.

Additional Requirements

Energy engineers must have an ability to take in, analyze, and comprehend large amounts of information and data, given the diversity and complexity of the numerous systems they work with on a daily basis. Organization is also key in building an effective frame of reference. Sound active listening, writing, speaking, and problem-solving skills are also beneficial, as is the willingness to work as an effective member of a large team.

EARNINGS AND ADVANCEMENT

Earnings of energy engineers depend on the individual's training and experience. Mean annual earnings of energy engineers were $80,100 in 2013. The lowest ten percent earned less than $40,000, and the highest ten percent earned more than $126,000.

Energy engineers may receive paid vacations, holidays and sick days; life and health insurance; and retirement benefits. These are usually paid by the employer.

Metropolitan Areas with the Highest Employment Level in This Occupation

Metropolitan area	Employment[1]	Employment per thousand jobs	Hourly mean wage
Houston-Sugar Land-Baytown, TX	89,620	32.50	$49.56
Los Angeles-Long Beach-Glendale, CA	68,050	17.12	$44.18
San Jose-Sunnyvale-Santa Clara, CA	52,920	56.90	$51.95
Washington-Arlington-Alexandria, DC-VA-MD-WV	52,590	22.21	$47.63
Seattle-Bellevue-Everett, WA	50,710	34.98	$42.51
Warren-Troy-Farmington Hills, MI	50,210	45.15	$37.72
Chicago-Joliet-Naperville, IL	49,070	13.26	$36.90
Dallas-Plano-Irving, TX	45,650	21.24	$40.75
New York-White Plains-Wayne, NY-NJ	45,300	8.64	$39.88
Boston-Cambridge-Quincy, MA	40,230	23.00	$41.96

[1] Does not include self-employed. Source: Bureau of Labor Statistics

EMPLOYMENT AND OUTLOOK

Architects and building engineers, of which energy engineers are a part, held about 110,000 jobs in 2013. Employment of energy engineers is expected to grow faster than the average for all occupations through the year 2022, which means employment is projected to increase 15 percent or more. Energy and its relationship to sustaining the environment is a rapidly growing field that will continue to create demand for new jobs for many years to come.

Employment Trend, Projected 2012–22

Building Engineers and Energy Engineers: 17%

Architects, Surveyors, and Cartographers: 15%

Total, all occupations: 11%

Note: "All Occupations" includes all occupations in the U.S. Economy. Source: U.S. Bureau of Labor Statistics, Employment Projections Program.

Related Occupations

- Civil Engineer
- Electrical & Electronics Engineer
- Energy Auditor
- Environmental Engineer
- Heating & Cooling Technician
- Mechanical Engineer
- Petroleum Engineer
- Renewable Energy Technician
- Solar Energy System Installer
- Water & Wastewater Engineer
- Wind Energy Engineer

Conversation With . . .
RICHARD W. SULLIVAN

PE, EM, CEP
Principal EE/PDR Business Programs Coordinator, 4 yrs
American Electric Power, Ohio
Engineer, 43 years

1. What was your individual career path in terms of education/training, entry-level job, or other significant opportunity?

I always enjoyed math but I had a high school geometry teacher who challenged me. I was struggling at that time and he asked me after class one day what my career path might be, and I said, "I'm thinking of engineering." He said, "Oh you can't do that; you're not good at math." I thought, "I'm going to show him." It made me even more determined.

Before I graduated with a degree in Industrial Engineering from Youngstown State University, I worked two summers for Ohio Edison. They took me on an all-expense paid, three-day bus tour of their different facilities such as power plants, and they encouraged me to consider working for them. When I interviewed on campus, I was told they were only hiring civil and mechanical engineers. A former summer boss of mine intervened after my name was published in the local paper for graduating at the top of my class. I ended up giving up another offer and going to work for Ohio Edison as a junior engineer in their Customer Service Department in Akron, Ohio. I went on to work in various positions, such as Senior Energy Application Engineer and Major Account Executive, with the parent company, First Energy. I retired in 2009, but had the opportunity to come work for AEP Ohio, a subsidiary of American Electric Power. They hired me to manage the Custom and Peak Demand Response programs for business customers. We have monetary incentives we provide to customers when they install more energy-efficient electric equipment, which can include a number of things such as lighting, HVAC equipment, motors, variable speed drives, transformers, controls on computers, and energy management systems. In addition to holding a professional engineer's (PE) license, I am a certified energy procurement (CEP) specialist and a certified energy manager (CEM). It really helped to have an engineering background to take the CEM test. Having the engineering degree opened the doors to many opportunities.

2. What are the most important skills and/or qualities for someone in your profession?

I'm dealing with customers on a regular basis, and they have to trust that I'm giving them the straight scoop. You need enthusiasm about the job and integrity to establish good working business relationships with co-workers, customers, or contractors.

3. **What do you wish you had known going into this profession?**

I wish I had known how much fun I could have with a career in energy. I'm a people person and there's a lot of that with my job.

4. **Are there many job opportunities in your profession? In what specific areas?**

I often hear that the demand for engineers has increased, not decreased. Engineers will find opportunities throughout the electric utility industry. To name a few, you could be a distribution engineer, dealing w/electrical distribution of power; transmission engineer, dealing with transmission-level voltage designs; Customer Service Engineer; or you could be in energy efficiency as I am.

5. **How do you see your profession changing in the next five years, what role will technology play in those changes, and what skills will be required?**

Changes in alternative energy sources will become more important because states are requiring that a certain portion of energy is alternative, such as wind or solar. Since most electric utility networks are aging, there also are going to be opportunities to upgrade those networks.

6. **What do you enjoy most about your job? What do you enjoy least about your job?**

Il enjoy meeting with customers and seeing different types of manufacturing. I find that very interesting. Business-relationship building is something I also enjoy.

Sometimes there's quite a bit of paperwork, such as 100-300 page applications from contractors. Those can take quite a while to review.

7. **Can you suggest a valuable "try this" for students considering a career in your profession?**

Shadowing opportunities to view jobs would be helpful, or co-op programs while you are going to school. The latter is a golden opportunity to experience the job; it's also an opportunity for the employer to look at you, as well.

SELECTED SCHOOLS

Many colleges and universities have bachelor's degree programs in civil engineering, architecture, or related subjects, sometimes with a specialization in energy engineering or building engineering. The student may also gain an initial grounding in the field at an agricultural, technical, or community college. For advanced positions, a master's degree is usually obtained. Below are listed some of the more prominent schools in this field.

Auburn University
The Quad Center
Auburn, AL 36849
334.844.6425
www.auburn.edu

California Polytechnic University, San Luis Obispo
Admissions Office
San Luis Obispo, CA 93407
805.756.2311
www.calpoly.edu

Drexel University
3141 Chestnut Street
Philadelphia, PA 19104
215.895.2000
www.drexel.edu

Penn State University
201 Shields Building
University Park, PA 16802
814.865.5471
www.psu.edu

University of Cincinnati
2600 Clifton Avenue
Cincinnati, Ohio 45220
513.556.6000
www.uc.edu

University of Colorado, Boulder
Regent Administrative Center 125
552 UCB
Boulder, CO 8309
303.492.6301
www.colorado.edu

University of Kansas
1450 Jayhawk Boulevard
Lawrence, KS 66045
785.864.2700
www.ku.edu

University of Nebraska
1400 R Street
Lincoln, NE 68588
402.472.7211
www.unl.edu

University of Oklahoma
660 Parrington Oval
Norman, OK 73019
405.325.0311
www.ou.edu

University of Texas, Austin
PO Box 8058
Austin, TX 78713
512.475.7387
www.utexas.edu

MORE INFORMATION

Air-Conditioning, Heating, and Refrigeration Institute
2111 Wilson Blvd., Suite 500
Arlington, VA 22201
703.524.8800
www.ahrinet.org

American Council for an Energy-Efficient Economy
529 14th Street NW, Suite 600
Washington, DC 20045-1000
202.507.4000
www.aceee.org

Association of Energy Engineers
4025 Pleasantdale Road
Suite 420
Atlanta, GA 30340
770.447.5083
www.aeecenter.org

Green Mechanical Council
1701 Pennsylvania Avenue NW
Suite 300
Washington, DC 20006
877.347.3360
www.greenmech.org

Office of Energy Efficiency & Renewable Energy
Department of Energy
1000 Independence Avenue, SW
Washington, DC 20585
800.342.5363
www.eere.energy.gov

John Pritchard/Editor

Environmental Engineer

Snapshot

Career Cluster: Engineering; Environment & Conservation; Science & Technology
Interests: Science, mathematics, environmental issues, research, data analysis
Earnings (Yearly Average): $85,520
Employment & Outlook: Faster Than Average Growth Expected

OVERVIEW

Sphere of Work

Environmental engineers use the chemical, biological, and mechanical sciences to quantify, analyze, and mitigate pollution and other dangers to the natural environment. They design, implement, and supervise the operation of environmental systems that gauge and clean up water and air pollution, waste and wastewater, and other public health risks. Environmental engineers investigate polluted areas, write environmental impact assessments, and provide technical expertise and advice on environmental cleanup projects. Environmental engineers usually

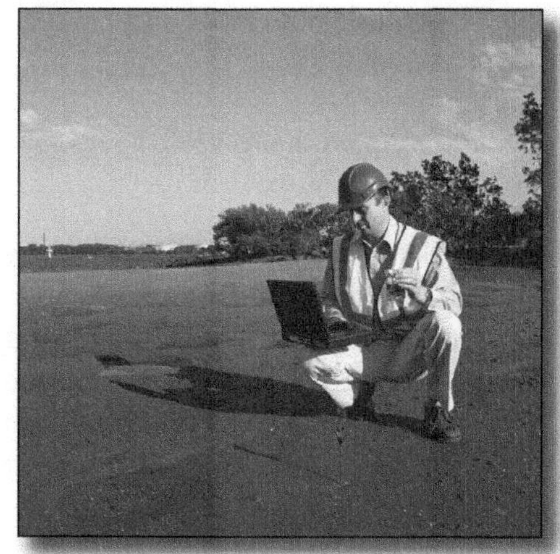

specialize in one area of the field, such as water pollution or solid waste management.

Work Environment

Environmental engineers perform a great deal of their work at construction areas, pollution cleanup sites, reservoirs and water supply pipelines, forests, waste storage facilities and landfills, and other areas in the field. Extensive travel may be required for fieldwork. In the field, there is a substantial risk of exposure to toxic chemicals and pollutants. Environmental engineers also work in engineering and industrial plants, laboratories, government agencies, architectural firms, and other controlled environments. These settings are typically clean, pleasant, and safe. Environmental engineers usually work a regular forty-hour week, although they may work additional hours when deadlines loom or emergencies occur.

Profile

Working Conditions: Work both Indoors and Outdoors
Physical Strength: Medium to Heavy Work
Education Needs: On-the-Job Training, High School Diploma or G.E.D., Technical Education, Apprenticeship
Licensure/Certification: Usually Not Required
Physical Abilities Not Required: N/A
Opportunities For Experience: Apprenticeship, Volunteer Work, Part Time Work
Holland Interest Score*: RCS

* See Appendix A

Occupation Interest

Environmental engineers are integral figures in the effort to protect the environment, natural resources, and wildlife from the threat of pollution and toxic substances. Environmental engineers rely on science and data (rather than political rhetoric or personal opinion) when they author assessments and other reports. In light of their evidence-based approach, they are seen as nonpartisan, reliable resources in the field of environmental protection and pollution abatement. Environmental engineering is considered an extremely "hands-on" area of specialization because it involves a significant amount of work in dirty conditions outdoors in all weather conditions. The field of environmental engineering continues to thrive with the growing popularity of "green" technologies and alternative energy. As a result, job prospects for environmental engineers are favorable.

A Day in the Life—Duties and Responsibilities

Environmental engineers examine industrial and municipal sites to ensure compliance with environmental regulations as well as efficiency in system operations. They assess safety issues and make recommendations to protect workers. Engineers test emissions and waste to ensure that the environment is not exposed to excessive amounts of toxic pollution. Environmental engineers also help design and implement environmental systems and programs. Some engineers design wastewater filtration, recycling, waste containment, air quality, and municipal water systems.

Environmental engineers also conduct research on the impact of industrial processes on the environment. They study acid rain, global climate change, air pollution, water quality, deforestation, wildlife population reductions, and other environmental issues. Environmental engineers write scholarly papers on these subjects as well as environmental impact assessments and reports for the government and private corporations. Many environmental engineers help lawmakers and government officials craft environmental policies and regulations and conduct research on the effectiveness of such policies.

Furthermore, environmental engineers frequently work with other scientists to build and improve large-scale environmental systems and programs. In this capacity, engineers help build roads and bridges, expand communities, and develop real estate. They develop and maintain plans, obtain permits, and implement operating procedures so that such large-scale projects proceed within standards that protect the natural environment as much as possible.

Duties and Responsibilities

- **Designing and developing systems and equipment that comply with environmental standards**
- **Consulting with environmental scientists, hazardous waste technicians, and other engineers and specialists**
- **Inspecting facilities to ensure observance with environmental regulations**
- **Educating organizations and government agencies on the necessary steps to clean up a contaminated site**
- **Creating and updating environmental investigation and recommendation reports**
- **Securing and maintaining necessary plans and permits for development of systems and equipment**
- **Overseeing the progress of environmental improvement programs**
- **Preparing reports and publishing articles**

WORK ENVIRONMENT

Physical Environment

Environmental engineers work in clean, bright office spaces, such as architectural firms, consulting businesses, and government offices. They also work in plants and manufacturing facilities where they risk exposure to hazardous materials and/or injury from heavy machinery. At construction sites and pollution cleanup scenes, there may also be a risk of injury and/or exposure to toxic chemicals..

Human Environment

Environmental engineers interact with government officials, environmentalists and environmental scientists, other engineers, laboratory technicians, construction managers and contractors, and architects..

Relevant Skills and Abilities

Analytical Skills

- Collecting and analyzing data
- Communication Skills
- Speaking and writing effectively

Interpersonal/Social Skills

- Being able to work independently and as a member of a team
- Having good judgment

Organization & Management Skills

- Initiating new ideas
- Paying attention to and handling details
- Managing time
- Promoting change
- Making decisions
- Meeting goals and deadlines
- Performing duties that change frequently

Research & Planning Skills

- Creating ideas
- Identifying problems
- Determining alternatives
- Identifying resources
- Solving problems
- Developing evaluation strategies
- Using logical reasoning

Technical Skills

- Performing scientific, mathematical and technical work
- Working with data or numbers

Technological Environment

Environmental engineers use a wide range of tools and technologies to perform their work. They use air velocity and temperature monitors, drills, spectrometers and photometers, and other measurement tools and detection equipment. They also use computer modeling and design software, including computer-aided design (CAD), photo-imaging, government compliance, scientific, and basic office programs.

EDUCATION, TRAINING, AND ADVANCEMENT

High School/Secondary

High school students should study a wide range of natural sciences, such as biology, chemistry, physics, and earth sciences to prepare for a career in environmental engineering. They should take as many mathematics courses as possible, including algebra, geometry, calculus, and trigonometry. Classes in social studies, political science, history, and other humanities can provide an understanding of current environmental issues. Computer science and drafting classes are also highly beneficial. Students should develop strong writing skills by taking English or composition classes.

Suggested High School Subjects

- Algebra
- Biology
- Calculus
- Chemistry
- College Preparatory
- Computer Science
- Drafting
- Earth Science
- English
- Forestry
- Geometry
- Mathematics
- Physics
- Social Studies
- Trigonometry

Famous First

The first environmental protection law enacted by a state was an 1865 law in New York. It concerned the defacement of "natural scenery" by advertisers who painted promotional messages on prominent stones or hung signs on trees. The act made violators subject to fines of up to $250, prison terms of up to six months, or both.

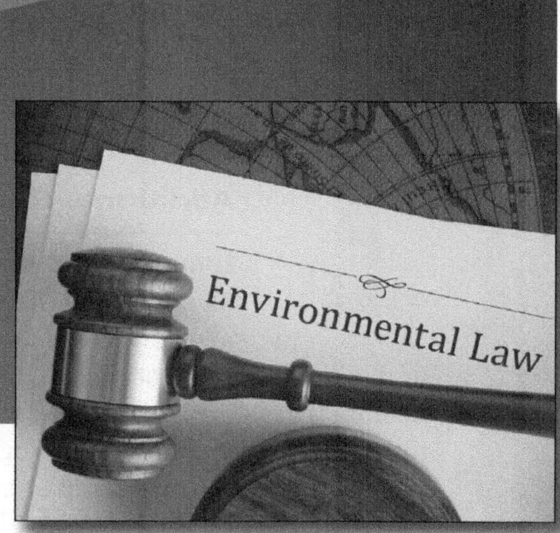

College/Postsecondary

Aspiring environmental engineers must earn at least a bachelor's degree in engineering. While pursuing this undergraduate degree, they are encouraged to take courses in natural and environmental studies. Engineers may improve their career prospects by obtaining advanced degrees in engineering with focus on an environmental field.

Related College Majors

- Engineering, General
- Environmental & Pollution Control Technology
- Environmental Health
- Environmental Science/Studies
- Environmental/Environmental Health Engineering

Adult Job Seekers

Qualified environmental engineers may apply directly to firms and government agencies that have openings. Job fairs, Internet listings, government employment web pages, and professional placement agencies also present opportunities for environmental engineers. Additionally, these individuals may join and network through professional organizations, such as the American Academy of Environmental Engineers.

Professional Certification and Licensure

Environmental engineers must receive licensure as a Professional Engineer (PE) from the state or states in which they work. This process entails passing a state examination as well as meeting educational and work experience requirements. Because the field of environmental engineering is broad, engineers may obtain training and certification in specialized fields. A number of engineering associations offer specialty certifications.

Additional Requirements

Inquisitive, innovative individuals often find success as engineers. Environmental engineers must be attentive to detail, able to understand complex systems, and adhere to set procedures and scientific standards. They should demonstrate strong research, writing, and analytical skills. An ability to use a wide range of technologies, including software applications, is essential for environmental engineers. Federal government-employed environmental engineers must be US citizens, and some must receive additional government security clearance as part of the hiring process.

Fun Fact

Want to help the environment? Consider becoming an environmental engineer. These engineer-ing professionals look for new ways to reduce air pollution and pesticides, and to develop water distribution systems, sewage treatment plants, recycling methods, and other pollution and pre-vention control systems.

Source: http://www.ic.sunysb.edu/Stu/hnaseer/photo.htm.

EARNINGS AND ADVANCEMENT

The mean annual salary of environmental engineers was $85,520 in 2013. The lowest ten percent earned less than $50,000, and the highest ten percent earned more than $122,000.

Environmental engineers may receive paid vacations, holidays and sick days; life and health insurance; and retirement benefits. These are usually paid by the employer.

Metropolitan Areas with the Highest Employment Level in This Occupation

Metropolitan area	Employment[1]	Employment per thousand jobs	Hourly mean wage
Boston-Cambridge-Quincy, MA	2,030	1.16	$38.98
Washington-Arlington-Alexandria, DC-VA-MD-WV	1,710	0.72	$49.64
Los Angeles-Long Beach-Glendale, CA	1,570	0.39	$50.92
New York-White Plains-Wayne, NY-NJ	1,550	0.30	$45.51
Atlanta-Sandy Springs-Marietta, GA	1,330	0.58	$36.89
Philadelphia, PA	1,230	0.67	$40.11
Sacramento--Arden-Arcade--Roseville, CA	1,200	1.43	$45.33
Houston-Sugar Land-Baytown, TX	1,040	0.38	$52.59
Seattle-Bellevue-Everett, WA	920	0.64	$43.98
Oakland-Fremont-Hayward, CA	850	0.84	$47.03

[1] Does not include self-employed. Source: Bureau of Labor Statistics

EMPLOYMENT AND OUTLOOK

Environmental engineers held about 53,000 jobs nationally in 2013. Employment of environmental engineers is expected to grow faster than the average for all occupations through the year 2022, which means employment is projected to increase 15 percent or more. Demand for environmental engineers will be created by a number of factors, including an increasing emphasis on preventing environmental problems before they exist, creating new ways to clean up existing hazards, the need to comply with environmental regulations, and the growth of public health concerns due to the expanding population.

Employment Trend, Projected 2012–22

Environmental Engineers: 15%

Total, all occupations: 11%

Engineers (All): 9%

Note: "All Occupations" includes all occupations in the U.S. Economy. Source: U.S. Bureau of Labor Statistics, Employment Projections Program.

Related Occupations

- Agricultural Engineer
- Biological Scientist
- Chemical Engineer
- Chemist
- Energy Engineer
- Environmental Science Technician
- Forester & Conservation Scientist
- Hazardous Waste Manager
- Petroleum Engineer
- Water & Wastewater Engineer
- Wind Energy Engineer

Related Military Occupations

- Environmental Health & Safety Officer
- Environmental Health & Safety Specialist

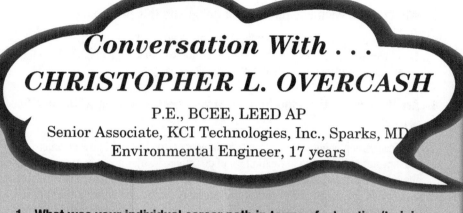

Conversation With . . .

CHRISTOPHER L. OVERCASH

P.E., BCEE, LEED AP
Senior Associate, KCI Technologies, Inc., Sparks, MD
Environmental Engineer, 17 years

1. What was your individual career path in terms of education/training, entry-level job, or other significant opportunity?

When I went to college, I started in mechanical engineering. Like all engineering majors, I took core courses for the first two years. I changed to environmental engineering after I took a cross-country trip with a friend who later became a Navy pilot. We flew all the way across the country and back in a small Cessna. I always had a love of the outdoors, and we got to see all of the landscapes across the entire country. That flipped the switch; I decided to become an environmental engineer so I could participate in affecting and preserving those landscapes. After I graduated from the University of Maryland, I started working in a branch of environmental engineering called industrial hygiene. I didn't really like the focus of that work so I got a job that dealt initially with hazardous waste assessment. As I progressed in my technical knowledge this broadened into water and wastewater work as well as marine environmental projects.

When I graduated, I had hoped to get a job that paid for me to get my master's degree and fortunately, my employer did that. I got my Master's in Environmental Engineering at Johns Hopkins University, and, in addition to my day-job, I teach environmental engineering part-time through Johns Hopkins' Engineering for Professionals program.

2. What are the most important skills and/or qualities for someone in your profession?

The key is to have that base education you get in school — mathematics and science — so you are able to think like an engineer. You have to be able to take those tools and put them to work to solve all sorts of different problems. Even though you are working in a certain track of engineering, you may need to bring in knowledge of another track. That's a plus of being an environmental engineer: it's a broad-based field, so you are more effective leading a design team. Also, you need to be able to think creatively to solve problems.

3. **What do you wish you had known going into this profession?**

   One thing you don't learn as an undergraduate is how to write to convey information. About ten years into your career, you're likely to be managing a team and you need to be able to convey information well in a written format.

4. **Are there many job opportunities in your profession? In what specific areas?**

   For environmental engineers, there are many opportunities right now in water-wastewater because the infrastructure of our original water and sewer systems in the U.S. are coming to the end of their life expectancy. In many large cities it's failing at a significant rate, and it's absolutely necessary for the continued strength of the U.S. economy that this be replaced and fixed. You've got to be able to flush toilets and have drinking water. Other branches of environmental engineering that continue to be strong -- although maybe not as strong -- are remediation of hazardous waste sites and air pollution control.

5. **How do you see your profession changing in the next five years, what role will technology play in those changes, and what skills will be required?**

   We've gone from pencils for drafting to CAD (computer assisted design), and CAD has continued to evolve such that design is becoming more and more automated. It's hard to say what leaps and bounds may happen in the next five years. CAD really drives efficiency for a project team; many junior engineers are filling the drafting role with CAD.

6. **What do you like most about your job? What do you like least about your job?**

   The thing I enjoy most is the variety of projects I get to work on. I do water-wastewater projects, marine-environmental projects such as dredging, and led the design of a visitor's dock at Thomas Point Lighthouse in the Chesapeake Bay. I designed a dredged material containment system to re-create a wetland-system on Grand Lake in Ohio. I also have completed projects to assess hazardous materials such as going to NASA in Bermuda to look at what materials were left there that could be contaminating the soil.

   Today I spend more time in the office than I would like now that I'm in a management role. When you're just coming up in the ranks, you spend a good portion of your time out in the field assessing project sites.

7. **Can you suggest a valuable "try this" for students considering a career in your profession?**

   Internships and shadowing a professional are key to figuring out what an engineer does. They are very different from building base knowledge as you do in college.

SELECTED SCHOOLS

Most colleges and universities have bachelor's degree programs in science and engineering, sometimes with a specialization in environmental engineering. The student may also gain an initial grounding in the field at an agricultural, technical, or community college. For advanced positions, a masters or doctoral degree is usually obtained. Below are listed some of the more prominent schools in this field.

Carnegie Mellon University
5000 Forbes Avenue
Pittsburgh, PA 15213
412.268.2000
www.cmu.edu

California Institute of Technology
1200 E. California Boulevard
Pasadena, CA 91125
616.395.6811
www.caltech.edu

Georgia Institute of Technology
North Avenue NW
Atlanta, GA 30332
404.894.2000
www.gatech.edu

Johns Hopkins University
3400 N. Charles Street
Baltimore, MD 21218
410.516.4050
engineering.jhu.edu

Stanford University
450 Serra Mall
Stanford, CA 94305
650.723.2300
www.stanford.edu

University of California, Berkeley
103 Sproul Hall
Berkeley, CA 94704
510.642.3175
berkeley.edu

University of Illinois—Urbana-Champaign
901 West Illinois Street
Urbana, IL 61801
217.333.0302
illinois.edu

University of Michigan—Ann Arbor
500 S. State Street
Ann Arbor, MI 48109
734.764.1817
www.umich.edu

University of Texas—Austin
301 E. Dean Keeton Street
Austin, TX 78712
512.471.7995
www.eng.utexas.edu

Virginia Tech
925 Price Forks Road
Blacksburg, VA 24061
540.231.3242
www.vt.edu

MORE INFORMATION

Air and Waste Management Association
1 Gateway Center, 3rd Floor
420 Fort Duquesne Boulevard
Pittsburgh, PA 15222-1435
800.270.3444
www.awma.org

American Academy of Environmental Engineers & Scientists
147 Old Solomons Island Road
Suite 303
Annapolis, MD 21401
410.266.3311
www.aaees.org

American Society for Engineering Education
1818 North Street NW, Suite 600
Washington, DC 20036
202.331.3500
www.asee.org

Association of Environmental & Engineering Geologists
100 Brandywine Boulevard
Zanesville, OH 43701
844.331.7867
www.aegweb.org

Institute of Professional Environmental Practice
600 Forbes Avenue
339 Fisher Hall
Pittsburgh, PA 15282
412.396.1703
www.ipep.org

Solid Waste Association of North America
1100 Wayne Avenue, Suite 700
Silver Spring, MD 20910
800.467.9262
www.swana.org

U.S. Army Corps of Engineers Research and Development Center
3909 Halls Ferry Road
Vicksburg, MS 39180-6199
866.373.2872
www.erdc.usace.army.mil

Michael Auerbach/Editor

Environmental Science Technician

Snapshot

Career Cluster: Engineering; Environment & Conservation; Science & Technology
Interests: Science, mathematics, environmental issues, research, data analysis
Earnings (Yearly Average): $45,470
Employment & Outlook: Faster Than Average Growth Expected

OVERVIEW

Sphere of Work

Environmental science technicians conduct tests in the laboratory and in the field to assess the levels and sources of air, water, and soil pollution. They set up and monitor experiments and calculate and record results using complex instruments, including state-of-the-art monitoring and testing equipment. Technicians are involved in regulatory compliance, waste management, and hazardous material management and control operations. Using the samples they collect at polluted sites, they assist in the location and elimination of pollution sources. Environmental science technicians typically work for scientific and technical services

businesses, environmental consultants, and state and federal government agencies.

Work Environment

Much of the work performed by environmental science technicians is conducted in laboratories. Such technicians also take samples directly from field sites. They frequently work in teams alongside environmental scientists. Technicians work with and around a wide range of technical equipment and systems at manufacturing facilities, refineries, military installations, and other sites that produce and emit pollution. Because of their direct work with pollution and environmental hazards, environmental science technicians are faced with potential health risks during the course of their work. They may work irregular hours, particularly when monitoring an ongoing issue or conducting a time-consuming experiment.

Profile

Working Conditions: Work both Indoors and Outdoors
Physical Strength: Light Work
Education Needs: Bachelor's Degree
Licensure/Certification: Recommended
Physical Abilities Not Required: N/A
Opportunities For Experience: Apprenticeship, Military Service
Holland Interest Score*: IRE

* See Appendix A

Occupation Interest

Environmental science technicians work to halt pollution before it affects the health of the general public. In many cases, environmental science technicians are sent to scenes of environmental disasters such as oil spills in order to assess the extent of environmental damage caused and to begin a course of action to contain and mitigate those issues. In other situations, environmental science technicians play an ongoing role in analyzing airborne emissions, wastewater discharge, and groundwater quality to comply with government environmental quality standards.

In addition to the potential for intervening in or preventing an environmental disaster, environmental science technicians use the latest in detection and sampling technology as well as advanced computers to analyze and record pollution levels.

A Day in the Life—Duties and Responsibilities

Environmental science technicians frequently work outdoors, sometimes in remote locations. They take air, water, and/or soil samples from areas affected by the waste emissions of a business, municipality, or government facility. Returning to the laboratory, technicians will set up and operate analytical and monitoring equipment to provide a clear study of those samples. They conduct experiments, calculate and record results, and often develop conclusions that are then used by the environmental scientists with whom they work. In the course of their daily activities, environmental science technicians maintain a detailed log of all experiments and operations conducted in the laboratory. They also run maintenance tests on the equipment to ensure that those devices are operating properly.

Many environmental science technicians are employed by companies that produce hazardous materials, waste, and airborne emissions. Many of these technicians are responsible for their companies' waste management and/or hazardous materials inventory programs. They file detailed reports on these topics for submission to state and federal government agencies as required by law.

Environmental science technicians often assist in researching and developing new ways to track and prevent pollution. These innovations are based on the specific data collected during the technicians' normal activities (as opposed to the theoretical concepts and models environmental scientists may use).

Duties and Responsibilities

- **Taking samples at polluted sites for testing in the laboratory**
- **Performing laboratory analysis of samples collected**
- **Preparing reports on sites and materials tested**
- **Advising officials and/or clients regarding pollution mitigation measures**

WORK ENVIRONMENT

Physical Environment

Environmental science technicians work in laboratories, where they operate and maintain scientific equipment, and in offices, where they write reports. These facilities may be found in government agencies, manufacturing plants, private consulting firms, or at universities. Technicians also work outdoors, where they collect samples. Whether indoors or outdoors, technicians work with toxic substances and waste materials; therefore, strict safety measures are enforced so that the risks associated with these pollutants are minimized.

Relevant Skills and Abilities

Analytical Skills
- Collecting and analyzing data

Communication Skills
- Speaking and writing effectively

Technical Skills
- Performing scientific, mathematical, and technical work
- Using laboratory equipment

Work Environment Skills
- Having a good awareness of safety issues
- Working both indoors and outdoors

Human Environment

Environmental science technicians often work in teams with peers as well as under environmental scientists. In their duties overseeing corporate waste management and other programs, environmental science technicians will also work with executives, government compliance officers and inspectors, and internal compliance officers.

Technological Environment

Central to an environmental science technician's responsibilities is the use and maintenance of analytical equipment and monitoring systems, such as air samplers, flow meters, decibel meters, water samplers, and sampling pumps. They also use a wide range of computers and software, such as computer-aided design (CAD) systems, map creation software, and other analytical and modeling software. They must also use basic software applications for reports and data management, such as spreadsheets and word processing systems.

EDUCATION, TRAINING, AND ADVANCEMENT

High School/Secondary

High school students interested in becoming environmental science technicians should focus on science courses such as biology, chemistry, and physics. They should also take relevant math courses, such as geometry, algebra, trigonometry, and calculus. Courses in communication can enhance aspiring technicians' writing skills.

Suggested High School Subjects

- Algebra
- Applied Biology/Chemistry
- Applied Communication
- Applied Math
- Biology
- Calculus
- Chemistry
- Computer Science
- English
- Geometry
- Physical Science
- Trigonometry

Famous First

The first noise pollution law was enacted by the state of New Jersey in 1971 and signed into law in 1972. The act authorized the state Department of Environmental Protection to set out rules and regulations regarding noise pollution and control. Later in 1972 a national noise pollution law was enacted; it was rescinded in 1981 under the Reagan administration.

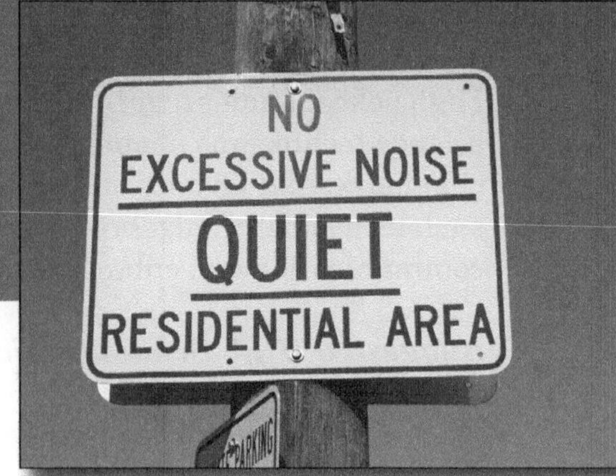

College/Postsecondary

Many environmental science technicians obtain an associate's or bachelor's degree in a field such as engineering, environmental science, or computer science. Courses in chemistry, physics, and math are also essential, as is work in a campus laboratory.

Related College Majors

- Chemical Engineering
- Civil Engineering
- Environmental Science/Studies
- Mechanical Engineering
- Natural Resources Conservation, General

Adult Job Seekers

Environmental science technicians may find employment by directly applying for jobs posted on corporate or government websites or through employment agencies. They may also benefit from joining a related professional trade organization such as the American Academy of Environmental Engineers.

Professional Certification and Licensure

Environmental science technicians should receive their Hazardous Materials Technician (also known as Hazardous Waste Operations and Emergency Response) certification through the U.S. Occupational Safety and Health Administration (OSHA). Professional certifications may also be obtained through trade organizations such as the National Registry for Environmental Professionals.

Additional Requirements

Environmental science technicians must be able to use scientific principles and rules to solve complex problems and issues. They should have strong organizational, communication, and analytical skills. Furthermore, technicians must have exceptional capability using mechanical devices and computer equipment.

EARNINGS AND ADVANCEMENT

Environmental science technicians increase their chances for advancement through experience and further education. Median annual earnings of environmental science technicians were $45,470 in 2013. The lowest ten percent earned less than $27,000, and the highest ten percent earned more than $70,000.

Environmental science technicians may receive paid vacations, holidays, and sick days; life and health insurance; and retirement benefits. These are usually paid by the employer.

Metropolitan Areas with the Highest Employment Level in This Occupation

Metropolitan area	Employment(1)	Employment per thousand jobs	Hourly mean wage
New York-White Plains-Wayne, NY-NJ	1,080	0.21	$24.08
Chicago-Joliet-Naperville, IL	860	0.23	$23.13
Boston-Cambridge-Quincy, MA	790	0.45	$17.27
Houston-Sugar Land-Baytown, TX	770	0.28	$26.39
Washington-Arlington-Alexandria, DC-VA-MD-WV	700	0.30	$22.23
Los Angeles-Long Beach-Glendale, CA	650	0.16	$24.43
Denver-Aurora-Broomfield, CO	580	0.46	$22.11
Phoenix-Mesa-Glendale, AZ	520	0.29	$23.51
San Diego-Carlsbad-San Marcos, CA	500	0.39	$22.12
Seattle-Bellevue-Everett, WA	490	0.34	$26.37

[1] Does not include self-employed. Source: Bureau of Labor Statistics

EMPLOYMENT AND OUTLOOK

Environmental science technicians held about 35,000 jobs nationally in 2013. Employment is expected to grow faster than the average for all occupations through the year 2022, which means employment is projected to increase 15 percent to 20 percent. Job growth will result from the need for environmental science technicians to regulate waste products; to collect air, water, and soil samples to measure levels of pollutants; to monitor compliance with environmental regulations; and to clean up contaminated sites. Environmental science technicians can expect job opportunities in government as well as private companies.

Employment Trend, Projected 2012–22

Environmental Science Technicians: 19%

Total, All Occupations: 11%

Science Technicians (All): 10%

Note: "All Occupations" includes all occupations in the U.S. Economy. Source: U.S. Bureau of Labor Statistics, Employment Projections Program.

Related Occupations

- Agricultural Engineer
- Biological Scientist
- Chemical Engineer
- Civil Engineer
- Environmental Engineer
- Hazardous Waste Manager
- Petroleum Engineer
- Water & Wastewater Engineer
- Wind Energy Engineer

Related Military Occupations

- Environmental Health & Safety Officer

SELECTED SCHOOLS

Many agricultural, technical, and community colleges offer programs related to environmental science and engineering. Interested students are advised to consult with their school guidance counselor or to research area postsecondary schools and training programs. For those interested in pursuing a bachelor's degree, refer to the list of schools in the "Environmental Engineer" chapter in the present volume.

MORE INFORMATION

American Academy of Environmental Engineers & Scientists
147 Old Solomons Island Road
Suite 303
Annapolis, MD 21401
410.266.3311
www.aaees.org

American Society for Engineering Education
1818 North Street NW
Suite 600
Washington, DC 20036
202.331.3500
www.asee.org

National Environmental Health Association
720 S. Colorado Boulevard
Suite 1000-N
Denver, CO 80246-1926
303.756.9090
www.neha.org

National Environmental, Safety & Health Training Association
2700 North Central Avenue
Suite 900
Phoenix, AZ 85004
602.956.6099
https://netforum.avectra.com

National Registry of Environmental Professionals
P.O. Box 2099
Glenview, IL 60025-6099
847.724.6631
www.nrep.org

Global Environment & Technology Foundation
2900 S. Quincy Street
Suite 375
Arlington, VA 22206
703.379.2713
www.getf.org

Michael Auerbach/Editor

Farmer/Farm Manager

Snapshot

Career Cluster: Agriculture; Business Administration; Natural Resources Development
Interests: Agriculture, business practices, being outside, working independently
Earnings (Yearly Average): $73,210
Employment & Outlook: Decline Expected

OVERVIEW

Sphere of Work

Farmers and farm managers, also called farm operators and agricultural managers, grow food for personal consumption and for wholesale and retail consumers. Farmers and farm managers oversee agricultural production and financial operations at farms, nurseries, ranches, and greenhouses. Farmers and farm managers grow crops, livestock, poultry, and aquatic animals. Although specific tasks vary by type of agricultural work, all farmers and farm managers are responsible for ensuring the care of crops and animals from conception to market. Farmers often perform the hands-on labor of planting, cultivating, operating farm machinery, harvesting, and

marketing and selling crops and animals. Farm managers hire, train, and supervise farm staff to complete these tasks.

Work Environment

Farmers and farm managers work in farms, nurseries, ranches, and greenhouses that they own or lease. Farmers and farm managers do not have set work hours and instead must work until tasks are complete. Crop farm work is seasonal. During non-growing seasons, crop farmers and farm managers focus on repairing farm machinery, planning next year's crops, and marketing and selling efforts. Animal farmers and farm managers work steadily throughout the year to care for their livestock, poultry, and aquatic animals.

Profile

Working Conditions: Work both Indoors and Outdoors
Physical Strength: Medium Work, Heavy Work
Education Needs: On-The-Job Training, High School Diploma with Technical, Education, Junior/Technical/Community College pprenticeship, Bachelor's Degree
Licensure/Certification: Usually Not Required
Physical Abilities Not Required: N/A
Opportunities For Experience: Internship, Apprenticeship, Volunteer Work, Part Time Work
Holland Interest Score*: ESR, REI, RIE

* See Appendix A

Occupation Interest

Individuals attracted to the farming profession tend to be physically strong and detail-oriented people. Successful farmers and farm managers exhibit stamina, resilience, organizational abilities, integrity and ethics, independence, and effective time management. Business acumen and familiarity with computer technology is becoming increasingly advantageous. Farmers and farm managers should enjoy physical labor and have a strong background in agriculture and business.

A Day in the Life—Duties and Responsibilities

Farmers and farm managers perform different daily occupational duties and responsibilities depending on their specialization and work environment. They may specialize in the production of crops, beef, poultry, pork, dairy, or aquaculture.

On crop farms, farmers and farm managers oversee activities related to the planting, tending, and harvesting of crops. These tasks may include preparing soil and managing its nutrient levels, using natural or chemical methods to eliminate pests, irrigating and draining fields, weather forecasting, and storing fuels and chemicals. Crop farmers and farm managers promote and sell crops to distributors and food-processing companies, retail customers in farmers markets or farm stands, or shareholders in a community-supported agriculture (CSA) program.

Animal farmers and farm managers oversee meat production operations. They raise beef cattle, chickens, turkeys, ducks, game birds, goats, or pigs. Animal farmers and farm managers must ensure proper breeding and birthing and feeding, housing, transportation, and slaughtering. Those who work with beef cattle and pigs medicate and vaccinate the animals as needed. On poultry farms, they also manage the hatchery, establish egg or meat-bird production effort, adjust the lighting in poultry buildings to promote molting or egg laying, and match stock size to seasonal demand. All animal farmers and farm managers are responsible for promoting and selling meat products.

Dairy farmers and farm managers direct tasks related to the production, collection, and sale of milk. They must ensure the proper care for milk cows. These farmers and farm managers oversee the establishment of a feed storage system for corn silage, alfalfa, hay, cottonseed, and soybeans. They also supervise the construction and maintenance of a milking parlor, a milking and milk storage system, and a manure management system. Dairy farmers and farm managers promote, transport, and sell dairy products.

Aquaculture farmers and farm managers oversee aquaculture production tasks. They or their staff stock ponds or floating nets with eggs, shellfish, or juvenile fish, feed fish stock, and protect fish stock from predators and contamination. Like their meat and dairy counterparts, these farmers and farm managers are responsible for the promotion and sale of their products.

In addition, all farmers and farm managers are responsible for purchasing supplies, maintaining farm machinery, ensuring the cleanliness of farm facilities, and educating themselves about government regulations and business trends affecting their industry.

Duties and Responsibilities

- Planning crops to be planted or livestock to be raised
- Preparing soil for planting
- Cultivating and irrigating crops
- Spraying crops with insecticides and fungicides
- Harvesting and marketing produce
- Tending and marketing livestock and poultry
- Handling business functions as needed to keep the operation running

OCCUPATION SPECIALTIES

Livestock Ranchers

Livestock Ranchers breed and raise livestock such as beef cattle dairy cattle, goats, horses, sheep and swine to sell meat, dairy products, wool and hair.

Poultry Farmers

Poultry Farmers raise chickens, turkeys or other fowl for meat or egg production.

Vegetable Farmers

Vegetable Farmers plan and plant vegetables according to weather, type of soil and size and location of the farm.

Tree-Fruit-And-Nut Crop Farmers

Tree-Fruit-And-Nut Crop Farmers plant and cultivate fruit producing trees.

Nursery Managers

Nursery Managers supervise plant nurseries which produce plants for sale to wholesale or retail customers.

Farm General Managers

Farm General Managers operate farms for corporations, cooperatives or other owners.

Fish Farmers

Fish Farmers spawn and raise fish for commercial purposes.

Horse Trainers

Horse Trainers train horses for riding or harness.

Organic Farmers/Farm Managers

Organic Farmers/Farm Managers grow crops, control pests and maintain soil health w
ithout the use, or the limited use, of synthetic fertilizers and pesticides.

WORK ENVIRONMENT

Physical Environment

Farmers and farm managers work in farms, nurseries, ranches, and greenhouses. Farming tends to be very physical and require extensive hard labor, walking, lifting, and bending. Farmers and farm managers are at high risk for back strain, pesticide exposure, and machine accidents.

Human Environment

Farms, nurseries, ranches, and greenhouses tend to be remotely located and isolated. However, farmers and farm managers interact with farm workers, families, customers, landholders, bankers, veterinarians, and government inspectors. The amount of human interaction often depends on the scale and business model of the farm operation. Farm managers typically report to a farmer or corporation.

Relevant Skills and Abilities

Interpersonal/Social Skills
- Cooperating with others
- Working as a member of a team

Organization & Management Skills
- Coordinating tasks
- Managing people/groups
- Performing duties which change frequently

Research & Planning Skills
- Analyzing information
- Developing evaluation strategies

Technical Skills
- Applying technology to a task
- Performing manual labor and technical work
- Using technology to process information
- Working with data or numbers
- Working with machines, tools or other objects

Technological Environment

In the course of their work, farmers and farm managers use farm machinery and equipment such as animal feeders, hay balers, mowers, trucks, irrigation systems, tractors, chain saws, and milking machines. In addition, farmers and farm managers use computers, Internet communication tools, accounting and farm management software, and spreadsheets to assist them with the business tasks of farming.

EDUCATION, TRAINING, AND ADVANCEMENT

High School/Secondary

High school-level study of agricultural science, biology, chemistry, and business can provide a strong foundation for work as a farmer or college-level study in the field. High school students interested in this career path may benefit from internships, apprenticeships, or part-time work with local farms that expose them to the diversity and challenges of farming responsibilities.

Suggested High School Subjects
- Agricultural Education
- Applied Biology/Chemistry

- Bookkeeping
- Business
- Economics
- English
- Forestry
- Mathematics

Famous First

The first tomatoes eaten by European descendants in America were from a batch grown in Virginia in 1745. Until that time, colonists thought tomatoes to be poisonous. It took a physician, John Siccary, to examine this red fruit of the nightshade plant and declare it edible to convince people of the tomato's worth. Later, Siccary's fellow Virginian Thomas Jefferson raised tomatoes on his plantation, Monticello, and publicized their safety.

College/Postsecondary

Although a postsecondary degree is not strictly necessary for farm work, aspiring farmers or farm managers should pursue the associate's degree or bachelor's degree in agriculture, farm management, agronomy, and dairy science. Formal postsecondary studies afford students a better understanding of the work and industry and provide greater opportunities for advancement. Postsecondary students can gain work experience and potential advantage in their future job searches by securing internships or part-time employment with local farms.

Related College Majors

- Agricultural Business & Management
- Agricultural Production Workers & Managers
- Agricultural Supplies Retailing & Wholesaling
- Farm & Ranch Management
- Horticulture Science
- Horticulture Services Operations & Management
- International Agriculture
- Plant Sciences

Adult Job Seekers

Adults seeking employment as farmers or farm managers should have, at a minimum, a high school diploma or associate's degree. Some farm manager jobs require extensive experience, on-the-job training, and a bachelor's or master's degree. Those seeking farm manager positions should educate themselves about the educational and professional requirements of their prospective employers.

Adult job seekers may benefit from joining professional associations to help with networking and job searching. Professional farming and agricultural associations, such as the American Farm Bureau Federation, the American Society of Agronomy and the American Society of Farm Managers & Rural Appraisers, generally offer job-finding workshops and maintain lists and forums of available jobs.

Professional Certification and Licensure

Certification and licensure is not required for farmers but may be required of farm managers as a condition of employment, salary increase, or promotion. The Accredited Farm Manager (AFM) certification, offered by the American Society of Farm Managers and Rural Appraisers, is the leading option for voluntary farm manager certification. The Accredited Farm Manager certification requires a minimum of four years of farm management experience, a bachelor's degree in agricultural science, a sample farm management plan, and the successful completion of a national exam covering farm business, finances, and law.

Additional Requirements

Successful farmers and farm managers will be knowledgeable about the profession's requirements, responsibilities, and opportunities. The US Environmental Protection Agency requires farmers and farm workers to be trained in agricultural pesticide safe practices. Operating licenses for farm vehicles may be required for some types of agricultural work.

Fun Fact

Could there be some good news down on the farm? Though the U.S. has seen a long-term trend of fewer farms, the decline of less than one percent between 2007 and 2012 was the third small-est decline since 1950, according to the 2012 Census of Agriculture. Crop sales increased 48 percent in the five years between the 2007 and 2012 censuses, and livestock sales increased 19 percent.

Source: http://www.agcensus.usda.gov/Publications/2012/Preliminary_Report/Highlights.pdf

EARNINGS AND ADVANCEMENT

Earnings depend on the size of the farm, type of crop grown or animal raised, the weather during the growing season, market prices, cost of materials, labor costs and management ability. Mean annual earnings of farmers and farm managers were $73,210 in 2013. The lowest ten percent earned less than $34,000, and the highest ten percent earned close to $120,000.

Farmers and farm managers may receive paid vacations, holidays, and sick days; life and health insurance; and retirement benefits. These are usually paid by the employer. Farmers and farm managers may also receive free housing, transportation and farm products. Self-employed farmers and farm managers must pay for their own benefits.

States with the Highest Employment Level in This Occupation

State	Employment[1]	Employment per thousand jobs	Hourly mean wage
California	780	0.05	$45.02
Iowa	260	0.18	$31.93
Texas	240	0.02	$33.88
Illinois	230	0.04	$31.16
Florida	230	0.03	$36.52

[1] Does not include self-employed. Source: Bureau of Labor Statistics

EMPLOYMENT AND OUTLOOK

Farmers and farm managers held about 95,000 jobs in 2012. About 80 percent were self-employed. Employment is expected to decline through the year 2022. This is due to the long-term trend toward the consolidation of farms into fewer and larger farms. The majority of job openings will result from the need to replace farmers who retire or leave the occupation for economic or other reasons.

Employment Trend, Projected 2012–22

Total, All Occupations: 11%

Other Management Occupations: 4%

Farmers and Farm Managers: -19%

Note: "All Occupations" includes all occupations in the U.S. Economy. Source: U.S. Bureau of Labor Statistics, Employment Projections Program.

Related Occupations

- Farm & Ranch Advisor
- Farm Worker
- Forester & Conservation Scientist
- Range Manager

Conversation With . . .
PETER JOHNSON

Farmer Owner Pete's Greens, Pete's Pastured Meats, Good Eats CSA, Craftsbury, Vermont
Farmer in business 17 years

1. What was your individual career path in terms of education/training, entry-level job, or other significant opportunity?

I've always been involved in growing things. Even as a kid, I had a small pumpkin operation. I got a bachelor's degree in environmental studies from Middlebury College and after college, I got right back into farming. I returned to my parents' land in Greensboro (Vermont) and cleared ¾ of an acre to start my farm. For the first four years, Pete's Greens produced only salad greens. Then we began to di-versify, which required land. I rented 10 acres from a friend, about six miles away. For five years, I looked for a farm to buy. I struck gold in 2003. It has 190 acres, a huge house and beautiful barn. Today Pete's Greens is a four-season or-ganic vegetable farm. In the Northeast, 80 acres of vegetables is a lot, but on a na-tional and international level, we're small.

The locavore movement has been huge for us. Our Good Eats CSA (Community Supported Agriculture) is probably the most profitable part of our business. Peo-ple buy a share and we deliver food to sites where they pick it up. We had a healthy, strong business before we started the CSA, but it's helped us grow.

2. What are the most important skills and/or qualities for someone in your pro-fession?

Endurance is probably the biggest one. For the kind of farm that I have, that relies on staying ahead of the curve. You have to have vision, be adaptable and be in-novative. But that's different from what a lot of farming requires. For most farm-ing, you have to have endurance, the ability to make good financial decisions, and be reliable and steady.

3. What do you wish you had known going into this profession?

I wish that I had been able to recognize the extremely low prices land was selling for and had been able to figure out a way to buy some of it, because not only was it cheap, but it was available. In our area, a new wave of agricultural ventures is driving up prices. I've been very much a part of that, and it's been incredible, but it's kind of hurting us now.

4. Are there many job opportunities in your profession? In what specific areas?

Oh yes, there are plenty of opportunities in farming for smart, capable, hardwork-ing, common sense people. Unfortunately, a lot of young Americans don't really have those traits. I don't know a farm that isn't always looking for help. Once you get there, you can very quickly move up. It's a very quick, very clear path to get close to the top. And actually, right now in Vermont, we have a wave of folks with really nice vegetable farms who are thinking about retiring. A lot of them are working on succession plans that don't involve people who are related to them. I read that the average age of a farmer across the country is 57. Some of them have kids that love it, and some have kids that don't want anything to do with it.

5. How do you see your profession changing in the next five years? What role will technology play in those changes, and what skills will be required?

We're all using our smart phones more and more. I monitor my cooler tempera-tures with it. I communicate with my customers with it. I sell things with it. In the future, we'll probably be using more GPS technology for fertilizing, watering, things like that, which is already common on bigger farms.

The ability to communicate in real time has really changed things. It's amazing. I hardly ever go into the office or use my computer anymore. I can be sitting on the tractor doing business.

We can't afford some of the automated equipment that much bigger farms use, so I've been looking to China and India for niche products.

6. What do you enjoy most about your job? What do you enjoy least about your job?

What I enjoy most is having a problem with an important crop and through re-search or intuition or some other means coming up with a solution that leads to genuine success with the crop down the road. It's difficult, but it's very gratifying. You can't get it in a book–books can help, information can help you–but no one's situation is exactly like yours in terms of soil, temperature, pests. You have to spend time in the field.

What I enjoy least is people management. It's not my strong suit. It's a really big part of my job.

7. Can you suggest a valuable "try this" for students considering a career in your profession?

Go find a farm and get a summer job. Oftentimes, you know pretty quickly whether this is something you're going to enjoy or not.

SELECTED SCHOOLS

Many agricultural, technical, and community colleges offer programs related to farming and farm management. Interested students are advised to consult with their school guidance counselor or to research area postsecondary schools and training programs. For those interested in pursuing a bachelor's degree, a state land-grant college is often the best place to start.

MORE INFORMATION

American Farm Bureau Federation
600 Maryland Avenue, SW
Suite 1000
Washington, DC 20024
202.406.3600
www.fb.org

American Society of Agronomy
Career Development & Placement Services
5585 Guilford Road
Madison, WI 53711
608.273.8080
www.agronomy.org

American Society of Farm Managers & Rural Appraisers
950 South Cherry Street, Suite 508
Denver, CO 80246-2664
303.758.3513
www.asfmra.org

Center for Rural Affairs
145 Main Street
PO Box 136
Lyons, NE 68038
402.687.2100
www.cfra.org

National Agri-Marketing Association
11020 King Street, Suite 205
Overland Park, KS 66210
913.491.6500
www.nama.org

National FFA Organization (Future Farmers of America)
P.O. Box 68960
6060 FFA Drive
Indianapolis, IN 46268-0960
317.802.6060
www.ffa.org

National Institute of Food and Agriculture
800 9th Street SW
Washington, DC 20024
202.720.4423
www.csrees.usda.gov

National Sustainable Agriculture Information Service
P.O. Box 3838
Butte, MT 59702
www.attra.org

USDA Farm Service Agency
1400 Independence Avenue, SW
Washington, DC 20250
www.fsa.usda.gov

Simone Isadora Flynn/Editor

Forester and Conservation Scientist

Snapshot

Career Cluster: Agriculture; Environment & Conservation; Science & Technology
Interests: Environmental issues, natural resources, working outdoors, solving problems
Earnings (Yearly Average): $59,000
Employment & Outlook: Slower Than Average Growth Expected

OVERVIEW

Sphere of Work

Foresters and conservation scientists oversee the development, use, and management of forests, rangelands, recreational areas, and other natural sites. Foresters develop plans and policies for safeguarding against forest fires, tree disease outbreaks, and insect infestations. Conservation scientists help landowners make sustainable use of timber, water, and other natural resources.

Both foresters and conservation scientists often work for government agencies, managing and enforcing regulations that pertain to sustainable development activities, such as controlled burns and land clearances, reforestation, and proper harvesting techniques. Foresters and conservation scientists often specialize in a particular subfield like wildlife management, soil science, procurement, or environmental law enforcement.

Profile

Working Conditions: Work both Indoors and Outdoors
Physical Strength: Light to Medium Work
Education Needs: Bachelor's Degree, Master's Degree
Licensure/Certification: Required
Physical Abilities Not Required: No Heavy Labor
Opportunities For Experience: Apprenticeship, Volunteer Work, Part Time Work
Holland Interest Score*: RIE, RIS

* See Appendix A

Work Environment

Foresters and conservation scientists typically work in a combination of outdoor, laboratory, and office settings. When doing outdoor fieldwork, they frequently hike deep into forests and other rural and underpopulated areas in order to conduct research, analyze trends, and assess environmental issues. In the laboratory, they study soil, plant, water, and other samples and collate data regarding long-term trends. In their offices, they write reports, conduct meetings, and coordinate with farmers, timber industry representatives, and government officials. Foresters and conservation scientists usually work a forty-hour week, although they may work erratic hours. When conducting fieldwork, they must outdoors (on many occasions by themselves) in all climates and conditions. During natural disasters such as forest fires, flooding, and other emergencies, foresters and conservation scientists work longer hours and spend most of their time outdoors.

Occupation Interest

Foresters and conservation scientists are key figures in the ongoing effort to promote sustainable development and protect ecosystems. They must balance using and harvesting wood, water, and other natural resources for economic purposes with protecting the environment. Because foresters and conservation scientists must resolve a wide range of environmental issues, the work performed by these individuals is rarely monotonous. Foresters and conservation scientists should enjoy spending a great deal of time outdoors in different areas of the forest or in open spaces.

A Day in the Life—Duties and Responsibilities

The responsibilities of foresters and conservation scientists vary based on individual area of expertise. For example, procurement foresters contact and gain permission from forest property owners to take inventory of the different types of timber standing within the territory, appraise the value of that inventory, and develop contracts for its procurement. Range conservation scientists, meanwhile, work with ranchers to determine the maximum number of cattle that can live in and feed off an area in a sustainable fashion.

Foresters negotiate the terms of a wide range of land use contracts and regulate how timber is cut and moved. They also supervise other forestry workers, direct fire suppression protocols, and analyze how development and tree removal affect tree growth rates and species durability. Conservation scientists, meanwhile, take soil samples to address soil erosion issues and provide counsel to farmers, ranchers, and landowners on how to engage in sustainable development and natural resource extraction. Conservation scientists also plan and implement plans for replanting trees and plants after development has taken place. In both cases, conservation scientists and foresters carefully study trends and resource quantities to ensure long-term use while minimizing the impact of such activities on the ecosystem in question.

Duties and Responsibilities

- **Planning and directing projects for all aspects of forest management, including seeding and replanting forests**
- **Making maps of soil and vegetation of forest areas**
- **Researching methods of processing timber for various uses**
- **Directing or participating in the control of forest fires and conducting fire-prevention programs**
- **Planning campsites and recreational facilities**
- **Monitoring habitats for conformance to state and federal environmental protection regulations**
- **Negotiating land-use contracts with outside interests**

OCCUPATION SPECIALTIES

Silviculturists

Silviculturists manage tree nurseries and thin forests. They also conduct research in forest propagation, life span of seeds and the effects of fire and animal grazing.

Range Managers

Range Managers protect rangelands to maximize their use without damaging the environment.

Soil Conservationists

Soil Conservationists assist farmers, ranchers, and others to conserve soil, water and related natural resources.

Forest Ecologists

Forest Ecologists conduct research upon the various environmental factors affecting forests.

WORK ENVIRONMENT

Physical Environment

Foresters and conservation scientists spend some time working in offices and laboratories, where they analyze samples, collate data, write reports, and hold meetings. These environments are clean, well-lit, and organized. Foresters and conservation scientists also conduct fieldwork in farm country, open ranges, and forests, which are rugged, at times remote, and subject to a wide range of weather conditions.

Relevant Skills and Abilities

Communication Skills
- Speaking and writing effectively

Interpersonal/Social Skills
- Being able to work independently and as a member of a team

Organization & Management Skills
- Making decisions
- Paying attention to and handling details
- Performing duties which change frequently

Research & Planning Skills
- Developing evaluation strategies
- Using logical reasoning

Technical Skills
- Performing scientific, mathematical and technical work

Work Environment Skills
- Driving a vehicle
- Working outdoors
- Working with plants or animals

Human Environment

Foresters and conservation scientists work with a wide range of public and private employees, including ranchers, loggers, land owners, business executives, government regulators, political leaders, and emergency and public safety officials.

Technological Environment

Foresters and conservation scientists use analytical and data collection technologies. Foresters use clinometers, increment borers, and bark gauges to measure tree height and growth, as well as aerial and remote sensors to map areas of land use and undeveloped forests. Conservation scientists use water testing kits, soil spectrometers, and other equipment to analyze the impact of development on natural resources. Both foresters and conservation scientists must use basic office software, scientific databases, and mapping programs.

EDUCATION, TRAINING, AND ADVANCEMENT

High School/Secondary

High school students should take courses in biology, chemistry, and the natural sciences. Geometry, algebra, and trigonometry are essential mathematics courses for foresters and conservation scientists. Additional training in computer science and agriculture are also useful, as is an understanding of environmental laws and sustainable development issues, which may be obtained through social studies or history courses. Furthermore, English and communications courses build the writing skills that future foresters and conservation scientists need.

Suggested High School Subjects

- Agricultural Education
- Algebra
- Biology
- Chemistry
- College Preparatory
- Computer Science
- English
- Forestry
- Geometry
- Science
- Trigonometry

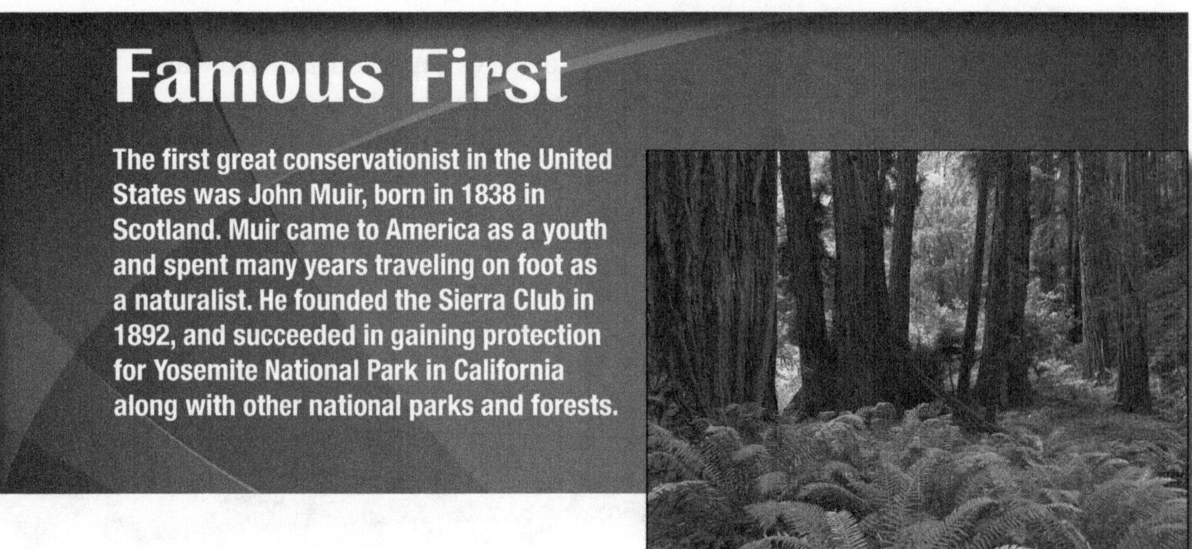

Famous First
The first great conservationist in the United States was John Muir, born in 1838 in Scotland. Muir came to America as a youth and spent many years traveling on foot as a naturalist. He founded the Sierra Club in 1892, and succeeded in gaining protection for Yosemite National Park in California along with other national parks and forests.

College/Postsecondary

Foresters and conservation scientists need a bachelor's degree, preferably in forestry, ecology, or environmental studies. A graduate degree can enhance a candidate's competitiveness and enable these individuals to attain senior-level research positions within these fields.

Related College Majors

- Agronomy & Crop Science
- Forest Harvesting & Production Technology
- Forestry
- Horticulture Services Operations & Management
- Natural Resources Conservation
- Plant Sciences
- Wildlife & Wildlands Management

Adult Job Seekers

Qualified foresters and conservation scientists may apply directly to private logging and lumber companies, research and testing consultancies, and federal and state government agencies that have posted openings. The US Department of Agriculture, which includes the US Forest Service and the Natural Resource Conservation Service, lists job openings on its website. Foresters and conservation scientists may also join and network through professional organizations and nonprofit groups, such as the Society of American Forests or the Conservation Science Institute.

Professional Certification and Licensure

A few states require that foresters obtain licensure or certification, for which they may need to satisfactorily pass a written test. Foresters and conservation scientists seeking to specialize in a particular field may take certification courses from nonprofit organizations and professional associations. The certification process usually involves a combination of education and professional experience.

Additional Requirements

Foresters and conservation scientists must have a strong attention to detail and exceptional data collection and analytical skills. They should have strong communication skills, be physically fit, and be willing to stand outdoors all day, even through inclement weather.

EARNINGS AND ADVANCEMENT

Earnings depend on the employer and the employee's education, experience, type of work performed and the level of responsibility. Recent graduates usually work under supervision and advance with experience. They may eventually qualify for managerial and supervisory positions.

According to a salary survey by the National Association of Colleges and Employers, graduates with a bachelor's degree in conservation and renewable natural resources received average annual starting salaries of $40,167 in 2012.

Mean annual earnings of foresters were $59,000 in 2013. The lowest ten percent earned less than $37,810, and the highest ten percent earned more than $80,072.

Median annual earnings of conservation scientists were $62,869 in 2012. The lowest ten percent earned less than $38,000, and the highest ten percent earned more than $83,000.
Foresters and conservation scientists may receive paid vacations, holidays, and sick days; life and health insurance; and retirement benefits. These are usually paid by the employer.

States with the Highest Employment Level in This Occupation

State	Employment[1]	Employment per thousand jobs	Hourly mean wage
California	1,190	0.08	$34.51
Minnesota	590	0.22	$28.42
Oregon	580	0.35	$30.47
Pennsylvania	470	0.08	$29.77
Wisconsin	450	0.17	$25.11

[1] Does not include self-employed. Source: Bureau of Labor Statistics

EMPLOYMENT AND OUTLOOK

Foresters and conservation scientists held about 35,000 jobs nationally in 2013. Most are employed by the federal government, mostly in the US Departments of Agriculture and Interior. Employment of foresters is concentrated in the Western and Southeastern States, where many national and private forests and parks, and most of the lumber and pulpwood-producing forests, are located.

Employment is expected to grow slower than the average for all occupations through the year 2022, which means employment is projected to increase 1 percent to 6 percent. Job growth should be strongest in consulting firms and scientific research and development services, where demand will occur because of a continuing emphasis on environmental protection, responsible land management and water-related issues. Opportunities will also be available in the federal government, as a large number of workers are expected to retire over the next decade. Opportunities will be best for those with advanced degrees or with several years of experience.

Related Occupations

- Agricultural Engineer
- Agricultural Scientist
- Biological Scientist
- Botanist
- Environmental Engineer
- Farmer/Farm Manager
- Fish & Game Warden
- Forestry Worker
- Landscape Architect
- Park Ranger
- Range Manager
- Soil Scientist
- Water & Wastewater Engineer
- Wildlife Biologist

Conversation With . . .
BRIAN M. DEEB

Procurement Forester, 7 years
Weaber Lumber, Lebanon, PA

1. What was your individual career path in terms of education/training, entry-level job, or other significant opportunity?

Originally, I wanted to be a marine biologist but realized I didn't want to be in school as long as that would take. Forestry is specialized biology, so I took a forestry course when I was at Penn State University, liked it, and received a four-year degree in Forest Science. I had interned with the Pennsylvania Dept. of Natural Resources for a summer. When I graduated, Weaber Lumber hired me as a forest tech, so I was in the field doing the physical work of cruising timber. My main job now is to secure raw material. I go out and talk with landowners; I am selling a service. I work on contracts and negotiate. Each landowner has a different objective for their woodlands, so my job is to evaluate the woodland to determine which management strategy best meets their objectives. Each property is different. I wouldn't advocate clear-cutting, for instance, for every tract but there's more biodiversity in a clearcut than an old growth forest and sometimes it's the way to go. We're in this for the long haul and want to preserve the resources.

Also, these jobs have big equipment with heavy trees coming down and sometimes things happen, like a truck takes out a neighbor's mailbox. Part of my job is to talk with the public and satisfy any concerns. I also deal with state and local regulations and obtain approvals and permits, as well as annual company audits for SFI, Sustainable Forestry Initiative Certification. Back when I was in college, I had a part-time job in retail sales, and that helped me learn to deal with people.

2. What are the most important skills and/or qualities for someone in your pro-fession?

I work from home, so I need to be self-sufficient. You also need to have physical stamina. I climb to the top of a mountain in all sorts of weather to evaluate a stand of timber.

3. What do you wish you had known going into this profession?

Il wish I'd know there would be as much public interaction. I got into forestry to go out in the woods. In procurement, I'm on the phone a lot. We also have to go to township and county meetings. I have to be able to express to a lot of different people what we're doing and why we're doing it. I wish I'd taken more public speaking classes in school.

4. **Are there many job opportunities in your profession? In what specific areas?**

   Speaking broadly, foresters go into three sectors: government or research forestry, where your main objective is research; a private timber broker; or foresters who work for a sawmill as an industrial forester. This is a small profession -- you may need to relocate — with an aging workforce. I graduated in '02 and am a member of the Society of American Foresters. Until recently, I was one of the youngest guys there. So I think in the next five-to-10 years, it could be a sector where there is a lot of turnover.

5. **How do you see your profession changing in the next five years? What role will technology play in those changes, and what skills will be required?**

   GPS and GIS (geographic information systems) are getting bigger. You can draw pretty accurate maps with this technology.

   Also, we're seeing more regulation. Counties and townships are putting in ordinances that make it harder to work. Plus, competing products are being made of materials other than wood; for example, composite decking has some wood product but it's mainly plastic and chemicals. In the future, a forester will need to work harder and negotiate more regulations.

6. **What do you enjoy most about your job? What do you enjoy least about your job?**

   I like being independent; I make my own schedule. I like being outside.

   What I like least is that you're not going to click with everyone you talk with. Sometimes I put a lot of work into a job and don't see a return. Sometimes it's hard not to take that personally.

7. **Can you suggest a valuable "try this" for students considering a career in your profession?**

   Find a state property where you can hike, get off the trail and hike to the top of the mountain around rocks and downed trees. That will give you some idea of what you need to do physically.

   Federal and state agencies offer seasonal work that will give you an idea of the skills you need to learn.

   See if you can shadow a forester.

SELECTED SCHOOLS

Many state colleges and universities have bachelor's degree programs related to forestry and conservation. The student may also gain an initial grounding in the field at an agricultural, technical, or community college. For advanced positions, a master's or doctoral degree is usually obtained. Below are listed some of the more prominent schools in this field.

Clemson University
109 Drive
Clemson, SC 29634
864.656.3311
www.clemson.edu

Colorado State University
1062 Campus Delivery
Fort Collins, CO 80523
970.491.6909
www.colostate.edu

Michigan State University
220 Trowbridge Road
East Lansing, MI 48824
517.355.1855
www.msu.edu

North Carolina State University
203 Peele Hall, Box 7103
Raleigh, NC 27695
919.515.2434
www.ncsu.edu

Oregon State University
104 Kerr Admin Building
Corvallis, OR 97331
541.734.4411
oregonstate.edu

Pennsylvania State University
University Park
State College, PA 16801
814.865.4700
www.psu.edu

University of Georgia
210 South Jackson Street
Athens, GA 30602
706.542.8776
www.nau.edu

University of Washington
4000 15th Avenue NE
Box 352100
Seattle, WA 98195
206.543.2730
www.cfr.washington.edu

University of Wisconsin
702 W. Johnson Street
Suite 1101
Madison, WI 53715
608.262.3961
www.wisc.edu

Virginia Tech
925 Price Forks Road
Blacksburg, VA 24061
540.231.3242
www.vt.edu

MORE INFORMATION

American Forests
P.O. Box 2000
Washington, DC 20013
202.737.1944
www.americanforests.org

Forest Guild
2019 Galisto Street
Suite N7
Santa Fe, NM 87505
505.983.8992
www.forestguild.org

National Association of State Foresters
Hall of the States
444 N. Capitol Street NW
Suite 540
Washington, DC 20001
202.624.5415
www.stateforesters.org

Society for Range Management
10030 West 27th Avenue
Wheat Ridge, CO 80215-6601
303.986.3309
www.rangelands.org

Society of American Foresters Career Information Department
5400 Grosvenor Lane
Bethesda, MD 20814-2198
301.897.8720
www.safnet.org

Soil and Water Conservation Society
945 SW Ankeny Road
Ankeny, IA 50021
515.289.2331
www.swcs.org

USDA Forest Service
1400 Independence Avenue SW
Washington, DC 20250-0002
800.832.1355
www.fs.fed.us

USDA Natural Resources
Conservation Service
P.O. Box 2890
Washington, DC 20013
202.720.3210
www.nrcs.usda.gov/programs

Michael Auerbach/Editor

Forestry Worker

Snapshot

Career Cluster: Agriculture; Environment & Conservation
Interests: Environment, working outdoors, physical labor
Earnings (Yearly Average): $28,860
Employment & Outlook: Slower Than Average Growth Expected

OVERVIEW

Sphere of Work

Forestry workers help maintain, grow, and protect forest and woodland areas. They plant seedlings, remove diseased trees, as well as tally, mark, and examine trees. Some maintain national and state park facilities or work at tree farms where they keep plants healthy by controlling growth, weeds, and insect, animal, or invasive plant infestation. Forestry workers may also be responsible for some equipment maintenance and repairs. .

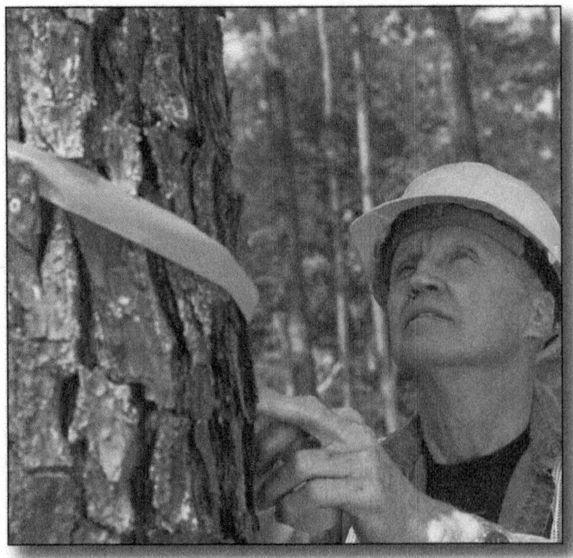

Work Environment

Forestry workers are outdoors most of the time, in all types of weather. The work is physically demanding and can require walking long distances or being in isolated areas.

Profile

Working Conditions: Work Outdoors
Physical Strength: Medium to Heavy Work
Education Needs: On-The-Job Training, High School Diploma with Technical Education, Junior/Technical/Community College
Licensure/Certification: Usually Not Required
Physical Abilities Not Required: N/A
Opportunities For Experience: Volunteer Work, Part Time Work
Holland Interest Score*: RES

* See Appendix A

Occupation Interest

Individuals attracted to forestry work are comfortable spending long hours outdoors and enjoy physical labor. They tend to be practical and decisive individuals who become adept at a range of skills, from helping to harvest trees for raw materials to planting seedlings for conservation as part of a reforestation crew. The variety of daily tasks can be one of the most satisfying parts of forestry work. In addition, forestry workers must be familiar with the wildlife in their environment. They should show good judgment and be motivated to learn about sustainable forestry practices.

It is useful for self-employed forestry workers to have business and managerial skills.

A Day in the Life—Duties and Responsibilities

Forestry workers help manage forests. The typical daily tasks of a forestry worker include removing fallen trees and branches that may have come down as a result of a storm or other disturbance, or cutting trees to clear forest roads and facilities. Forestry workers plant seedlings for new growth, control soil erosion, and use power and hand saws to remove dead or diseased trees. They are also responsible for protecting environments from invasive species of insects, animals, or plants, which may require the application of herbicides.

Some forestry workers are employed by state and federal government agencies and help maintain campsites, forest trails, roads, campsite restrooms, and kitchen facilities in recreational areas. Those who work for private businesses sometimes help with controlled burning, which helps prevent the spread of wild fires. Forestry workers also set boundary lines and measure, mark, and count trees.

Tree farms also hire forestry workers to cultivate and harvest specialty plants, such as ornamental or Christmas trees. At tree farms, foresters are responsible for shaping Christmas trees, promoting foliage growth in some areas and pruning in others. They also spend time controlling the growth of weeds and undergrowth.

Duties and Responsibilities

- **Measuring and marking trees**
- **Collecting and recording data on tree conditions**
- **Working at seasonal tasks such as planting trees, spraying and patrolling park and forest areas**
- **Working with foresters and wildlife specialists on habitat projects**
- **Leading crews to contain or put out forest fires**
- **Assisting in the enforcement of recreation rules**
- **Answering questions on park or forest regulations and facilities, numbers and types of wildlife and tree species**
- **Preventing forest fires**

OCCUPATION SPECIALTIES

Forester Aides

Forester Aides may perform any of the forestry technician duties in addition to conducting research studies and investigating problems of growth, improvement, productivity and management of forest resources.

WORK ENVIRONMENT

Physical Environment

Forestry workers work outdoors in all kinds of weather. They must be in good health and able to handle heavy lifting. Forestry work may be seasonal, and weather conditions vary. Forestry workers may have to trek through dense foliage and deal with falling trees and branches, insects, wildlife, harmful plants, and high noise levels from saws and machinery. Forestry workers must follow proper safety measures by wearing hard hats, safety eye glasses, proper clothing, boots, and ear protection.

Relevant Skills and Abilities

Communication Skills
- Speaking effectively

Interpersonal/Social Skills
- Being able to remain calm
- Cooperating with others
- Working as a member of a team

Organization & Management Skills
- Coordinating tasks
- Following instructions
- Handling challenging situations
- Making decisions
- Managing people/groups
- Paying attention to and handling details
- Performing duties which change frequently

Research & Planning Skills
- Developing evaluation strategies
- Using logical reasoning

Technical Skills
- Performing technical work
- Working with your hands

Human Environment

A forestry worker's human environment varies. Sometimes forestry workers work in teams, where communication, good judgment, and teamwork are essential. In isolated areas or when working alone, the ability to work independently is required.

Technological Environment

Forestry workers work with hand tools and machinery used for reforestation and timber cutting. Herbicides, pesticides, and controlled burns are also methods used to manage forests. All of these tools and techniques present potential hazards and will require training.

EDUCATION, TRAINING, AND ADVANCEMENT

High School/Secondary

A high school diploma is usually required in order to become a forestry worker. Expertise comes with on-the-job training, which generally takes place in the field. Students can become apprentices in a variety of training programs, do volunteer work through forest conservation groups, do seasonal or part-time work in state parks or national forests, and find opportunities through state- or nationally-funded programs—for example the Youth Conservation Corps (YCC).

Suggested High School Subjects

- Agricultural Education
- Algebra
- Applied Biology/Chemistry
- Applied Math
- Biology
- Chemistry
- College Preparatory
- English
- Forestry
- Science

Famous First

The first book on forestry in the United States was Franklin B. Hough's 1882 *Elements of Forestry.* It was "Designed to afford information concerning the planting and care of forest trees for ornament or profit and giving suggestions upon the creation and care of woodlands with the view of securing the greatest benefit for the longest time, particularly adapted to the wants and conditions of the United States."

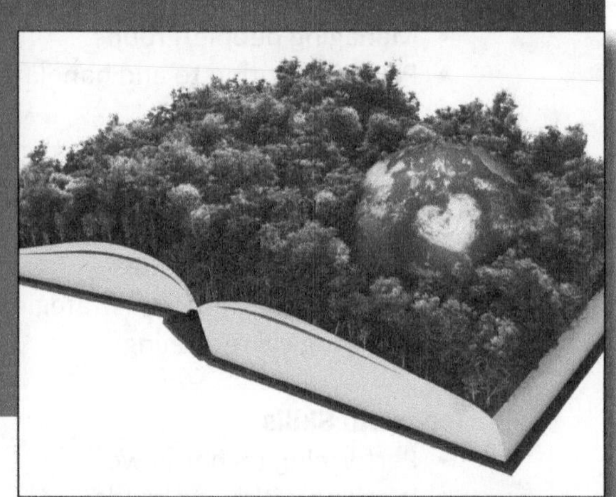

Postsecondary

Students with a high school diploma can study in two-year vocational schools for associate's degrees in courses such as forest management, forest harvesting, and conservation. Opportunities to participate in extracurricular experiences that offer forestry and logging activities may be available through educational institutions or state agencies.

Forestry workers who wish to advance in their profession and become foresters should combine on-the-job experience with a bachelor's degree in forestry or a similar field.

Related College Majors

- Forest Harvesting & Production Technology
- Forestry
- Natural Resources Conservation
- Natural Resources Law Enforcement & Protection
- Natural Resources Management & Policy
- Wildlife & Wildlands Management

Adult Job Seekers

Adults seeking forestry work do not necessarily need a college degree, but employers do prefer candidates with prior forestry work experience. Depending on the individual's area of interest in forestry, there are different ways to find that experience. State and national parks often have opportunities for entry-level forestry workers. In other areas, where forestry workers are cutting timber and carrying out conservation techniques, there may be opportunities for apprenticeships. Some businesses offer logging and forestry training programs that teach the use of machinery and equipment.

Professional Certification and Licensure

Although there are no certification requirements, forestry workers employed by government agencies usually must pass the civil service exam. Certification programs have been developed by a number of organizations. These certifications have to do with labels used in the wood products market that indicate sustainable practices. With any volunteer certification process, it is in the candidate's best interest to consult credible professional associations within the field and follow professional debate as to the relevancy and value of any certification program.

Additional Requirements

Prospective forestry workers should be strong, with the physical ability to lift and manipulate large items such as logs, trees, branches, saws, and other machinery used in forestry tasks. They should also possess a familiarity with plant, animal, and insect species that may pose a threat to environments and habitats.

Fun Facts

The slogan "Only you can prevent forest fires," was created by the Ad Council in 1947. In 2001, after an outbreak of wildfires, the slogan was updated to "Only you can prevent wildfires." The words are uttered by Smokey Bear, who is often referred to–incorrectly–as Smokey the Bear.

Source: www.adcouncil.org/Our-Campaigns/The-Classics/Wildfire-Prevention and smokeybear.com

Lightning sets about 10,000 forest fires every year in the United States, which start when lightening strikes dry grass, shrubs, leaves, branches, or brush. These fires cause upward of $100 million in losses.

Source: http://www.science-facts.com/14/destruction-caused-by-lightning/

EARNINGS AND ADVANCEMENT

Earnings depend on the geographic location of the employer, and the employee's experience, level of responsibility and type of work performed. Workers in Alaska and the Northwest earned much more than those in the South, where the cost of living is generally lower.

Forestry workers had mean annual earnings of $28,860 in 2013. The lowest ten percent earned less than $17,000, and the highest ten percent earned more than $45,000. Forestry workers may be required to purchase some or all of their supplies, such as uniforms or protective clothing.

Forestry workers may receive paid vacations, holidays, and sick days; life and health insurance; and retirement benefits. These are usually paid by the employer.

States with the Highest Employment Level in This Occupation

State	Employment[(1)]	Employment per thousand jobs	Hourly mean wage
California	1,700	0.12	$10.00
Washington	560	0.20	$12.58
South Dakota	430	1.06	$12.89
Georgia	390	0.10	$13.55
Louisiana	280	0.15	$15.54

Source: Bureau of Labor Statistics

EMPLOYMENT AND OUTLOOK

Forestry workers held about 10,000 jobs nationally in 2013. Most forestry workers work for the government, usually at the state and local levels. Employment is expected to grow slower than the average for all occupations through the year 2022, which means employment is projected to increase 2 percent to 6 percent. As more and more land in this country is designated for the protection of natural resources and wildlife habitats, demand for forestry workers will increase. In addition, job openings will result from replacing workers who leave the field or retire.

Employment Trend, Projected 2012–22

Total, All Occupations: 11%

Forestry Workers: 4%

Farming, Fishing, and Forestry Occupations (All): 11%

Note: "All Occupations" includes all occupations in the U.S. Economy. Source: U.S. Bureau of Labor Statistics, Employment Projections Program.

Related Occupations

- Farm Worker
- Forester & Conservation Scientist
- Lumber Production Worker
- Nursery Worker
- Park Ranger

Conversation With . . .
CHRISTOPHER R. KING

Forestry Technician, 5 years
USFS Southern Research Station

1. What was your individual career path in terms of education/training, entry-level job, or other significant opportunity?

I started in liberal arts -- philosophy and sociology -- and sort of burned out. I was into the outdoors, took a big jump, and enrolled in the University of Tennessee Forestry Program. It was a perfect fit. In my junior year I got a forestry technician job designed for forestry students and I have continued as a technician for the USDA Forest Service's Forest Inventory and Analysis (FIA) program at the Southern Research Station in Knoxville, TN. I have a B.S. in Forestry and I have nearly completed my M.S. degree in Forestry at U.T.

2. What are the most important skills and/or qualities for someone in your profession?

Forestry technician jobs can focus on anything from wildfire, silviculture, or even grassland management to a vast array of research efforts in both field and office. Typically, any accredited four-year forestry degree will prepare you for work as a technician. I work in a research position in an office that collects research data to get an idea of where the resources are and keep track of the diversity we have in our region. My work takes place mostly in the office with occasional assistance to field crews. It requires a solid understanding of Geographic Information Systems (GIS) and general forestry concepts (dendrology, silviculture, ecology, mensuration). One must be able to communicate and collaborate well with coworkers and the public. I'm also red-card certified, which means the Forestry Service can send me out to fight fires. You want to be in decent physical condition to work as a forestry technician.

3. What do you wish you had known going into this profession?

A better understanding of the challenges in the job market. Try to specialize your education so you are qualified for the position you want. For example, if your passion is silviculture (the agriculture of trees), take advanced courses in that subject and get involved with any related research efforts around campus. It also would have been useful to have better understood the federal and state agency structure and politics, as well as research funding. Also, GIS was a weak point in my education but I was able to take some extra coursework and that helped. Everybody from private industry to agencies needs somebody who can do GIS.

4. Are there many job opportunities in your profession? In what specific areas?

I've always heard that forestry jobs are hard to find but they are out there. A lot of people are retiring, plus there are not a huge number of college graduates with forestry majors. It is challenging to find what you want. You may need to move to get your foot in the door. It also helps to start with a temporary position.

5. How do you see your profession changing in the next five years, what role will technology play in those changes, and what skills will be required?

I've seen many paper-based methods convert to digital methods. Field crews collect data in the woods using data recorder devices. Tasks in natural resources research, such as mapping, land cover analysis, and data analysis, are done at a computer now. Useful skills in the future will be GIS, programming (languages and methods), model building, statistical analysis, and publishing. Another important skill set is interpersonal communication. There is a huge increase in collaboration with the public, other agencies, or interest groups.

6. What do you enjoy most about your job? What do you enjoy least about your job?

I enjoy communicating research findings to the public, as well as educating people about natural resources use and conservation. Being focused on new projects and ideas always seems to make me feel satisfied in my position. I also enjoy the community that exists in my field, and being able to have a large variety of professional friendships and connections.

Sometimes, as with many jobs, tasks must be done that are monotonous. That is the least enjoyable part of my position. Different types of forestry technician jobs may have more or less of this type of work. For example, I do a lot of filing; we have archives that must be constantly organized.

7. Can you suggest a valuable "try this" for students considering a career in your profession?

Network! The Society of American Foresters is a terrific group to be involved in. Join your university's Forestry Club or the equivalent. Get to know the faculty in your departments and talk to your professors. Don't hesitate to reach out to professionals in your field for advice on jobs, research, etc. Attend conferences and special training events whenever you can. This can boost your résumé and help build a professional network, which can be instrumental in finding a job. Participation in these extracurricular activities can also be very enjoyable. I find they often re-invigorate my interests and remind me why I entered the field.

SELECTED SCHOOLS

Many agricultural, technical, and community colleges offer programs related to forestry. Interested students are advised to consult with their school guidance counselor or to research area postsecondary schools and training programs. For those interested in pursuing a bachelor's degree, a state land-grant college is probably the best place to start. See also the list of schools in the chapter "Forester and Conservation Scientist" in the present volume..

MORE INFORMATION

American Forest and Paper Association
1111 19th Street NW, Suite 800
Washington, DC 20036
800.878.8878
info@afandpa.org
www.afandpa.org

American Forests
P.O. Box 2000
Washington, DC 20013
202.737.1944
www.americanforests.org

American Loggers Council
P.O. Box 966
Hemphill, TX 75948
409.625.0206
www.americanloggers.org/

Forest Resources Association
600 Jefferson Plaza, Suite 350
Rockville, MD 20852
301.838.9385
www.forestresources.org

Northeastern Loggers Association
3311 State Route 28
P.O. Box 69
Old Forge, NY 13420
800.318.7561
www.northernlogger.com

Society of American Foresters
Career Information Department
5400 Grosvenor Lane
Bethesda, MD 20814-2198
301.897.8720
safweb@safnet.org
www.safnet.org

USDA Forest Service
1400 Independence Avenue SW
Washington, DC 20250-0002
800.832.1355
www.fs.fed.us

Susan Williams/Editor

Geographer

Snapshot

Career Cluster: Environment & Conservation; Science & Technology
Interests: Research, data analysis, map making, environment
Earnings (Yearly Average): $75,070
Employment & Outlook: Faster Than Average Growth Expected

OVERVIEW

Sphere of Work

Geographers are social scientists who study the earth's climate, topography, features, and natural phenomena, as well as the interaction between humans and their environment and the effects of that interaction on both people and places. Geographers contribute to a better understanding of natural resources, wildlife, climate, and vegetation. They help provide clues about how diseases spread, how public policy impacts certain areas, and how public services may be more effectively distributed within a given geographic area.

Work Environment

Geographers work in government agencies, universities and colleges, and private corporations and consulting firms. These settings are clean, pleasant, and highly organized. Geographers also work in the field, surveying mountain ranges, forest ecosystems, and animal habitats. In this arena, geographers may be required to travel great distances, cross or fly over remote and rugged terrain, and work in varying weather conditions. Other geographers work in cities and neighborhoods, among certain social and economic groups. Geographers usually work forty-hour weeks, although they may work erratic hours due to travel, evening meetings, and individual research.

Profile

Working Conditions: Work both Indoors and Outdoors
Physical Strength: Light Work
Education Needs: Bachelor's Degree, Master's Degree, Doctoral Degree
Licensure/Certification: Recommended
Physical Abilities Not Required: No Heavy Labor
Opportunities For Experience: Internship, Part-Time Work
Holland Interest Score*: IRE

* See Appendix A

Occupation Interest

Geographic research helps medical professionals deliver care to certain neighborhoods, political leaders to gauge the effectiveness of public policy among individual demographics, and residents to consider the effects of development on natural habitats. They help warn people about climate shifts, changes in animal populations, and the spread of disease. Geographers who work in academic settings frequently work flexible hours, which enables them to teach students while conducting their own individual pursuits. They frequently travel to and experience new cultures and natural sites.

A Day in the Life—Duties and Responsibilities

Physical geographers study the physical features and trends of a particular region, such as glaciers (glaciology) or oceans (oceanography), while cultural geographers study the particular economic, social, and political characteristics of people living within a certain area. Other areas of study, including urban and transportation geography, medical geography, and economic geography, are found within cultural geography.

Geographers design and create maps of certain physical and cultural groupings, using data obtained through surveys, aerial and satellite photographs, field observations, and other methods. They develop, utilize, and maintain Geographical Information System (GIS) hardware (including video cameras, plotters, and printers) and software. They also search existing GIS databases to compile their findings. They use this data to write reports and present their findings to clients and the public.

The work performed by geographers depends on their particular area of expertise. As consultants, they provide information to private landowners and government officials about land and natural resource management, sustainable development practices, environmental risks, cultural and ethnic population shifts, and urban development.

Geographers also work with cartographers to modify maps, geographic charts, and diagrams (used for military as well as public purposes) using GIS, global positioning systems (GPS), and related software. Furthermore, geographers who work with private businesses and corporations frequently perform market analyses, recommend sites for production facilities, and locate new markets for goods and services. Additionally, geographers work with climatologists and weather services to track weather patterns, climate changes, and other issues related to the natural environment.

Many geographers are also educators, teaching university courses and conducting guest lectures, seminars, and conferences. Some geographers work with emergency medical professionals, such as epidemiologists, to track the spread of disease outbreaks and other health issues.

Duties and Responsibilities

- **Studying the physical and climatic aspects of an area or region**
- **Studying the human activities within an area, such as ethnic distribution and political organization**
- **Acting as an advisor or consultant to governments and international organizations**
- **Constructing and interpreting maps, graphs, and diagrams**
- **Writing reports and research papers**
- **Teaching classes in colleges and universities**

OCCUPATION SPECIALTIES

Physical Geographers

Physical Geographers study the origin, nature, and distribution of land and surface features of the earth including climate, soils, and plant and animal life. They survey the physical characteristics of a region by conducting studies of its features. They may conduct environmental studies and prepare environmental impact reports.

Human Geographers

Human Geographers analyze the organization of human activity and its relationships with the physical environment. Human geographers often combine issues from other disciplines into their research, which may include economic, social, or political topics. In their research, some human geographers rely primarily on statistical techniques, and others rely on non-statistical sources, such as field observations and interviews.

WORK ENVIRONMENT

Physical Environment

Geographers spend a significant part of their time working in offices, where they analyze photographs, collate survey results and data, write reports, and conduct meetings. These environments are clean, bright, and organized. Geographers also conduct fieldwork in urban, rural, and unpopulated locations, which may present safety hazards and unpleasant weather conditions or may be difficult to reach.

Human Environment

Depending upon geographers' areas of specialty, they may interact with government officials, business executives, marketing professionals, university students and professors, sociologists, climatologists, environmental scientists, political scientists, and epidemiologists.

Relevant Skills and Abilities

Analytical Skills
- Collecting and analyzing data

Communication Skills
- Speaking and writing effectively

Interpersonal/Social Skills
- Being flexible

Organization & Management Skills
- Coordinating tasks
- Managing people/groups

Research & Planning Skills
- Analyzing a situation or problem
- Developing evaluation strategies
- Using logical reasoning

Technical Skills
- Performing scientific and technical work

Technological Environment

In the field, geographers use various sampling and detection devices, including soil core sample apparatuses, wind direction sensors, aerial photographic equipment, and GIS and GPS systems. In their offices, geographers use a wide range of computer systems, such as map creation programs, analytical and scientific software, graphic and photo imaging systems, and databases and office suites.

EDUCATION, TRAINING, AND ADVANCEMENT

High School/Secondary

High school students should take classes such as history, social studies, government and economics. They must also take mathematics courses, including geometry, algebra, and statistics. Additionally, computer science classes are essential, as are courses that build writing and communication skills, such as English.

Suggested High School Subjects
- Algebra
- Applied Math

- College Preparatory
- Computer Science
- Drafting
- Earth Science
- Economics
- English
- Geography
- Geometry
- Government
- History
- Photography
- Social Studies
- Statistics

Famous First

The first and only Geographer of the United States was Thomas Hutchins, appointed in 1785. Hutchins was a military cartographer from New Jersey who served with the British Army before switching to the American side during the Revolution. He helped survey and map large tracts of the southern United States before becoming US Geographer General. His first and last assignment in that post was to map a section of the Northwest Territories.

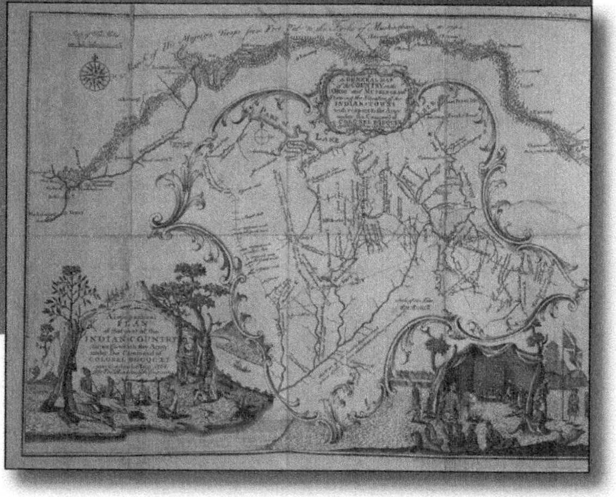

College/Postsecondary

Most employers, including the federal government, require that candidates have at least a bachelor's degree in geography. However, a master's degree in geography and/or a field of relevance to the geographer's area of specialty is preferred. Geographers who also teach courses at the university level, as well as those who seek senior-level positions, must have a doctorate.

Related College Majors

- Anthropology

- Earth Science
- Political Science
- Sociology
- Urban/Regional Planning

Adult Job Seekers

Qualified geographers may find open positions through university placement offices. They may also apply for open positions with the federal government by applying directly to agencies or through the federal government job listings website. Additionally, they can find jobs by joining and networking through professional geography organizations, such as the American Geographical Society and the National Geographic Society.

Professional Certification and Licensure

Geographers who apply for government jobs, particularly with the federal government, may be required to take and pass a civil service examination. Some professional associations provide voluntary certifications in GIS and other geography tools that can enhance a geographer's candidacy for an open position.

Additional Requirements

Geographers should be capable of analyzing complex issues and concepts, possess strong logical and mathematical skills, and have a natural interest in earth sciences and the study of people. They must demonstrate exceptional research and writing skills. Furthermore, geographers should have strong computer skills as well as an understanding of other aspects of the area in which they specialize, such as sociology and meteorology.

Fun Fact

The American Geographical Society was founded in 1851. Women were included as active members from its founding, since its constitution stated under "membership" that "any person of good standing and character may be admitted."

Source: www.amergeog.org

EARNINGS AND ADVANCEMENT

Earnings depend on the individual's experience, academic background and the geographic location of the employer. Mean annual earnings of geographers were $75,070 in 2013. The lowest ten percent earned less than $43,000, and the highest ten percent earned more than $105,000.

Geographers may receive paid vacations, holidays, and sick days; life and health insurance; and retirement benefits. These are usually paid by the employer.

Metropolitan Areas with the Highest Employment Level in This Occupation

Metropolitan area	Employment[1]	Employment per thousand jobs	Hourly mean wage
Chicago-Joliet-Naperville, IL	80	0.02	$43.97
Salt Lake City, UT	60	0.09	$25.54
Denver-Aurora-Broomfield, CO	50	0.04	$34.57
Austin-Round Rock-San Marcos, TX	40	0.05	$28.76
Portland-Vancouver-Hillsboro, OR-WA	40	0.04	$40.15
Sioux Falls, SD	40	0.27	$34.19

[1] Does not include self-employed. Source: Bureau of Labor Statistics

EMPLOYMENT AND OUTLOOK

Geographers held about 1,700 jobs nationally in 2012. Employment of geographers is expected to grow much faster than the average for all occupations through the year 2022, which means employment is projected to increase 29 percent or more. Geographers will have opportunities to utilize their skills to advise government, businesses, real-estate developers, utilities and telecommunications firms on where to build new roads, buildings, power plants, and cable lines. Geographers also will advise on environmental matters, such as where to build a landfill or preserve wetland habitats. As the use of GIS technology expands, geographers will find numerous job opportunities applying GIS technology in non-traditional areas, such as emergency assistance, where GIS can track locations of ambulances, police and fire rescue units and their proximity to the emergency. GIS technology will also be utilized in areas of growing importance, such as homeland security and defense.

Employment Trend, Projected 2012–22

Geographers: 29%

Social Scientists (All): 11%

Total, All Occupations: 11%

Note: "All Occupations" includes all occupations in the U.S. Economy. Source: U.S. Bureau of Labor Statistics, Employment Projections Program.

Related Occupations

- Anthropologist
- Geologist & Geophysicist
- Mining & Geological Engineer
- Oceanographer
- Sociologist

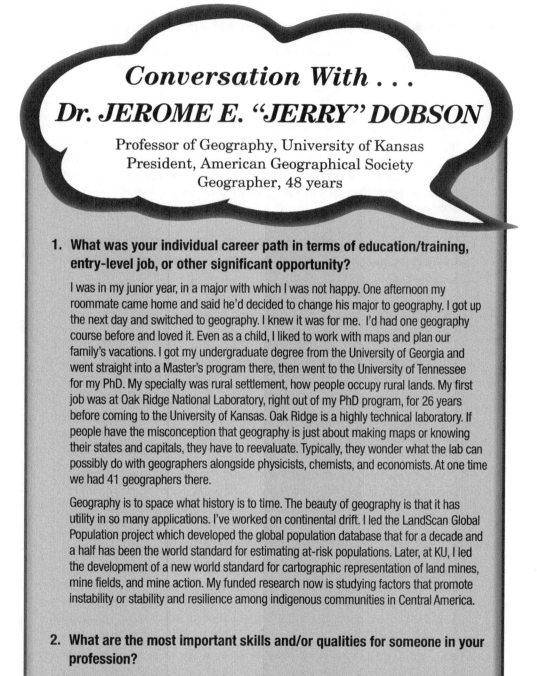

Conversation With . . .
Dr. JEROME E. "JERRY" DOBSON

Professor of Geography, University of Kansas
President, American Geographical Society
Geographer, 48 years

1. What was your individual career path in terms of education/training, entry-level job, or other significant opportunity?

I was in my junior year, in a major with which I was not happy. One afternoon my roommate came home and said he'd decided to change his major to geography. I got up the next day and switched to geography. I knew it was for me. I'd had one geography course before and loved it. Even as a child, I liked to work with maps and plan our family's vacations. I got my undergraduate degree from the University of Georgia and went straight into a Master's program there, then went to the University of Tennessee for my PhD. My specialty was rural settlement, how people occupy rural lands. My first job was at Oak Ridge National Laboratory, right out of my PhD program, for 26 years before coming to the University of Kansas. Oak Ridge is a highly technical laboratory. If people have the misconception that geography is just about making maps or knowing their states and capitals, they have to reevaluate. Typically, they wonder what the lab can possibly do with geographers alongside physicists, chemists, and economists. At one time we had 41 geographers there.

Geography is to space what history is to time. The beauty of geography is that it has utility in so many applications. I've worked on continental drift. I led the LandScan Global Population project which developed the global population database that for a decade and a half has been the world standard for estimating at-risk populations. Later, at KU, I led the development of a new world standard for cartographic representation of land mines, mine fields, and mine action. My funded research now is studying factors that promote instability or stability and resilience among indigenous communities in Central America.

2. What are the most important skills and/or qualities for someone in your profession?

Think spatially. Be able to analyze patterns and connections and understand how everything flows and interacts. If a person likes maps, he or she likely will have those other skills; the map is not the skill, the skill is understanding what the map is showing.

3. What do you wish you had known going into this profession?

I wish I had taken more computer science early in my career. GIS is the marriage of computer science and geography. I have heard people in computer science say it is easier to train a geographer in computer science than vice versa.

4. Are there many job opportunities in your profession? In what specific areas?

Geography has one of the highest average salaries and lowest unemployment rates and is one of the fastest-growing job-creating industries. Whatever you do, whether it's human geography or physical geography, make sure you have GIS. That's what will get you the job.

5. How do you see your profession changing in the next five years, what role will technology play in those changes, and what skills will be required?

The biggest change we're seeing in geography is a shift from commercial GIS to more friendly and cheaper "popular geographics." It's booming.

6. What do you enjoy most about your job? What do you enjoy least about your job?

I enjoy travel, anywhere in the world. I tend to go places that are a little more on the edge, such as Honduras, Eritrea, and the Balkans. Liberia was a failed state when I spent five weeks there in 1981. Now it's in a health crisis, but I would go back in a heartbeat.

Also, there are many circumstances in which I get to meet famous, accomplished people through the America Geographical Society's Flyer's and Explorer's Globe. We've had it since the 1920s, and it was signed by almost every famous explorer and record-breaking aviator of the 20th Century. Since 2000, I have presided over half a dozen ceremonies when, for instance, Neil Armstrong -- the first person on the Moon -- and Valentina Tereshkova -- the first woman in space -- signed. In 2012, my wife and were I invited to the annual meeting of the Board of Trustees of the Russian Geographic Society with Vladimir Putin presiding. Also present were the presidents of BP and BP Russia, chancellors of universities and heads of national academies. I was there because geography, in general, is appreciated far more in other countries than it is in the U.S. My AGS counterpart in Russia? His day job is Secretary of Defense.

What I like least is America's great folly of rejecting geography. I'm talking about the education and academic system. Universities have been killing off geography departments regularly since 1948. Or, they rename departments so they are no longer called geography. Or they add something like "geography and atmospheric science" which implies that the earth's atmosphere is not part of the earth's geography. Geography is the most integrated of all disciplines. A 2012 survey polled the U. S. public on their knowledge of and values toward geography and found that they love it.

7. Can you suggest a valuable "try this" for students considering a career in your profession?

If you want to experiment, see if you can create something that's worth posting on mapstory.com.

SELECTED SCHOOLS

Most colleges and universities have bachelor's degree programs in geography or subjects related to geography. The student may also gain an initial grounding in the field at an agricultural, technical, or community college. For advanced positions, a doctoral degree is commonly obtained. Below are listed some of the more prominent graduate schools in this field.

Arizona State University
School of Geographical Sciences
Coor Hall, 5th Floor
PO Box 875302
Tempe, AZ 85287
480.965.7533
geoplan.asu.edu

Boston University
Earth and Environment
685 Commonwealth Avenue
Boston, MA 02215
617.353.2525
www.bu.edu/earth

Clark University
Department of Geography
Jefferson Academic Center
Room 210
950 Main Street
Worcester, MA 01610
508.793.7324
www.clark.edu

Ohio State University
Department of Geography
1036 Derby Hall
154 North Oval Mall
Columbus, OH 43210
614.292.2514
www.geography.ohio-state.edu

Penn State University
Department of Geography
302 Walker Building
University Park, PA 16802
814.865.3433
www.geog.psu.edu

University of California, Santa Barbara
Department of Geography
1832 Ellison Hall
Santa Barbara, CA 93106
805.893.3663
www.geog.ucsb.edu

University of California, Los Angeles
Department of Geography
1255 Bunche Hall
Los Angeles, CA 90095
310.825.1070
www.geog.ucla.edu

University of Colorado, Boulder
Geography Department
Guggenheim 110, 260 UCB
Boulder, CO 80309
303.492.2631
geography.colorado.edu

University of Maryland, College Park
Department of Geography
2181 LeFrak Hall
College Park, MD 20740
301.405.4050
www.geog.umd.edu

University of Wisconsin, Madison
Department of Geography
550 North Park Street
Madison, WI 53706
www.geography.wisc.edu

MORE INFORMATION

American Geographical Society
32 Court Street, Suite 201
Brooklyn, NY 11201-4404
718.624.2212
www.amergeog.org

American Society for Photogrammetry and Remote Sensing
5410 Grosvenor Lane, Suite 210
Bethesda, MD 20814-2160
301.493.0290
www.asprs.org

Association of Collegiate Schools of Architecture
1710 16th Street, NW
Washington, DC 20009-3198
202.234.1450
www.aag.org

GeoPlace
P.O. Box 4290
Port Jervis, NY 12771
847.381.4621
www.geoplace.com

International Map Trade Association
23052-H Alicia Parkway
Suite 602
Mission Viejo, CA 92692
949.458.8200
www.imtamaps.org

National Council for Geographic Education
1145 Seventeenth Street, NW, Room 7620
Washington, DC 20036
202.857.7695
www.ncge.org

National Geographic Society
Geography Education
1145 17th Street, NW
Washington, DC 20036-4688
800.647.5463
www.nationalgeographic.com

Society of Woman Geographers
415 East Capitol Street SE
Washington, DC 20003
202.546.9228
www.iswg.org

Michael Auerbach/Editor

Geologist and Geophysicist

Snapshot

Career Cluster: Environment & Conservation; Natural Resources Development; Science & Technology
Interests: Seismology, hydrology, earth science
Earnings (Yearly Average): $108,420
Employment & Outlook: Faster Than Average Growth Expected

OVERVIEW

Sphere of Work

Geologists and geophysicists—also called geoscientists—study the composition, natural history, and other aspects of the earth. Geologists analyze rocks, plant and animal fossils, soil, minerals, and precious stones. They work for government agencies, oil and petroleum corporations, construction companies, universities, and museums. Geophysicists use physics, chemistry, mathematics, and geology to study the earth's magnetic fields, oceans, composition, seismic forces, and other elements. Most geologists and geophysicists

specialize in sub-fields such as mineralogy, hydrology, paleontology, seismology, and geochemistry. Geologists and geophysicists may be employed by organizations that intend to locate new oil deposits, predict earthquakes and volcano activity, or analyze environmental degradation.

Work Environment

Most geologists and geophysicists spend a significant portion of their time in the field conducting research. Fieldwork often involves traveling great distances into remote, rugged environments. Some geologists and geophysicists travel to foreign countries to pursue field research opportunities. Geologists and geophysicists must also work in all weather conditions. When performing field research, geologists and geophysicists typically work long and irregular hours. When not conducting fieldwork, geologists and geophysicists are at work in offices and laboratories, studying samples, writing papers, and analyzing and interpreting data.

Profile

Working Conditions: Work both Indoors and Outdoors
Physical Strength: Light Work, Medium Work
Education Needs: Master's Degree, Doctoral Degree
Licensure/Certification: Required
Physical Abilities Not Required: No Heavy Labor
Opportunities For Experience: Military Service, Part-Time Work
Holland Interest Score*: IRE, IRS

* See Appendix A

Occupation Interest

Geophysicists and geologists play an important role in protecting people from natural disasters – their work in seismology, hydrology, and other fields can help people avoid flood damage, prepare for seismic activity, or escape the impending eruption of a volcano. These geoscientists also help businesses, universities, and government agencies locate safe locations for construction, find dinosaur remains, and identify new areas in which to dig for oil, metals, or precious stones. The work performed by geophysicists and geologists changes frequently, and new research contributes to a growing body of knowledge about the history and characteristics of the earth. This occupation attracts inquisitive individuals with an interest in earth sciences and a desire to help others.

A Day in the Life—Duties and Responsibilities

The work performed by geologists and geophysicists varies based on their area of expertise. For example, some mineralogists prepare cross-sectional diagrams and geographic surveys of areas from which precious stones and metals may be located and extracted. Others set up and maintain seismic monitors in and around active volcanic areas. Some geophysicists and geologists spend a great deal of time in the laboratory, while others spend the vast majority of time in the field.

Most often, geologists and geophysicists plan and conduct geological surveys, field studies, and other technical analyses. They take small samples of stones, soil, and sediment, or use sensory equipment to sample magnetic waves, tremors, and subterranean water flows. Using these samples and data, geologists and geophysicists compile technical reports, academic papers, charts, maps, and policy recommendations. Geologists and geophysicists rely on computer modeling software, sensory data recorders, and other pieces of hardware and software to ensure that data is complete and organized. Scientists who study the compositions of rocks, minerals, and other resources must also conduct laboratory experiments using chemicals and other analytical tools.

Geologists and geophysicists employed by educational institutions may also need to write research proposals and grant applications in addition to performing their own research. Some geologists and geophysicists are also university professors, overseeing lectures and laboratory sections in addition to performing their own independent research.

Duties and Responsibilities

- **Examining rocks, minerals, and fossil remains**
- **Determining and explaining the sequence of the earth's development**
- **Interpreting research data**
- **Recommending specific studies or actions**
- **Preparing reports and maps**
- **Managing and cleaning up toxic waste**
- **Exploring for natural resources (e.g., oil and natural gas)**

OCCUPATION SPECIALTIES

Petroleum Geologists

Petroleum Geologists study the earth's surface and subsurface to locate gas and oil deposits and help develop extraction processes.

Mineralogists

Mineralogists examine, analyze and classify minerals, gems and precious stones and study their occurrence and chemistry.

Paleontologists

Paleontologists study the fossilized remains of plants and animals to determine the development of past life and history of the earth.

Hydrologists

Hydrologists study the distribution and development of water in land areas and evaluate findings in reference to such problems as flood and drought, soil and water conservation and inland irrigation.

Oceanographers

Oceanographers study the physical aspects of oceans such as currents and their interaction with the atmosphere. They also study the ocean floor and its properties.

Seismologists

Seismologists interpret data from seismographs and other instruments to locate earthquakes and earthquake faults. Stratigraphers Stratigraphers study the distribution and arrangement of sedimentary rock layers by examining their contents.

WORK ENVIRONMENT

Physical Environment

Geologists and geophysicists spend much of their time in the field. Fieldwork is typically conducted in remote areas and may require long travel across rugged terrain to reach. These geoscientists must work outdoors in a wide range of climates and weather conditions. When not in the field, geologists and geophysicists work in offices and laboratories, which are clean, comfortable work environments.

Relevant Skills and Abilities

Analytical Skills
- Collecting and analyzing data

Communication Skills
- Editing written information
- Writing concisely

Interpersonal/Social Skills
- Cooperating with others
- Working as a member of a team

Organization & Management Skills
- Paying attention to and handling details

Research & Planning Skills
- Analyzing information
- Creating ideas
- Gathering information
- Solving problems

Technical Skills
- Applying the technology to a task
- Performing scientific, mathematical and technical work
- Working with machines, tools or other objects

Work Environment Skills
- Working outdoors

Human Environment

Depending on their area of specialty, geologists and geophysicists work with a number of different individuals. Among the people with whom they interact are engineers, other geoscientists, laboratory assistants, environmental scientists, oceanographers, chemists, geographers, business executives, and government officials.

Technological Environment

Geologists and geophysicists need to use a wide range of technology to complete their work. Geological compasses, electromagnetic instruments, water flow measurement instruments, soil core sampling tools, sonar, magnetic field measurement devices, geographic information systems software (GIS), global positioning systems (GPS), map creation systems, and scientific databases are only some of the tools and technologies used by individuals in this field.

EDUCATION, TRAINING, AND ADVANCEMENT

High School/Secondary

High school students should study chemistry, physics, environmental science, and other physical science courses. Math classes, such as algebra, geometry, and trigonometry, are essential in geology and geophysics. History, computer science, geography, English, foreign language, and photography courses can also be highly useful for future geologists and geophysicists.

Suggested High School Subjects

- Algebra
- Applied Math
- Chemistry
- College Preparatory
- Earth Science
- English
- Geography
- Geometry
- History
- Photography
- Physical Science
- Science
- Trigonometry

Famous First

The first woman geologist was Florence Bascom (1862-1945). Bascom was also the first woman to earn a PhD at Johns Hopkins University. She was appointed assistant geologist to the US Geological Survey in 1896. In addition to this work, she founded the geology department at Bryn Mawr College in Pennsylvania and edited the magazine *American Geologist*.

College/Postsecondary

Geologists and geophysicists generally need a master's degree in geology, paleontology, mineralogy, or a related geosciences subject for entry-level jobs. Those who wish to pursue a senior-level research position or employment at an educational institution will need to obtain a doctorate.

Related College Majors

- Geography
- Geological Engineering
- Geophysical Engineering
- Geophysics & Seismology
- Ocean Engineering
- Oceanography

Adult Job Seekers

Qualified geologists and geophysicists may apply directly to postings by government agencies and private business organizations. University geology departments may also have access to entry-level openings. Geoscience journals frequently post openings in this field, and professional geology and geophysics societies and associations create opportunities for job searching and networking.

Professional Certification and Licensure

Some states require geologists and geophysicists who work for government agencies to obtain state licensure. An examination and proof of academic and professional experience are typically required for these licenses. Geologists and geophysicists may choose to pursue voluntary certification in specialized areas of expertise.

Additional Requirements

Geologists and geophysicists should be physically fit, as they frequently work in remote and rugged areas and sometimes carry heavy equipment and samples. They should also have familiarity with computer systems, GIS, GPS, and other technologies. Strong communication and interpersonal skills, writing abilities, and a sense of teamwork are important for geologists and geophysicists, as are an inquisitive nature and the desire to spend time working outdoors.

Fun Fact

Landslides occur in all of the 50 states in the U.S. Washington, Oregon, and California's mountainous and coastal regions are the major areas where landslides occur. Eastern U.S. mountain and hill regions are also susceptible.

Source: http://geology.com/usgs/landslides

EARNINGS AND ADVANCEMENT

Earnings depend on the individual's particular position, occupational specialty, amount of experience and level of education. Although the petroleum, mineral, and mining industries offer higher salaries, changes in oil and gas prices result in less job security in this area. According to the National Association of Colleges and Employers, starting annual salaries for graduates with a bachelor's degree in geology and related sciences averaged $47,243 in 2012.

Mean annual earnings of geologists and geophysicists were $108,420 in 2013. The lowest ten percent earned less than $49,000, and the highest ten percent earned more than $175,000.

Geologists and geophysicists may receive paid vacations, holidays, and sick days; life and health insurance; and retirement benefits. These are usually paid by the employer.

Metropolitan Areas with the Highest Employment Level in This Occupation

Metropolitan area	Employment[1]	Employment per thousand jobs	Hourly mean wage
Houston-Sugar Land-Baytown, TX	7,070	2.57	$80.54
Denver-Aurora-Broomfield, CO	1,830	1.43	$55.31
Seattle-Bellevue-Everett, WA	800	0.55	$40.17
Los Angeles-Long Beach-Glendale, CA	790	0.20	$47.98
Santa Ana-Anaheim-Irvine, CA	710	0.49	$43.56
Dallas-Plano-Irving, TX	700	0.33	$68.12
Sacramento--Arden-Arcade--Roseville, CA	670	0.80	$44.78
Oklahoma City, OK	660	1.11	$65.30
San Francisco-San Mateo-Redwood City, CA	620	0.59	$53.07
San Diego-Carlsbad-San Marcos, CA	600	0.46	$39.80

[1] Does not include self-employed. Source: Bureau of Labor Statistics

EMPLOYMENT AND OUTLOOK

Geologists and geophysicists held about 38,000 jobs nationally in 2012. In addition, many more individuals held geoscience faculty positions in colleges and universities. About one-fourth were employed in architectural and engineering firms, and another one-fourth worked for oil and gas extraction companies. State agencies, such as state geological surveys and state departments of conservation, and the Federal Government, mostly within the U.S. Department of the Interior for the U.S. Geological Survey (USGS) and within the U.S. Department of Defense, also employed significant groups of these workers.

Employment of geologists and geophysicists is expected to grow faster than the average for all occupations through the year 2022, which means employment is projected to increase 15 percent to 20 percent.

In the past, employment of geologists and other geoscientists has been cyclical and largely affected by the price of oil and gas. In recent years, a growing worldwide demand for oil and gas and new exploration and recovery techniques have returned some stability to the petroleum industry, with a few companies increasing their hiring of geoscientists. Geoscientists who speak a foreign language and who are willing to work abroad should enjoy the best opportunities.

Employment Trend, Projected 2012–22

Geologists and Geophysicists: 16%

Total, All Occupations: 11%

Scientific Occupations (All): 10%

Note: "All Occupations" includes all occupations in the U.S. Economy. Source: U.S. Bureau of Labor Statistics, Employment Projections Program.

Related Occupations

- Geographer
- Metallurgical/Materials Engineer
- Mining & Geological Engineer
- Oceanographer
- Petroleum Engineer
- Surveyor & Cartographer

Related Military Occupations

- Oceanographer

Conversation With . . .
RON PYLES

Geotechnical Engineer
Principal Engineer, 15 Years
VP, Kim Engineering, Baltimore MD

1. What was your individual career path in terms of education/training, entry-level job, or other significant opportunity?

I first was exposed to construction, and went to a junior college in Upstate New York for construction management. Then I decided to go on to a four-year school where I took civil engineering. While there, I found the geotechnical discipline, which offered more of a challenge, and took as many courses in that area as I could. I went on to work for three years to make sure I was interested in geotech, and then I earned a Master's in Civil Engineering specializing in geology.

Being a geotechnical engineer is not being a geologist per se. My field merges geology and engineering, and I mostly deal with foundations that a specific building requires, or pilings, groundwater problems, retaining walls, and that sort of thing.

Geotechnical engineering, in my opinion, is more creative than other engineering disciplines. When you think of the different formations associated with the massive earth movements that formed some of this geology, it takes a lot of force. You need to know geology. For example, if a region is limestone, which creates sinkholes, you need to know that and recommend specific techniques to build within and/or explore the karst terrain. If you're in an area where massive erosion occurred in past geologic times, and everything is consolidated because it's overburdened, then bearing capacities for foundations or walls can be much higher. Areas of Maryland, Washington, DC and Virginia, for example, have specific types of clays. These clays have specific characteristics, with high plasticity, and they may swell or shrink with moisture changes. You need to know that.

To specialize in geotechnical engineering, you should pursue advanced degrees. In geology that's not necessary, although it's always good to have an advanced degree.

2. What are the most important skills and/or qualities for someone in your profession?

Good writing skills are critical, because we produce reports that other engineers and developers read. You need good verbal communications skills with clients. It can be a high-risk business if you're not careful with your quality of work, so you need to be cognitive of legal aspects. Being organized is a plus. And, you need to be able to manage people if you are directing subordinates.

3. **What do you wish you had known going into this profession?**

In our work we deal with the substrate but once they build a foundation, they cover up the substrate. You can't stand there and appreciate your work.

4. **Are there many job opportunities in your profession? In what specific areas?**

There is very good demand relative to employment. Geotechical engineering is good, and geologists interfacing with the geotechical field have pretty good overall demand as well.

5. **How do you see your profession changing in the next five years, what role will technology play in those changes, and what skills will be required?**

Many of our theories have not changed a lot over the years. As technology has progressed we've obtained newer advanced equipment to assess the soils. An example would be the geophysical device that sends electrical waves to measure the resistance of those waves as they pass through the earth. We use that to find sinkholes and rock levels.

6. **What do you enjoy most about your job? What do you enjoy least about your job?**

Most enjoyable is exploring new areas from a geology viewpoint and soils aspect relative to proposed construction. Each site offers sort of a surprise because you don't know what's under the ground. You have the ability to assess and confirm the geology of the site, then look forward to the lab analysis.

This is a pretty demanding business, and there can be demanding turnaround. Unfortunately, sometimes clients can be hard to deal with.

7. **Can you suggest a valuable "try this" for students considering a career in your profession?**

Visit construction sites and field trips with a geologist or engineer. There are a lot of areas where you can get exposed to geologic formations; field trips are obviously an excellent way to get some exposure. Also, consider interning. Each summer my company has an intern program. We bring in 3-4 interns from colleges who are taking engineering and they can learn more about what we do.

SELECTED SCHOOLS

Most colleges and universities have bachelor's degree programs in geology or related subjects. The student may also gain an initial grounding in the field at an agricultural, technical, or community college. For advanced positions, a master's or doctoral degree is commonly obtained. Below are listed some of the more prominent graduate schools in this field.

California Institute of Technology
Division of Geological and Planetary Sciences
1200 East California Boulevard
Mail Code 170-25
Pasadena, CA 91125
626.395.6123
www.gps.caltech.edu

Massachusetts Institute of Technology
Earth, Atmospheric, and Planetary Sciences
77 Massachusetts Avenue
Cambridge, MA 02139
617.253.2127
eapsweb.mit.edu

Penn State University
Geosciences Department
503 Deike Building
University Park, PA 16802
814.867.4760
www.geosc.psu.edu

Stanford University
Geological and Environmental Sciences
450 Serra Mall, Building 320
Stanford, CA 94305
650.723.0847
pangea.stanford.edu/**departments/ges**

University of Arizona
Department of Geosciences
1040 E. 4th Street
Tucson, AZ 85721
520.621.6000
www.geo.arizona.edu

University of California, Berkeley
Earth and Planetary Science
307 McCone Hall
Berkeley, CA 94720
510.642.3993
eps.berkeley.edu

University of Colorado, Boulder
Department of Geological Sciences
UCB 359
Boulder, CO 80309
303.492.8141
www.colorado.edu/geolsci

University of Michigan, Ann Arbor
Earth and Environmental Sciences
2534 C.C. Little Building
1100 North University Avenue
Ann Arbor, MI 48109
734.763.1435
www.lsa.umich.edu/earth

University of Texas, Austin
Department of Geological Sciences
2275 Speedway Stop C9000
Austin, TX 78712
512.471.5172
www.jsg.utexas.edu/dgs

University of Wisconsin, Madison
Department of Geoscience
1215 West Dayton Street
Madison, WI 53706
608.262.8960
www.geoscience.wisc.edu

MORE INFORMATION

American Association of Petroleum Geologists
P.O. Box 979
Tulsa, OK 74101-0979
800.364.2274
www.aapg.org

American Geosciences Institute
4220 King Street
Alexandria, VA 22302-1502
703.379.2480
www.americangeosciences.org

Environmental and Engineering Geophysical Society
1720 South Bellaire, Suite 110
Denver, CO 80222-4303
303.531.7517
www.eegs.org

Geological Society of America
P.O. Box 9140
Boulder, CO 80301-9140
303.357.1000
www.geosociety.org

Paleontological Society
P.O. Box 9044
Boulder, CO 80301
855.357.1032
www.paleosoc.org

Seismological Society of America
201 Plaza Professional Building
El Cerrito, CA 94530
510.525.5474
www.seismosoc.org

Society of Exploration Geophysicists
P.O. Box 702740
Tulsa, OK 74170-2740
918.497.5500
www.seg.org

United States Geological Survey
12201 Sunrise Valley Drive
Reston, VA 20192
703.648.5953
www.usgs.gov

Michael Auerbach/Editor

Hazardous Materials Technician

Snapshot

Career Cluster: Environment & Conservation; Government & Public Administration; Public Safety & Security
Interests: Engineering, chemistry, environment, working with dangerous materials
Earnings (Yearly Average): $42,220
Employment & Outlook: Faster Than Average Growth Expected

OVERVIEW

Sphere of Work

FHazardous materials (hazmat) technicians work in the collection and disposal of toxic chemicals, nuclear waste, and similar substances. They work for government agencies and private waste management companies. Hazmat technicians design, organize, and implement policies and strategies for safe disposal and storage of chemical and nuclear waste from energy facilities, manufacturing plants, hospitals, and scientific institutions, among others. They are also called to spill sites to oversee quick and complete toxic waste cleanups when accidents occur. Most hazmat technicians

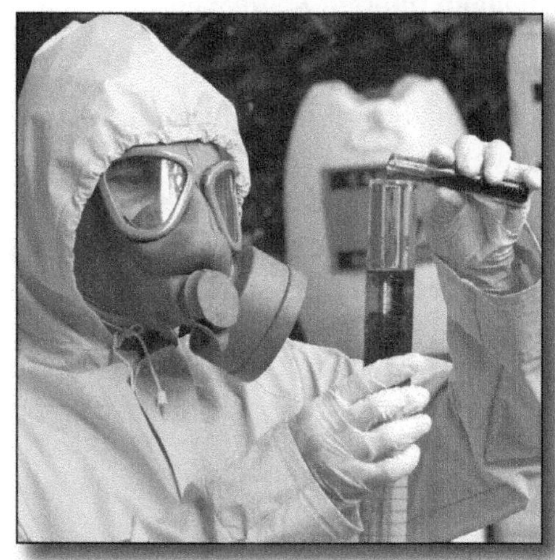

have training in specific areas, such as engineering, chemistry, or the basics of nuclear physics.

Work Environment

Many hazmat technicians work in government agency labs or offices, such as the Environmental Protection Agency, the Department of Energy, or the Department of Defense. Others are employed by waste management companies as consultants or workers, or by manufacturing corporations that need full-time waste management teams. All of these work environments are bound by strict protocols and policies designed to protect hazmat technicians and their teams, as well as the general public. However, there remains a consistent danger of exposure to nuclear or chemical waste during the course of the job, particularly when working at a landfill or spill site. Most hazmat technicians work a standard forty-hour week, although they are likely to be called upon to put in extra hours when spills occur.

Profile

Working Conditions: Work both Indoors and Outdoors
Physical Strength: Light to Medium Work
Education Needs: Junior/Technical/ Community College, Bachelor's Degree
Licensure/Certification: Required
Physical Abilities Not Required: N/A
Opportunities For Experience: Military Service, Part-Time Work
Holland Interest Score*: IRE

* See Appendix A

Occupation Interest

Hazmat technicians work to protect the general public from exposure to toxic substances. They also play an integral role in protecting the environment by ensuring the proper storage and disposal of these substances. In addition to routine cleaning, storage, and disposal of dangerous materials, hazmat technicians often help companies and agencies establish protocols that can prevent accidents. Hazmat technicians remain in high demand by the government and private corporations, which means that the field is a vibrant one, with frequent job opportunities and growth. Although the work is challenging, compensation for hazmat technicians is highly competitive, particularly in the private sector.

A Day in the Life—Duties and Responsibilities

The daily duties and responsibilities of hazmat technicians vary based on the field in which they specialize. For example, waste management engineers frequently design storage facilities and systems, while chemists may focus more on the effects of leaks on local drinking supplies and soil deposits.

Hazmat technicians generally focus on two types of waste materials. The first type is excess chemical material, which may include compounds used in experiments and manufacturing by-products. Hazmat technicians who specialize in this type of waste are responsible for formulating protocols for its proper on-site disposal, training waste technicians in proper storage practices, and scheduling transfers of the material to landfills and other facilities for safe disposal. When spills occur, waste technicians quickly initiate cleanup protocols, organizing teams and equipment and coordinating with the proper personnel to maintain public safety.

The second type of waste, nuclear fuel left over from power plants, medical facilities, or military activities, requires a similar approach. However, nuclear waste must be stored in specially designed storage facilities, which may be located great distances away from the site that produced them. Technicians must coordinate the collection, transfer, and storage of these containers.

Hazmat technicians must keep detailed logs and documentation of all relevant activities and oversee teams of waste technicians and other personnel. They also commonly provide consultation to company executives, government officials, and other parties on the dangers of the waste materials they create and the need for emergency protocols and proper storage and disposal practices.

Duties and Responsibilities

- **Setting up and following strict protocols regarding the handling of hazardous materials**
- **Working as part of a hazardous materials removal team**
- **Coordinating efforts with other departments and outside agencies**
- **Keeping abreast of new regulations regarding hazardous materials**
- **Analyzing cost and effectiveness of various methods of disposing of hazardous materials**
- **Recommending ways of collecting, moving, storing, and disposing of hazardous materials**

OCCUPATION SPECIALTIES

Asbestos and Lead Abatement Technicians

Asbestos and Lead Abatement Technicians remove asbestos and lead, respectively, from buildings and structures, particularly those that are being renovated or demolished. Most of this work is in older buildings that were originally built with asbestos insulation and lead-based paints—both of which are now banned.

Emergency and Disaster Response Technicians

Emergency and Disaster Response Technicians clean up hazardous materials in response to natural or man-made disasters and accidents, such as those involving trains, trucks, or other vehicles transporting hazardous materials. Timely and thorough cleanups help to control and prevent more damage to accident or disaster sites.

Nuclear Safety and Decontamination Technicians

Nuclear Safety and Decontamination Technicians measure, record, and report radiation levels; operate high-pressure cleaning equipment for decontamination; and package radioactive materials for removal or storage. When a facility is being closed or decommissioned (taken out of service), these technicians clean the facility and decontaminate it from radioactive materials.

Treatment and Disposal Technicians

Treatment and Disposal Technicians prepare and transport hazardous materials for treatment, storage, or disposal. To ensure proper treatment of materials, workers must follow U.S. Environmental Protection Agency (EPA) or U.S. Occupational Safety and Health Administration (OSHA) regulations. They move materials from contaminated sites to incinerators, landfills, or storage facilities. They also organize and track the location of items in these facilities.

WORK ENVIRONMENT

Physical Environment

Hazmat technicians work on site at manufacturing plants, medical and scientific centers, government agencies, and energy facilities. Each of these locations has strict rules and protocols for handling waste materials, although physical risks are involved despite careful practices.

Human Environment

Hazmat technicians interact with a wide range of individuals, including waste managers, business executives, engineers, scientists, government officials, public safety and law enforcement officers, truck drivers, and members of the general public. .

Relevant Skills and Abilities

Interpersonal/Social Skills
- Cooperating with others
- Working as a member of a team

Organization & Management Skills
- Organizing information or materials
- Paying attention to and handling details

Work Environment Skills
- Being focused on safety
- Working in hazardous situations

Technological Environment

Hazmat technicians work with a variety of equipment and technology, including respirators, gas masks and face shields, protective outerwear, Geiger counters, nuclear reactors and related equipment, ventilation systems, soil and water sampling equipment, and personal computers. They must also use a number of different computer programs, including scientific software, computer-aided design (CAD) software, databases, and basic office suites.

EDUCATION, TRAINING, AND ADVANCEMENT

High School/Secondary

High school students should study sciences such as chemistry, geology, biology, and environmental science. They should also hone their communications skills through English and similar classes. Mathematics courses help prepare individuals for the technical aspects of the job.

Suggested High School Subjects

- Applied Biology/Chemistry
- Biology
- Chemistry
- Earth Science
- English
- Health Science Technology
- Mathematics
- Physical Science

Famous First

The first deep underground storage facility for nuclear waste was the site at Carlsbad, New Mexico, opened in 1998. It can hold hundreds of thousands of barrels of radioactive plutonium and other materials for up to 10,000 years in its natural vaults dug into salt beds 2,150 feet below the desert surface.

College/Postsecondary

Hazmat technicians should have at least an associate's degree in a relevant field, such as waste management, pollution control, nuclear technology, or chemistry.. A bachelor's degree will enhance a job candidate's qualifications in a competitive marketplace.

Related College Majors

- Chemistry
- Civil Engineering
- Engineering
- Environmental & Pollution Control Technology
- Environmental Health
- Environmental Science/Studies
- Environmental/Environmental Health Engineering
- Geology

Adult Job Seekers

Qualified individuals may apply directly to business organizations, energy companies, consulting firms, and government agencies. Candidates may also join and network through professional trade associations such as the Air and Waste Management Association or the National Solid Wastes Management Association.

Professional Certification and Licensure

Hazmat technicians should obtain certification and federal licensure in the area in which they work. For example, individuals working in emergency and disaster response, hazardous materials storage, or waste treatment must obtain training through an Occupational Safety and Health Administration (OSHA)–approved program. Different states may also require additional certification to work in this field.

Additional Requirements

Hazmat technicians should have a strong attention to detail, excellent analytical skills, and exceptional mechanical abilities. They must be quick thinkers and strong leaders, able to organize teams and direct personnel to respond rapidly to spills and other issues. Furthermore, hazmat technicians must be able to communicate clearly in both writing and speech, often to people who may not be familiar with technical concepts.

Fun Fact

Think "hazardous waste," and a hulking industrial complex spewing chemicals may come to mind, but the EPA estimates that the average U.S. household generates more than 20 pounds of household hazardous waste a year. Examples include paint thinners, grease solvents, insecticides, antifreeze, and even nail polish.

Source: www.epa.gov/region9/waste/solid/house.html

EARNINGS AND ADVANCEMENT

Advancement is obtained through experience on the job and/or additional education in waste management. Mean annual earnings of hazmat technicians were $42,220 in 2013. The lowest ten percent earned less than $26,000, and the highest ten percent earned more than $66,000.

Hazmat technicians may receive paid vacations, holidays, and sick days; life and health insurance; and retirement benefits. These are usually paid by the employer.

Metropolitan Areas with the Highest Employment Level in This Occupation

Metropolitan area	Employment[1]	Employment per thousand jobs	Hourly mean wage
New York-White Plains-Wayne, NY-NJ	1,760	0.34	$31.00
Houston-Sugar Land-Baytown, TX	1,450	0.52	$14.72
Oakland-Fremont-Hayward, CA	1,160	1.16	$18.97
Chicago-Joliet-Naperville, IL	1,030	0.28	$22.37
Los Angeles-Long Beach-Glendale, CA	1,000	0.25	$22.31
Philadelphia, PA	830	0.45	$21.74
Cleveland-Elyria-Mentor, OH	770	0.76	$19.30
San Diego-Carlsbad-San Marcos, CA	660	0.51	$17.99
Atlanta-Sandy Springs-Marietta, GA	660	0.28	$17.88
Boston-Cambridge-Quincy, MA	660	0.37	$18.67

[1] Does not include self-employed. Source: Bureau of Labor Statistics

EMPLOYMENT AND OUTLOOK

Hazmat technicians held about 38,000 jobs nationally in 2012. Employment is expected to grow faster than the average for all occupations through the year 2022, which means employment is projected to increase 10 percent to 15 percent. Employment growth of hazmat technicians will stem from the numerous disposal and cleanup sites throughout the United States, and the expansion of regulatory and compliance programs in solid and hazardous waste disposal and water pollution. Federal, state and local governments employ hazmat technicians. Consulting firms also employ hazmat technicians to prepare environmental impact reports.

Employment Trend, Projected 2012–22

Hazmat Technicians: 14%

Other Construction and Related Occupations: 12%

Total, All Occupations: 11%

Note: "All Occupations" includes all occupations in the U.S. Economy. Source: U.S. Bureau of Labor Statistics, Employment Projections Program.

Related Occupations

- Biological Scientist
- Chemical Engineer
- Chemist
- Environmental Engineer
- Environmental Science Technician
- Geologist & Geophysicist
- Inspector & Compliance Officer
- Nuclear Quality Control Inspector
- Water & Wastewater Enginee

Related Military Occupations

- Environmental Health & Safety Officer
- Environmental Health & Safety Specialist

Conversation With . . .
WESLEY SEIGLER

Hazardous Waste Manager, 6 years
University of South Carolina, Columbia, SC

1. What was your individual career path in terms of education/training, entry-level job, or other significant opportunity?

It wasn't straight. I started as a pre-med major, then realized, 'I don't want to do this.' I was always more interested in the environmental side of things and ended up getting a bachelor's degree in biology.

My first job was in a local environmental testing lab, where I tested effluent discharge from water treatment plants. I transitioned to a lab where I extracted oils, pesticides, herbicides and heavy metals from effluent discharge

Then I worked in air regulation, first as the poor sucker on top of smokestacks, then as manager of the lab that analyzed those emissions.

A couple of years later, I got a job doing research and development in a manufacturing plant.

Then I went back to the environmental field, doing project management. About seven years ago, I finally wound up here. I started as a technician. Then the hazardous waste position became available and I trained for it.

If you had asked me 15 years ago if I'd ever be in hazardous waste, I would have said no way. But I really do enjoy it. You never know where life takes you.

2. What are the most important skills and/or qualities for someone in your pro-fession?

You have to be versatile.You can't limit yourself to one disposal method for everything and you can't take the easiest approach. You don't necessarily have to incinerate hazardous waste. You don't necessarily have to landfill it. There's a lot of research involved. We actually recycle a lot of chemicals. That's a very big part of this job. You also have to maintain integrity. Integrity, above all, is the key.

3. What do you wish you had known going into this profession?

Starting out, I wish I'd realized how important grunt work was in the scheme of things. A lot of times, you're doing really hard work that seems so small but it's actually very important

4. Are there many job opportunities in your profession? In what specific areas?

I think there are. A lot of large corporations and universities are recognizing they have a big impact on the environment and they're going to be looking for people who have an overall understanding of environmental regulations and policies and how to manage them.

They also need someone who can communicate the risk and regulatory policies both to upper management and to the people down in the field and on the floor. That way, everyone has an overall understanding of what it means to be in compliance with regulations.

A lot of corporations use what's called an environmental management system which is basically a tracking system for all their risks to human health and the environment and activities. A hazardous waste manager has to rank risks in order to spend more time and attention monitoring those with higher levels.

5. How do you see your profession changing in the next five years? What role will technology play in those changes, and what skills will be required?

One thing to remember in terms of hazardous waste is that our population is getting bigger and everyone loves the newest thing in technology. But all of that comes with an environmental cost. These products use a lot of chemicals and create waste. We have to understand how we can manage all of this better. I don't think the demand will go away.

I think a lot of people will be more concerned about what they're exposed to and push for "greener" chemicals. It's going to be critical to manage chemicals from the moment they're produced to the moment they're disposed of.

6. What do you enjoy most about your job? What do you enjoy least about your job?

I enjoy the diversity. Every day is different. We have a lot of labs here and every lab is different, with different research intents and using different materials. I like that I'm allowed to manage this material in an environmentally friendly way. We recycle about 91 percent of all of our waste.

The paperwork is not so enjoyable. There's a lot of regulatory reporting. Sometimes I get buried under it but that's just part of the game.

7. Can you suggest a valuable "try this" for students considering a career in your profession?

Find an organization like the Sierra Club or even the Peace Corps that does a lot of really good environmental projects and volunteer or just research a project. If there's a household hazardous waste collection day in your community, volunteer. You can also do an assessment of the chemicals in your own house and learn how best to dispose of them.

SELECTED SCHOOLS

Many agricultural, technical, and community colleges offer programs in waste management, sometimes with a concentration in hazardous materials removal. Interested students are advised to consult with their school guidance counselor or to research area postsecondary schools and training programs. For those interested in pursuing a bachelor's degree, a state land-grant college or technical institute is probably the best place to start.

MORE INFORMATION

Air & Waste Management Association
1 Gateway Center, 3rd Floor
420 Fort Duquesne Boulevard
Pittsburgh, PA 15222-1435
412.232.3444
www.awma.org

Institute of Hazardous Materials Management
11900 Parklawn Drive, Suite 450
Rockville, MD 20852
301.984.8969
www.ihmm.org

National Environmental, Safety & Health Training Association
5320 North 16th Street, Suite 114
Phoenix, AZ 85016
602.956.6099
netforum.avectra.com/eweb

National Waste & Recycling Association
4301 Connecticut Avenue NW
Suite 300
Washington, DC 20008
800.424.2869
wasterecycling.org

U.S. Department of Energy
Office of Environmental Management
1000 Independence Avenue SW
Washington, DC 20585
800.342.5363
www.emcbc.doe.gov

U.S. Occupational Safety and Health Administration
200 Constitution Avenue NW
Washington, DC 20210
800.321.6742
www.osha.gov

Michael Auerbach/Editor

Landscape Architect

Snapshot

Career Cluster: Architecture & Construction; Environment & Conservation
Interests: Environment, technology, design, communicating with others
Earnings (Yearly Average): $68,570
Employment & Outlook: Average Growth Expected

OVERVIEW

Sphere of Work

Landscape architects are designers of exterior space. Much of the work they do is both decorative and functional. They plan the surrounding landscape for new buildings, deciding where to place walkways, lawns, trees, gardens, retaining walls, fountains, reflecting pools, and other natural and manmade objects. They also design bike trails, golf courses, playgrounds, highway and waterfront beautification projects, and other public spaces. In addition to planning aesthetically pleasing environments, they prepare environmental impact statements, solve environmental problems such as flooding or mudslides, and restore habitats back to their original condition.

Work Environment

Landscape architects work in government and in the private sector. Many landscape architects are self-employed or work in small architectural firms. They interact with clients, architects, urban planners, engineers, and other professionals involved in construction and development. They also often supervise the contractors and gardeners who carry out their landscaping plans. They frequently work long or odd hours to meet deadlines.

Profile

Working Conditions: Work both Indoors and Outdoors
Physical Strength: Light Work
Education Needs: Bachelor's Degree, Master's Degree
Licensure/Certification: Required
Physical Abilities Not Required: No Heavy Labor
Opportunities For Experience: Internship, Apprenticeship, Volunteer Work, Part-Time Work
Holland Interest Score*: AIR

* See Appendix A

Occupation Interest

Landscape architecture attracts people who value the harmony between humans and nature that can be achieved through thoughtful planning and manipulating the environment. They are imaginative, artistic problem-solvers who are solidly grounded in science and technology. They are both detail-oriented and able to envision large-scale projects. Successful landscape architects use their excellent communication skills to convey their design ideas to others.

A Day in the Life—Duties and Responsibilities

The duties and responsibilities of landscape architects are many and varied. Larger jobs usually involve carrying out a preliminary assessment, or feasibility study, performed in collaboration with the architect, engineers, and environmental scientists. At that time, the landscape architect might take photographs or a video of the area to be developed. He or she might also have to submit applications to government agencies for zoning permits and environmental approval.

After a site has been approved, the landscape architect studies the area's topographic features. The landscape architect then offers suggestions on how best to situate the project's buildings, walkways and roadways, and natural elements based on environmental factors such as sunlight and drainage. He or she then designs the landscape to complement the design of the building, harmonize with the surrounding environment, and accommodate the spatial needs of various stakeholders. Much of the design work is done with a computer-aided design (CAD) program, but it may also be sketched by hand. The landscape architect might also prepare a video simulation or build a 3-D model of the design. He or she then puts together a proposal that also includes a cost analysis, written reports, permits, and other materials.

On large projects, the approval process typically involves many meetings with the developer over the course of several months. During this time, the landscape architect might give several presentations to a board of shareholders or a government commission. He or she also submits construction designs to local building commissioners for approval.

Once approved, the landscape architect refines the drawings and details specific construction guidelines. After construction begins, he or she may return to the site to oversee the work.

Duties and Responsibilities

- **Preparing site plans, working drawings, specifications and cost estimates for land developments**
- **Presenting design sketches to clients and community interest groups**
- **Outlining in detail the methods of construction**
- **Drawing up a list of necessary materials**
- **Inspecting construction work in progress to make sure specifications are followed**
- **Conferring with clients, engineering personnel and architects on overall programs for project**
- **Compiling and analyzing data on site conditions such as geographic location, soil, vegetation and rock features, drainage and location of structures**

WORK ENVIRONMENT

Physical Environment

Landscape architects work in offices but also spend much time at job sites. Undeveloped sites may have safety issues such as uneven terrain, mud, or plant and animal pests, while those under construction may involve loud noise, fumes, chemicals, or other hazards.

Relevant Skills and Abilities

Communication Skills

- Expressing thoughts and ideas clearly
- Speaking and writing effectively

Creative/Artistic Skills

- Being skilled in art or design

Organization & Management Skills

- Making decisions
- Paying attention to and handling details

Research & Planning Skills

- Using logical reasoning

Technical Skills

- Performing technical work

Human Environment

Unless they are self-employed, landscape architects usually work in firms or departments with other architects, assistants, and staff, under supervision by the head architect or director. They may supervise drafters, surveyors, gardeners, and other employees or contractors. Their clients range from homeowners to residential and commercial developers to boards of directors.

Technological Environment

Landscape architects use computers equipped with CAD software, word processing, geographic information systems (GIS), and spreadsheets, among other programs. They might also use photo imaging, illustration, modeling, and other computer graphics or design software. In addition to conventional office equipment, they use large format copiers and a variety of drafting and art tools and supplies. They may also use surveying equipment.

EDUCATION, TRAINING, AND ADVANCEMENT

High School/Secondary

A well-rounded college preparatory program that emphasizes math, science, and courses that introduce CAD, such as mechanical drawing or drafting, will provide the best foundation for a career in landscape design. Especially relevant courses include geometry, trigonometry, environmental science, biology, geology, and botany. Speech communication and English courses help develop communication skills, while drawing, sculpture, photography, computer graphics, and other art courses encourage creativity. Part-time jobs in gardening, lawn care, or construction, or volunteering at a nature center or arboretum can provide valuable hands-on work experience.

Suggested High School Subjects

- Applied Biology/Chemistry
- Applied Math
- Arts
- Blueprint Reading
- Drafting
- English
- Landscaping
- Mathematics
- Mechanical Drawing
- Ornamental Horticulture
- Photography

Famous First

The first American landscape architect of note was Frederick Law Olmstead (1822-1903), designer of Central Park and Prospect Park in New York City as well as numerous other notable municipal parks, state parks, and college campuses. Olmsted was also active in the conservation movement, and during the Civil War he headed the US Sanitary Commission, which oversaw care of sick and wounded soldiers.

College/Postsecondary

A bachelor's degree in landscape architecture is the minimum requirement for licensing as a landscape architect; some employers require an advanced degree. The undergraduate degree in landscape architecture often takes five years and includes courses in surveying, CAD and modeling, ecology, horticulture, earth sciences, landscape planning, design, and construction, and management. Some programs require, or strongly suggest, an internship and offer hands-on opportunities as part of the curriculum.

Related College Majors

- Architectural Environmental Design
- Landscape Architecture

Adult Job Seekers

Adults with a background in horticulture, gardening, botany, geology, urban planning, or another related discipline would have an advantage when entering this career. Those with a bachelor's degree in a related field may be able to enroll directly in a three-year master's degree program, thus saving time and money. Qualified landscape architects should consider membership in professional associations, which often provide opportunities for networking, job-finding, and professional development.

Advancement opportunities depend on the place of employment and its size. Experienced landscape architects are given more difficult and higher-profile jobs. They may become project managers, partners in their firms, or establish their own firms. Some move into consulting or academic positions.

Professional Certification and Licensure

All states license landscape architects. In most cases, candidates are required to have a bachelor's degree from a Landscape Architectural Accreditation Board (LAAB) accredited program as well as one to four years of experience and a passing score on the Landscape Architect Registration Examination (LARE). Some states also administer their own test and have slightly different requirements for experience and education. Continuing education is a common requirement for license renewal. Interested individuals should check the requirements of their home state.

Additional Requirements:

Landscape architects must be familiar with local zoning regulations and environmental codes. Those who wish to establish their own landscape design firms should have business skills and motivation as well as experience in the field.

Fun Fact

A tree shading an outdoor air conditioner unit can increase its efficiency by as much as ten percent.

Source: signatureconcretedesign.com

EARNINGS AND ADVANCEMENT

Earnings of landscape architects depend on the type, size, and geographic location of the employer and the individual's education and experience. Mean annual earnings for landscape architects were $68,570 in 2013. The lowest ten percent earned less than $39,000, and the highest ten percent earned more than $104,000.
Landscape architects may receive paid vacations, holidays, and sick days; life and health insurance; and retirement benefits. These are usually paid by the employer.

Metropolitan Areas with the Highest Employment Level in This Occupation

Metropolitan area	Employment[1]	Employment per thousand jobs	Hourly mean wage
Seattle-Bellevue-Everett, WA	680	0.47	$30.19
Washington-Arlington-Alexandria, DC-VA-MD-WV	570	0.24	$39.84
Minneapolis-St. Paul-Bloomington, MN-WI	550	0.30	$26.51
Denver-Aurora-Broomfield, CO	530	0.42	$34.96
Santa Ana-Anaheim-Irvine, CA	440	0.30	$33.82
Boston-Cambridge-Quincy, MA	420	0.24	$43.54
Philadelphia, PA	420	0.23	$30.06
San Diego-Carlsbad-San Marcos, CA	410	0.32	$34.44
Oakland-Fremont-Hayward, CA	390	0.39	$42.97
Atlanta-Sandy Springs-Marietta, GA	350	0.15	$31.22

[1] Does not include self-employed. Source: Bureau of Labor Statistics

EMPLOYMENT AND OUTLOOK

There were approximately 24,000 landscape architects employed nationally in 2012. About one-fourth were self-employed. Employment of landscape architects is expected to grow about as fast as the average for all occupations through the year 2022, which means employment is projected to increase 10 percent to 16 percent. Employment will grow because of the expertise of landscape architects will be sought after in the planning and development of new construction. Growing interest in city and regional environmental planning, increased development of open space into recreation areas, wildlife refuges and parks and continued concern for the environment should also spur demand for landscape architects.

Employment Trend, Projected 2012–22

Architects, Surveyors, and Cartographers (All): 15%

Landscape Architects: 14%

Total, All Occupations: 11%

Note: "All Occupations" includes all occupations in the U.S. Economy. Source: U.S. Bureau of Labor Statistics, Employment Projections Program.

Related Occupations

- Architect
- Floral Designer
- Forester & Conservation Scientist
- Gardener & Groundskeeper
- Urban & Regional Planner

Conversation With . . .
JON CONNER

Vice President and Practice Leader
Landscape Architecture, JMT, Sparks MD
Landscape Architect, 28 years

1. What was your individual career path in terms of education/training, entry-level job, or other significant opportunity?

I started in the School of Architecture at the University of Maryland but after two years figured out that wasn't my cup of tea. I was more of a logical thinker and not quite so prepared for the artistic side of that profession. So, moving to design outside of buildings placed me in a design environment that was more scientifically-based. That's how I found my comfort level. I got my degree in horticulture with a landscape design option from the College of Agriculture. I was at my first job about five years and decided to get my Master's in Landscape Architecture at Morgan State University. I then moved here to JMT, which is historically a transportation engineering firm

Our projects range from conceptual planning to final design. We do many streetscape projects, which include not only planting design but also design for sidewalks, urban plazas and parks. We led the planning team to site stations in neighborhoods for the Baltimore City Red Line. We've done studies and reports and management plans for scenic byways, understanding what's particularly special about an historic road or corridor. I plan and design pedestrian and bicycle facilities.

In general, landscape architecture has historically suffered from an identity crisis because people tend to place emphasis on the word "landscape" and not the word "architecture." Landscape Architects can focus on ecological and stream restoration, historic preservation, parks and recreation, or even schools. I chose to pursue the transportation realm.

2. What are the most important skills and/or qualities for someone in your pro-fession?

You need to be well-equipped in terms of graphic capabilities. You communicate with drawings, and you still need to be able to sketch something out to depict what you're thinking. As you get into the working world, you have to be a good communicator and comfortable presenting in front of people.

3. **What do you wish you had known going into this profession?**

   I wish I had known that landscape architecture was more diverse. It would have allowed me to hone in more quickly on a niche that I was interested in pursuing.

4. **Are there many job opportunities in your profession? In what specific areas?**

   Job prospects and the future are really bright because of the growing emphasis on sustainability and green solutions. Engineers, architects, and private institutions hire us because of our experience understanding how the built environment must co-exist with the natural environment. Many times we are brought in to serve as the quarterback for a project because we understand how the full range of project issues and systems fit into the overall ecosystem of an area.

5. **How do you see your profession changing in the next five years? What role will technology play in those changes, and what skills will be required?**

   We'll see even more emphasis on sustainable solutions. Also, computer graphics are a big part of our production work, so being able to graphically depict views of what you want to build is important. Higher end software products that can depict ideas — something that's completely photorealistic — are used in higher levels of design. Any of the computer mapping and graphic applications are essential.

6. **What do you enjoy most about your job? What do you enjoy least about your job?**

   My job is rewarding because in the broadest sense it gives me an opportunity to make a difference to improve places where people live, work, play and learn. One of my more rewarding projects came when we asked to re-invent Main Street in Rehoboth Beach, DE, a popular East Coast beach town. The main street was showing years of design decisions geared towards moving cars, and was not particularly attractive or safe for pedestrians and bicyclists. Much of the infrastructure was deteriorating and in need of replacement. It cost the city $35 million and took six years, but now there's a traffic circle when you come into town -- with a replica of the local Cape Henlopen Lighthouse -- that slows traffic down for pedestrians and bicyclists. It says, "I have arrived." The overhead utilities went underground as part of that project.

   My least favorite thing, probably because most of our work is with the public sector, is the bureaucracy. It can be mind-numbing at times, and you see how much money gets wasted just trying to move designs to construction.

7. Can you suggest a valuable "try this" for students considering a career in your profession?

Think of one or more of your favorite places to go, go there, and think what is it about that place that makes it one of your favorite places. Is it the sheer natural beauty, or something designed? There's a full range: you might go to the Grand Canyon and be in awe of natural beauty, or you might go to Disney World, an artificial environment created by man.

Also look for opportunities such as the one offered by my company, which participates in the local chapter of the American Society of Landscape Architects' annual job shadow program. That lets students experience what we do. We take them out to a couple of job sites and look at projects that are under construction as well as reviewing designs that are "on the boards."

A good resource is ASLA.org, which has a section called "Become a Landscape Architect."

SELECTED SCHOOLS

Many colleges and universities have bachelor's degree programs in art and architecture, design, and related subjects; some offer concentrations in landscape architecture. The student may also gain an initial grounding in the field at an agricultural, technical, or community college. For advanced positions, a master's is commonly obtained. Below are listed some of the more prominent schools in this field.

Cal Poly, Pomona
3801 W. Temple Avenue
Pomona, CA 91768
909.869.7659
www.csupomona.edu

Cornell University
410 Thurston Avenue
Ithaca, NY 14850
607.255.5241
www.cornell.edu

Kansas State University
119 Anderson Hall
Manhattan, KS 66506
785.532.6250
www.k-state.edu

Louisiana State University
1146 Pleasant Hall
Baton Rouge, LA 70803
225.578.1175
www.lsu.edu

Purdue University
445 Stadium Mall
West Lafayette, IN 47907
765.494.1776
www.purdue.edu

Ohio State University
281 West Lane Avenue
Columbus, OH 43210
614.292.3980
www.osu.edu

Texas A&M University
PO Box 30014
College Station, TX 77842
978.845.1060
www.tamu.edu

University of Georgia
Terrell Hall
210 South Jackson Street
Athens, GA 30602
706.542.8776
www.uga.edu

University of Pennsylvania
1 College Hall, Room 1
Philadelphia, PA 19104
215.898.7507
www.upenn.edu

Virginia Tech
925 Prices Forks Road
Blacksburg, VA 24061
540.231.6267
www.vt.edu

MORE INFORMATION

American Institute of Architects
1735 New York Avenue NW
Washington, DC 20006-5292
800.242.3837
www.aia.org

American Nursery and Landscape Association
1000 Vermont Avenue NW, Suite 300
Washington, DC 20005
202.789.2900
www.anla.org

American Society of Landscape Architects
636 Eye Street NW
Washington, DC 20001-3736
888.999.2752
www.asla.org

Association of Collegiate Schools of Architecture
1735 New York Avenue, NW
Washington, DC 20006
202.785.2324
www.acsa-arch.org

Council of Landscape Architectural Registration Boards
3949 Pender Drive, Suite 120
Fairfax, VA 22030
571.432.0332
www.clarb.org

Landscape Architecture Foundation
818 18th Street NW, Suite 810
Washington, DC 20006
202.331.7070
www.lafoundation.org

Society of American Registered Architects
14 E. 38th Street
New York, NY 10016
888.385.7272
www.sara-national.org

Sally Driscoll/Editor

Marine Biologist

Snapshot

Career Cluster: Environment & Conservation; Science & Technology
Interests: Biology, science, marine wildlife and habitats, animal behavior, oceanography
Earnings (Yearly Average): $60,365
Employment & Outlook: Faster Than Average Growth Expected

OVERVIEW

Sphere of Work

Marine biologists study the habitats of sea, animal, and plant life in saltwater environments. There are many specialties within marine biology, including those focused in the areas of conservation, fisheries management, animal behavior, microbiology, and more. Marine biologists work all over the world; the occupation is one of the most all-encompassing fields of oceanography. Marine biologists study a range of species—from sea turtles to sharks, as well as sponges, plankton, and microorganisms. Studies may concentrate on

the behavior of species, the chemical makeup of water, the ocean's geology, plants, and biological habitats such as coral reefs.

Often, potential marine biologists are interested in mammals. Research jobs in this specialty are extremely popular, and therefore, the field of marine biology is competitive. Most marine biologists will have completed field work in their chosen concentration, such as internships at aquariums or natural history museums, and perhaps even spent a semester at sea.

Profile

Working Conditions: Work both Indoors and Outdoors
Physical Strength: Light Work, Medium Work
Education Needs: Master's Degree, Doctoral Degree
Licensure/Certification: Required
Physical Abilities Not Required: No Heavy Labor
Opportunities For Experience: Military Service, Part-Time Work
Holland Interest Score*: IRE, IRS

* See Appendix A

Work Environment

Marine biologists' workplaces vary, and include but aren't limited to laboratory environments, underwater expeditions, fishing boats, and aquariums. In any of these environments, strong communication skills are essential, as is an eye for detail. Marine biologists often work with other researchers or professionals from other disciplines, which requires that marine biologists have great task flexibility. For instance, in underwater expeditions, it is useful to be licensed in scuba diving, while observation, education, and public speaking may be essential skills in an aquarium or museum environment.

Occupation Interest

Marine biologists not only have a strong background in science, but also a healthy respect for the scientific process and for new discovery. Marine biologists deal directly with marine life and they must collaborate with co-workers to achieve established research goals. This requires open-mindedness, a continual willingness to learn, and respect for all marine organisms.

A Day in the Life—Duties and Responsibilities

Since the oceans cover about 70 percent of the earth, study of this environment is wide-ranging. Research is a significant component of what a marine biologist does. Studying wildlife in natural environments may be a part of that—a marine biologist could be part of a research team on a boat studying animal behavior, or could be employed by the federal fisheries as an observer on a fishing boat, monitoring fish catches. Some marine biologists' research may take them to Arctic waters or to the tropics. Other researchers may work in a laboratory, studying the chemical composition of water in a certain area or mapping the DNA of ocean microorganisms.

Marine biologists often record their findings, write and present reports and scientific papers, provide analysis, and perform administrative tasks relevant to their place of employment. Often, the research focuses on collecting, examining, and analyzing preserved specimens for experiments. In museum, aquarium, or zoo settings, a marine biologist may be asked to perform public outreach functions or participate in fundraising.

For researchers in the field, the hours may vary widely, from long days during a particularly successful fishing trip to quieter days with less activity as a boat travels to offshore fishing grounds. Researchers in an academic or corporate laboratory might have a more reliable schedule of 40-plus hours a week.

Duties and Responsibilities

- **Conducting scientific research into oceanic plants and animals**
- **Observing and recording living species in their natural habitats**
- **Studying interactions of plants and animals with their ocean environment and other species**
- **Examining organisms in the laboratory**
- **Interpreting data and writing reports**
- **Conducting environmental impact studies**
- **Exploring the commercial uses of saltwater plants and animal**

OCCUPATION SPECIALTIES

Icthyologists

Icthyologists study wild fishes, such as sharks and tuna.

Cetologists

Cetologists study marine mammals, including whales and dolphins.

Aquaculturists

Aquaculturists use their knowledge of fish and breeding to raise fish, lobster, clams, oysters and shrimp on commercial farms.

WORK ENVIRONMENT

Physical Environment

Marine biologists work primarily in laboratories, on boats, at the seashore, underwater, and in aquariums and marine museums. Working on boats is stressful at times, as people aboard the ship share tight quarters yet enjoy little privacy. Depending on the location of a research facility, climate and access to research facilities can be a challenge for some scientists. Laboratory research positions are often in academic, clinical, or corporate settings. Most marine biologists work in locations close to or on oceans.

Human Environment

Sometimes marine biologists are away from home for weeks, working in harsh weather conditions. For this reason, they must be hardy, focused, and strong multitaskers. They are also required to be open-minded in their interactions with others, as they may live in cramped quarters for long periods of time with people from various walks of life. Those in academic fields must be open to a range of learning styles and levels of understanding. Effective communication and interpersonal skills are a necessity.

Relevant Skills and Abilities

Analytical Skills
- Collecting and analyzing data

Communication Skills
- Speaking and writing effectively

Interpersonal/Social Skills
- Being able to work independently
- Being patient

Research & Planning Skills
- Identifying a research problem
- Laying out a plan
- Solving problems

Unclassified Skills
- Being curious

Work Environment Skills
- Working in a laboratory setting
- Working outdoors

Technological Environment

The technological equipment available for marine biologists to use in their research varies according to the setting, research funding, and need. Those mapping the genome of microorganisms, for example, use complex laboratory equipment and computers; those working in a not-for-profit aquarium have more limited resources, and therefore have limited access to sophisticated laboratory or computer equipment. Marine biologists may work with oceanographic instruments to help them navigate their way through the experiments relating to oceans, fisheries, federal or state government agencies, and private research institutions. Researchers on ocean vessels may be expected to have some familiarity with the sailing or operation of a boat or ship as a member of the crew.

EDUCATION, TRAINING, AND ADVANCEMENT

High School/Secondary

High school students seeking a career in marine biology should build a solid foundation in the natural sciences, especially biology. Developing an understanding of and a respect for the scientific process is desirable. When ready to explore college options, students should research colleges that have a strong science department with up-to-date lab facilities, opportunities for relevant internships, and an affiliation with a research facility. High school students should make use of career guidance counselors, who can help to navigate through the choices that best meet future career goals. They might also avail themselves of extracurricular programs or activities that can enhance their familiarity with saltwater habitats.

Suggested High School Subjects

- Applied Biology/Chemistry
- Applied Math
- Biology
- Chemistry
- College Preparatory
- Computer Science
- English
- Physics

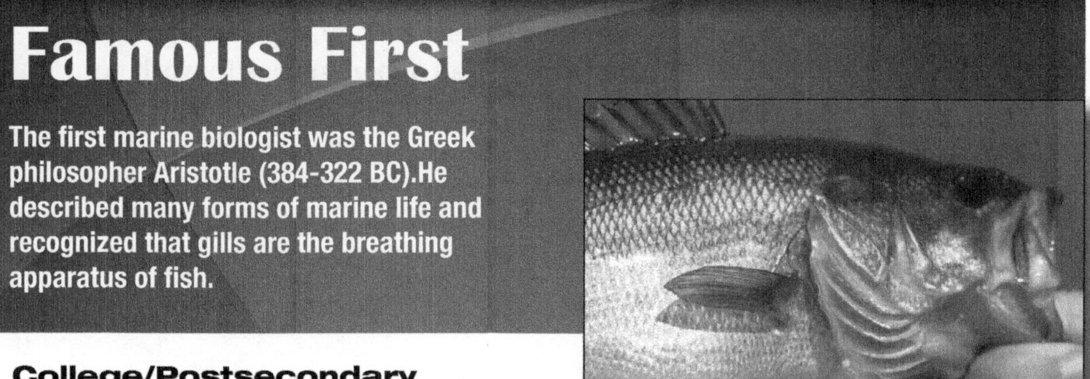

Famous First
The first marine biologist was the Greek philosopher Aristotle (384-322 BC).He described many forms of marine life and recognized that gills are the breathing apparatus of fish.

College/Postsecondary

Marine biologists need a bachelor's degree in either marine biology or a related subject, such as biology, botany, biochemistry, chemistry, ecology, microbiology, or zoology. Those with bachelor's degrees and postgraduate degrees can expect to find opportunities appropriate to their education and experience, as technicians, educators, or researchers with employers such as industrial and private-sector companies, marine stations, research foundations, zoos, aquariums, federal agencies, or not-for-profit environmental advocacy organizations.

Related College Majors

- Marine/Aquatic Biology

Adult Job Seekers

Over the long term, advancement in marine biology requires graduate-level training. Most graduate students begin their careers in aquariums or marine centers. Even though graduate-level students may start out by cleaning tanks and feeding animals, after gaining some experience and showing initiative they can move on to the level of a marine center curator position and beyond. Doctoral graduates often conduct independent research or teach at the college level.

Professional Certification and Licensure

There is no license requirement to become a marine biologist, but most organizations require at least an undergraduate degree to meet the qualifications of existing positions. A master's degree is required for independent research roles, and a doctorate degree qualifies marine biologists to conduct professional work in their field.

Additional Requirements

Those interested in a career in marine biology should seek out internships and opportunities to work on or near the ocean in order to gain experience that enhances their academic studies. Experience and comfort in and on the water is essential, and it is useful to obtain a scuba diving license. Marine biologists should have good people skills and the ability to tolerate a wide variety of environmental conditions, such as rough seas, extreme temperatures, and inclement weather.

Fun Fact

Over 30,000 known species of fish exist, and over 1000 fish species are threatened by extinction.

Source: http://www.sciencekids.co.nz/sciencefacts/animals/fish.html

EARNINGS AND ADVANCEMENT

Full-time marine biologists are salaried employees of governmental institutions or private research and conservation organizations. Some of these professionals choose to enter academia and become college professors. Advancement in the government and private sectors is typically from entry level biologist to senior researcher or administrative executive. College professors climb the ladder of academia from instructor to full professor. Some marine biologists become full-time consultants and are thus self-employed.

Earnings of marine biologists depend on the geographic location of the employer, the type of job and the education and experience of the employee. According to a salary survey by the National Association of Colleges and Employers, beginning annual salaries for graduates with a bachelor's degree in biological science were $36,338 in 2012. Median annual earnings of marine biologists were $62,610 in 2013. The lowest ten percent earned less than $38,000, and the highest ten percent earned more than $95,000.

Marine biologists may receive paid vacations, holidays, and sick days; life and health insurance; and retirement benefits. These are usually paid by the employer.

Metropolitan Areas with the Highest Employment Level in This Occupation

Metropolitan area	Employment[1]	Employment per thousand jobs	Hourly mean wage
Seattle-Bellevue-Everett, WA	750	0.52	$38.59
San Diego-Carlsbad-San Marcos, CA	610	0.47	$30.21
Portland-Vancouver-Hillsboro, OR-WA	520	0.50	$35.14
Los Angeles-Long Beach-Glendale, CA	430	0.11	$36.33
Sacramento--Arden-Arcade--Roseville, CA	350	0.42	$44.24
Anchorage, AK	290	1.65	$31.56
Tampa-St. Petersburg-Clearwater, FL	290	0.25	$22.09
Minneapolis-St. Paul-Bloomington, MN-WI	280	0.16	$26.57
Boise City-Nampa, ID	240	0.89	$28.27
Olympia, WA	220	2.24	$30.04

[1] Does not include self-employed. Source: Bureau of Labor Statistics

EMPLOYMENT AND OUTLOOK

Zoologists and wildlife biologists, of which marine biologists are a part, held about 20,000 jobs nationally in 2012. Nearly one-half were employed by federal, state and local governments. Employment is expected to grow slower than the average for all occupations through the year 2022, which means employment is projected to increase 3 percent to 9 percent. Employment growth is due to the increasing desire to be environmentally aware and preserve natural wildlife and fauna. Health-related research and environmental impact studies will be in more demand, as will searching for commercial applications of sea-life.

Employment Trend, Projected 2012–22

Total, All Occupations: 11%

Science Occupations (All): 10%

Marine Biologists and Other Wildlife Biologists: 5%

Note: "All Occupations" includes all occupations in the U.S. Economy. Source: U.S. Bureau of Labor Statistics, Employment Projections Program.

Related Occupations

- Biological Scientist
- Biomedical Engineer
- Botanist
- Oceanographer
- Wildlife Biologist

Conversation With . . .
CARRIE KENNEDY

Coastal Fisheries Program Manager, Maryland
Dept. of Natural Resources
Fisheries Biologist, 15 years

1. What was your individual career path in terms of education/training, entry-level job, or other significant opportunity?

Before sixth grade, I got to do a summer program at the University of Wisconsin called College for Kids. My course was the World of Animals and we studied fish, bugs and frogs. Right after that, my family went on vacation to Hawaii where I went snorkeling. I've been pretty much singularly focused on fish since then.

I took other opportunities to gain hands-on experience. In high school, I went to Hawaii with Girl Scouts from around the world in a program called Wider Opportunity. We had marine biology classes in the morning. In the afternoon we'd go snorkeling and look at the things we'd learned about in the morning. I went on to St. Mary's College of Maryland and earned a BA in biology. Through contacts at the college, I had a couple of good internships at research labs. After I graduated, I wanted to get a graduate degree but first went to the Maryland Dept. of Natural Resources because I wanted to get experience to help focus on what I should specialize in grad school. After a few years, I left DNR to go to work for a summer at North Carolina State University for a grad student. It was a really good learning experience because it helped me understand I didn't want to be an academic. I wanted to be in fisheries management. I ended up back at Maryland DNR, and had to start again as a seasonal biologist at the bottom of the totem pole.

I worked with the striped bass stock assessment folks out in the field tagging striped bass and working with watermen, and went on to coordinate the commercial striped bass permitting system. Now I oversee the program that samples all of our fish in Maryland's Coastal Bays and Atlantic Ocean. We put trawls and seine nets out there to sample our fisheries resources, and we work with commercial and recreational fishermen to set regulations.

2. What are the most important skills and/or qualities for someone in your profession?

You need to have strong math skills, and to be able to look at a dataset and to understand what the data are telling you and what the next step is: what does it mean in the bigger picture?

3. **What do you wish you had known going into this profession?**

I thought I was going to be a field biologist, out on a boat with fish for my entire career, and that I was going to love it. I was surprised when I started understand that was not as fulfilling as I thought it would be. To make real change I needed to be in the office more, working on policy. Having an impact means you can't be outside all the time.

4. **Are there many job opportunities in your profession? In what specific areas?**

It is fairly competitive. It is really important to start getting experience early. I don't think there a ton of positions or a ton of new ones being created, and that has largely to do with money. Unfortunately, natural resource management is not a top priority of the vast majority of US citizens, so that means that -- while it is a priority -- it's not at the top of the funding list.

5. **How do you see your profession changing in the next five years, what role will technology play in those changes, and what skills will be required?**

We are moving toward ecosystem-based management and this is a particular challenge because there are still a lot of unknowns. We are very used to single-species management.

Also, fisheries management is really people management. We can control what the people do, not what the fish do. Communication is huge. So technologies that improve our partnership with our stakeholders, such as communication in real time information, are going to be the next big thing.

6. **What do you enjoy most about your job? What do you enjoy least about your job?**

I still really enjoy getting outside with field work, and I also really enjoy working with recreational and commercial fishermen toward the common goal of sustainable fisheries. The part I enjoy the least is knowing that sometimes hard decisions are going to affect our recreational and commercial fishermen, and those impacts can be significant.

7. **Can you suggest a valuable "try this" for students considering a career in your profession?**

Getting an internship at a state wildlife or fisheries management agency will expose you to the fun field work, although some people find out they don't like being dirty, or being wet all day. You're also probably going to have the opportunity to go and listen to what meetings are all about. Plus, you've made some connections and gained good experience.

SELECTED SCHOOLS

Virtually all colleges and universities have bachelor's degree programs in biology; some have concentrations in wildlife biology or marine biology. The student may also gain an initial grounding in the field at an agricultural, technical, or community college. For advanced positions, a master's or doctoral degree is usually obtained. Below are listed some of the more prominent graduate schools in this field.

Boston University
Department of Biology
5 Cummington Mall
Boston, MA 02215
617.353.2432
www.bu.edu/biology

Duke University
Nicholas School of the Environment
Box 90328
Durham, NC 27708
919.613.8070
nicholas.duke.edu

Stanford University
Department of Biology
Gilbert Hall
Stanford, CA 94305
650.723.2413
biology.stanford.edu

Stony Brook University
School of Marine and Atmospheric Sciences
Stony Brook, NY 11794
631.632.8700
www.somas.stonybrook.edu

University of California, San Diego
Scripps Institute of Oceanography
9500 Gilman Drive
La Jolla, CA 92093
858.534.3624
scripps.ucsd.edu

University of California, Santa Barbara
Ecology, Evolution, and Marine Biology
4314 Life Sciences Building
Santa Barbara, CA 93106
805.893.2974
www.eemb.ucsb.edu

University of Maine
School of Marine Sciences
5706 Aubert Hall, Room 360
Orono, ME 04469
207.581.4381
www.umaine.edu

University of Oregon
Oregon Institute of Marine Biology,
63466 Boat Basin Road
PO Box 5389
Charleston, OR 97420
541.888.2581
oimb.uoregon.edu

University of Texas
Marine Science Institute
750 Channel View Drive
Port Aransas, TX78373
361.749.6711
utmsi.utexas.edu

University of Washington
Marine Biology Program
1122 NE Boat Street
116 Fisheries Sciences Building, Box 355020
Seattle, WA 98195
206.543.7426
depts..washington.edu/marbio

MORE INFORMATION

MarineBio
1995 Fairlee Drive
Encinitas, CA 92024
713.248.257
marinebio.ogr

Marine Biological Laboratory
7 MBL Street
Woods Hole, MA 02543
508.548.3705
www.mbl.edu

Marine Technology Society
5565 Sterrett Place, #108
Columbia, MD 21044
410.884.5330
www.mtsociety.org

National Aquarium Society (NAS)
Commerce Building, Room B-077
14th and Constitution Avenue NW
Washington, DC 20230
202.482.2825
www.nationalaquarium.org

National Association for Research in Science Teaching (NARST)
12100 Sunset Hills Road, Suite 130
Reston, VA 20190-3221
703.234.4138
www.narst.org

Nature Conservancy
4245 North Fairfax Drive, Suite 100
Arlington, VA 22203-1606
800.628.6860
nature.org

Oceanic Society
Fort Mason Quarters 35
San Francisco, CA 94123
800.326.7491
www.oceanicsociety.org

Susan Williams/Editor

Meteorologist

Snapshot

Career Cluster: Environment & Conservation; Science & Technology
Interests: Weather, climate patterns, science, atmospheric science, analyzing and interpreting data
Earnings (Yearly Average): $88,140
Employment & Outlook: Faster Than Average Growth Expected

OVERVIEW

Sphere of Work

Meteorology is the scientific study of the earth's atmosphere and the natural forces that shape weather and climate patterns. Using atmospheric forecasting and research, meteorologists explain and forecast how the atmosphere affects the earth. Meteorologists in all specialties use instruments to record the short- and long-term effects of climate and variations in weather patterns. They use their skills and experience to produce and deliver forecasts and other weather-related information to the public via radio and television broadcasts, among

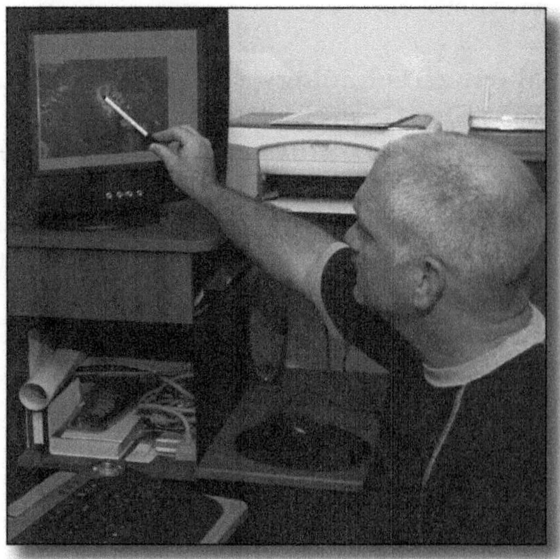

other mediums. Meteorologists can also use their forecasting skills to help city planners locate and design construction projects, such as airports and factories.

Work Environment

Meteorologists collaborate with other scientists and researchers in basic disciplines such as chemistry, physics, mathematics, oceanography, and hydrology. They can operate in any environment, from weather centers to field offices to ships at sea. The government is the largest employer of meteorologists in the United States; meteorologists work for government agencies such as the Department of Defense, Department of Energy, and Department of Agriculture, while many serve as civilians in the military. Broadcast meteorologists typically work for television and radio stations. Some meteorologists are self-employed and consult for large corporations.

Profile

Working Conditions: Work both Indoors and Outdoors
Physical Strength: Light Work
Education Needs: Bachelor's Degree, Master's Degree, Doctoral Degree
Licensure/Certification: Recommended
Physical Abilities Not Required: No Heavy Labor
Opportunities For Experience: Internship, Military Service
Holland Interest Score*: IRS

* See Appendix A

Occupation Interest

Many people are drawn to meteorology because they are keen to address the challenge of forecasting natural events throughout the world. As such, meteorologists should be interested in the world around them and want to understand the scientific principles that explain the patterns of atmospheric behavior. They must also be comfortable working with computer and satellite technology and other research instruments, and analyzing and interpreting data; forecasting is continually changing and improving, resulting in more accurate predictions over longer spans of time (such as five- or ten-day outlooks).

A Day in the Life—Duties and Responsibilities

Meteorologists must be able to direct, plan, and oversee the work of others, and be able to use reasoning and logic to come to conclusions about forecasting weather. In a typical day, they consult charts and graphs and apply mathematical concepts to help them perceive differences in paths between still or moving objects and picture three-dimensional objects from drawings or photos. Meteorologists base their decisions on measurable data as well as on personal judgment.

Meteorologists from around the world work together daily. They take atmospheric measurements several times a day from surface weather stations and on board ships at sea. They then analyze and interpret weather data that is generated and gathered by upper air stations and satellites, and through weather reports and radar, to prepare forecasts for the media and public. They use computer modeling and simulation to assist in creating these forecasts. Meteorologists also analyze charts and photos and data and information related to barometric pressure, temperature, humidity, and wind velocity. They issue storm warnings and advise pilots on atmospheric conditions such as turbulence, winds aloft, and cloud formations. They also provide relevant forecasts for sea transportation. Some meteorologists make tailored predictions for specific clients, such as city managers and agricultural stakeholders.

Duties and Responsibilities

- **Analyzing and interpreting meteorological data gathered by surface and upper air stations, satellites and radar**
- **Studying and interpreting reports, maps, photographs and charts to make both long and short –term weather predictions**
- **Preparing weather forecasts for the media and other users**
- **Interpreting charts, maps and other data in relation to such areas as barometric pressure, temperature, humidity, wind velocity and areas of precipitation**
- **Conducting research for long-range forecasting**
- **Directing forecasting services at a weather station**

WORK ENVIRONMENT

Physical Environment

Meteorologists work in a variety of physical locations. They can work in large field offices near airports or big cities, or they may operate from smaller sites in remote areas. Those in smaller, remote stations often work alone. Other meteorologists are on board ships, doing field work where visual weather observations are required. Some are located at television and radio stations. Meteorologists work primarily indoors. Weather support units at US military bases include global weather centers and command and control centers at sea.

Relevant Skills and Abilities

Analytical Skills
- Collecting and analyzing data

Communication Skills
- Speaking and writing effectively

Organization & Management Skills
- Making decisions
- Paying attention to and handling details

Research & Planning Skills
- Creating ideas
- Developing evaluation strategies
- Using logical reasoning

Technical Skills
- Performing scientific, mathematical and technical work

Human Environment

Weather stations and offices are located nationwide. Meteorologists work with a variety of other scientists in addition to lay people, such as broadcast journalists, who may simply report on the weather; meteorologists should therefore be aware of other peoples' roles and level of knowledge so that technology terms can be explained at the appropriate level. Strong communication skills are essential.

Technological Environment

Meteorologists use highly sophisticated tools to collect and analyze data. Radar systems, aircraft, satellites, and weather balloons gather information from the atmosphere. Computers are used to analyze the collected data and create simulations, models, and forecasts.

EDUCATION, TRAINING, AND ADVANCEMENT

High School/Secondary

Since the field of meteorology is highly scientific, the most prepared high school students will have taken calculus-level mathematics, chemistry, physics, earth sciences, and computer science. Mathematical proficiency is required in every aspect of physical science. It is also necessary to have a strong command of written and spoken English as well as other languages for following international developments.

Suggested High School Subjects

- Algebra
- Applied Math
- Chemistry
- College Preparatory
- Computer Science
- English
- Geography
- Geometry
- Mathematics
- Literature
- Physical Science
- Physics
- Science
- Statistics
- Trigonometry

Famous First

The first weather forecasting service to use the telephone was launched in New York City in 1938. Although newspaper forecasts and radio broadcasts were available at the time, the telephone provided on-demand reports through the city's Weather Bureau. A steel tape recorder developed by Bell Telephone and capable of responding to 30,000 inquiries per day was the central component of the system.

College/Postsecondary

Many universities offer a bachelor's degree in meteorology or atmospheric science. Meteorology is calculus-based, which means the academic coursework is designed to maximize its use. Recommended courses include physics, chemistry, geography, hydrology, oceanography, differential equations, linear algebra, numerical analysis, and computer science. Some university programs focus more on broad-based meteorological studies, others in more specialty areas. Undergraduate programs provide the foundation needed to move into specialties, such as agricultural meteorology. Those interested in pursuing a career in meteorology should consider applying for relevant internships.

While a bachelor's degree is the norm, the best jobs are available to those with graduate-level education. Advanced degrees are highly useful, and often required, for atmospheric research. Those with a master's degree are qualified to work as operational meteorologists for the government or in private-sector organizations. Alternatively, they may work as assistants to researchers, who have doctoral degrees. Those who wish to teach at the university level must have at least a master's degree.

Related College Majors

- Atmospheric Sciences & Meteorology
- Earth Science
- Oceanography

Adult Job Seekers

When it is not possible to attend a college or university, it is useful to consider joining US military branches, such as the US Air Force or US Navy, for training in observation and forecasting. For those returning to the workforce, internal apprenticeships, mentorships, internships, community work with a relevant government agency, and volunteering with meteorologists can be highly valuable for gaining experience in the field of meteorology. Federal agencies often provide some on-the-job training.

Meteorologists often start as weather forecasting trainees at weather centers or airports. As meteorologists become more experienced, they may turn to supervising research analysis as administrators and mentoring meteorological technicians. Experienced meteorologists can advance to senior management and supervisory positions.

Professional Certification and Licensure

Meteorologists are encouraged to acquire certification according to their job function. The American Meteorological Society (AMS) currently has two certification programs: the Certified Broadcast Meteorologist Program (CBM) and the Certified Consulting Meteorologist Program (CCM). Candidates for the CBM must complete an undergraduate degree in meteorology, an examination, and a work review to be certified. The CCM program requires a specified level of education, at least five years of experience in meteorology or a related field, and successful completion of an examination. Certification renewal depends on continuing education in the field. Consult credible professional associations within the field and follow professional debate as to the relevancy and value of any certification program.

Additional Requirements

Aspiring meteorologists must have a thorough understanding of calculus-based mathematical concepts, and they must always be willing to learn new methods of collecting, analyzing, interpreting, and delivering useful data. Broadcast meteorologists must also be willing to work long or flexible hours, which may include nights, weekends, and holidays, to meet forecast deadlines.

Fun Fact

The fastest a raindrop can fall is 18 mph. Between evaporation and falling as precipitation, a droplet of water may travel thousands of miles. A molecule of water will stay in earth's atmosphere an average of 10-12 days. One billion tons of rain falls on the earth every minute of each day.

Source: http://www.science-facts.com/quick-facts/amazing-weather-facts

EARNINGS AND ADVANCEMENT

Earnings of meteorologists depend on experience, ability, level of education and on the type of employer. Mean annual earnings of meteorologists were $88,140 in 2013. The lowest ten percent earned less than $50,000, and the highest ten percent earned more than $129,000. Meteorologists employed by the federal government earned average annual salaries of $97,350 in 2013.

Meteorologists may receive paid vacations, holidays, and sick days; life and health insurance; and retirement benefits. These are usually paid by the employer. Some employers also pay expenses for additional education.

Metropolitan Areas with the Highest Employment Level in This Occupation

Metropolitan area	Employment[1]	Employment per thousand jobs	Hourly mean wage
Boulder, CO	1,540	9.44	$45.99
Washington-Arlington-Alexandria, DC-VA-MD-WV	680	0.29	$45.44
Boston-Cambridge-Quincy, MA	310	0.18	$38.05
Chicago-Joliet-Naperville, IL	290	0.08	n/a
Bethesda-Rockville-Frederick, MD	250	0.45	$45.08
Houston-Sugar Land-Baytown, TX	240	0.09	$29.92
Sacramento--Arden-Arcade--Roseville, CA	190	0.22	$51.95
Oklahoma City, OK	190	0.31	$47.26
Miami-Miami Beach-Kendall, FL	180	0.17	$37.73
San Diego-Carlsbad-San Marcos, CA	160	0.13	$38.46

[1] Does not include self-employed. Source: Bureau of Labor Statistics

EMPLOYMENT AND OUTLOOK

There were approximately 11,000 meteorologists and atmospheric scientists employed nationally in 2012. The federal government employs the most meteorologists, around one-third, primarily in National Weather Service stations within the National Oceanic and Atmospheric Administration (NOAA). Employment is expected to grow about as fast as the average for all occupations through the year 2022, which means employment is projected to increase 10 percent to 15 percent. New jobs will be created in private industry as firms, especially those in climate-sensitive industries, recognize the value of having their own weather forecasting and meteorological services. Most of the job openings in this small occupation will arise from the need to replace those who change occupations or retire.

Employment Trend, Projected 2012–22

Total, All Occupations: 11%

Science Occupations (All): 10%

Meteorologists and Atmospheric Scientists: 10%

Note: "All Occupations" includes all occupations in the U.S. Economy. Source: U.S. Bureau of Labor Statistics, Employment Projections Program.

Related Occupations

- Astronomer
- Oceanographer
- Physicist

Related Military Occupations

- Meteorological Specialist
- Meteorologist

Conversation With . . .
DON SCHWENNEKER

TV Meteorologist, 20 years
WTVD-TV, Raleigh, NC

1. What was your individual career path in terms of education/training, entry-level job, or other significant opportunity?

I didn't get my job in the traditional way. I actually started in radio and TV production running cameras and shooting and editing video. I had always performed in choir and theatre and one day I was asked to audition for a part-time weather job. Once I started talking about the weather, I loved it! So I went back to school part-time while working full time and earned my meteorology certification from Mississippi State University. If someone wants to be an on-air meteorologist, they should go to college for Meteorology and while there, take classes in speech and broadcasting.

2. What are the most important skills and/or qualities for someone in your profession?

You have to be able to think on your feet and roll with change. Some days are slow and sunny, some days we have severe weather moving through our viewing area. It's never the same day twice (unless you work in Hawaii). Good math and science skills are also important when it comes to actually making the forecast. Computer skills are essential in making the graphics seen on TV.

3. What do you wish you had known going into this profession?

I thought I could stay in the same place and work for 30 years. I didn't think I would move as much as I have. If you start in smaller markets and want to make a living that will support a family, you have to keep moving to bigger cities to increase the pay. I don't regret it; I've lived in some amazing places!

4. Are there many job opportunities in your profession? In what specific areas?

In TV, the need for meteorologists is steady. But supply for meteorologists in general continues to exceed demand. According to the National Oceanic and Atmospheric Administration, U.S. colleges and universities confer meteorology degrees on approximately 600-1000 students every year. One study suggested the need for new meteorologists is only half that. Most people who go into meteorology do so because of a love of all things weather, and not because of the paycheck.

5. **How do you see your profession changing in the next five years, what role will technology play in those changes, and what skills will be required?**

   I think TV meteorology is shrinking. You can get a forecast from many different sources. I think our point of difference is severe weather. When you have a tornado bearing down on you, you don't want to rely on a computer for accurate weather information. That may change in 10-20 years, but for now, I think that is where we can still be relevant. As far as skills go, computer skills will continue to become more and more relevant. Knowing where to go online to get official and often complex meteorological data and how to work with it will be key.

6. **What do you enjoy most about your job? What do you enjoy least about your job?**

   TV weather is anything but routine. I love that my job is different every day. Some days it's sunny and quiet, some days I'm chasing a storm. Some days I'm working on the weather computer all day, some days I get to go out and speak to 150 school kids. As far as my least favorite thing about my job, it has to be the hours. We work when most people are home watching TV. There aren't a lot of 8am-5pm jobs in TV meteorology.

7. **Can you suggest a valuable "try this" for students considering a career in your profession?**

   Try making a Power Point of today's weather. On your first page, show some current temperatures. You can get those off your local National Weather Service page. On the second and third pages show some pictures of the weather, either ones you've taken, or one's you've borrowed off the internet. On the last page, make a forecast. Then practice talking about each of the pages. Once you are comfortable, give the forecast to a family member or friend and ask them what you can do better. Don't be afraid to hear criticism! If you are planning on working in a field where you speak to people, there's always a critic.

SELECTED SCHOOLS

Virtually all colleges and universities have bachelor's degree programs in biology; some have concentrations in wildlife biology or marine biology. The student may also gain an initial grounding in the field at an agricultural, technical, or community college. For advanced positions, a master's or doctoral degree is usually obtained. Below are listed some of the more prominent graduate schools in this field.

Colorado State University
Department of Atmospheric Science
200 West Lake Street
1371 Campus Delivery
Fort Collins, CO 80523
970.491.8682
www.atmos.colostate.edu

Cornell University
Earth and Atmospheric Sciences
Snee Hall
Ithaca, NY 14853
607.255.3474
www.eas.cornell.edu

Massachusetts Institute of Technology
Earth, Atmospheric, and Planetary Sciences
77 Massachusetts Avenue
Cambridge, MA 02139
617.253.2127
eapsweb.mit.edu

Penn State University
Department of Meteorology
503 Walker Building
University Park, PA 16802
814.865.0478
ploneprod.met.psu.edu

Texas A&M University
Department of Atmospheric Science
MS 3150
College Station, TX 77843
979.845.7688
atmo.tamu.edu

University of California, Los Angeles
Atmospheric and Oceanic Sciences
Los Angeles, CA 90095
310.825.1217
www.atmos.ucla.edu

University of Maryland, College Park
Atmospheric and Oceanic Science
College Park, MD 20742
301.405.5391
www.atmos.umd.edu

University of Miami
Rosenstiel School of Marine and Atmospheric Science
4600 Rickenbacker Causeway
Miami, FL 33149
305.421.4000
www.rsmas.miami.edu

University of Oklahoma
School of Meteorology
120 David Boren Boulevard,
Suite 5900
Norman, OK 73072
405.325.6561
som.ou.edu

University of Washington
Department of Atmospheric
Science
408 ATG Building
Box 351640
Seattle, WA 98195
206.543.4250
www.atmos.washington.edu

MORE INFORMATION

American Geosciences Institute
4220 King Street
Alexandria, VA 22302-1502
703.379.2480
www.americangeosciences.org

American Meteorological Society
45 Beacon Street
Boston, MA 02108-3693
617.227.2425
www.ametsoc.org

National Weather Association
228 W. Millbrook Road
Raleigh, NC 27609-4303
919.845.7121
www.nwas.org

National Oceanographic and
Atmospheric Administration
1401 Constitution Avenue, NW,
Room 5128
Washington, DC 20230
www.noaa.gov

University Corporation for
Atmospheric Research
3090 Center Green Drive
PO Box 3000
Boulder, CO 80301
www2.ucar.edu

Susan Williams/Editor

Nursery Worker

Snapshot

Career Cluster: Agriculture; Environment & Conservation
Interests: Gardening, planting and harvesting, agricultural science, horticulture, customer service
Earnings (Yearly Average): $20,080
Employment & Outlook: Slower Than Average Growth Expected

OVERVIEW

Sphere of Work

Nursery workers, also known as greenhouse workers, agricultural workers, horticultural workers, farm laborers, or harvesters, perform the physical labor necessary to operate nurseries and greenhouses. Nurseries and greenhouses are indoor spaces where plants are raised and tended until the plants reach the size and strength to be replanted in outdoor environments. Nursery workers support the production of food crops, ornamental plants, trees, sod, bulbs, and shrubs.

Work Environment

Nursery workers work predominately indoors in nurseries or greenhouses. They do not generally have set work hours but instead must work until the task (e.g. planting, harvesting, or irrigating) is completed. Nurseries and greenhouses generally employ nursery workers on a seasonal basis. Nursery workers work the majority of their hours in the spring and summer. During the fallow seasons, autumn and winter, nursery workers may be employed to maintain or repair machinery and equipment.

Profile

Working Conditions: Work both Indoors and Outdoors
Physical Strength: Medium Work
Education Needs: On-the-Job Training, High School Diploma with Technical Education, Junior/Technical/Community College,
Licensure/Certification: Usually Not Required
Physical Abilities Not Required: N/A
Opportunities For Experience: Internship, Part-Time Workk
Holland Interest Score*: REC

* See Appendix A

Occupation Interest

Individuals attracted to the nursery worker occupation tend to be physically strong and love nature. Those individuals who excel as nursery workers exhibit physical stamina, friendliness, patience, and self-direction. Nursery workers should enjoy physical work and have a background in agriculture.

A Day in the Life—Duties and Responsibilities

The nursery workers are employed in retail nurseries and greenhouses, wholesale nurseries and greenhouses, private nurseries and greenhouses, and mail order or catalogue nursery and greenhouses businesses. Duties tend to vary by employer.

The primary nursery and greenhouse tasks are planting, tending, and harvesting crops. Nursery workers first shape planting beds, till and test the soil, and manage soil nutrient content with fertilizers, peat moss, and other soil conditioning agents. Seeds, bulbs, or transplanted seedlings may be planted in the prepared bed. Sometimes nursery workers graft plants together to create hybrids or new varieties. Once the plants begin to grow, nursery workers weed and irrigate the planting beds and wrap burlap sacking around tree roots. The nursery workers also monitor and manage the greenhouse light and temperature control systems to ensure healthy growth. Nursery workers use natural and chemical methods to manage pests, and they dispose of any pest- and blight-contaminated trees or plants. At the appropriate times, they prune, thin, and harvest grains, fruits, vegetables, flowers, and nuts from the plants, often to encourage future fruitfulness. Nursery workers may be involved in making the planting decisions for upcoming years as well.

Nursery workers assist in their establishment's maintenance and customer service activities. They safely store fuels and chemicals. As needed, they repair greenhouse and nursery irrigation, lighting, heating, and cooling systems. Nursery workers may prepare mail order shipments of plants and seeds and load trucks with crops and plants for transport to wholesale or retail customers. They keep the nursery and greenhouse clean and ready for customers' visits. This may require digging up mature trees ready for sale, cutting and rolling sod, and potting and labeling plants with their common or scientific name. Nursery workers also promote the nursery business and sell crops, plants, trees, shrubs, and related items to the general public and wholesale buyers.

In addition, all nursery workers are responsible for educating themselves about the rights (work conditions, pay, and safety) of agricultural workers.

Duties and Responsibilities

- **Planting seeds, bulbs or plant cuttings**
- **Setting the fertilizer timing and metering devices that control frequency and amounts of nutrients to be introduced into the irrigation system**
- **Applying herbicides, fungicides and pesticides on plants to destroy any undesirable growth and pests**
- **Pollinating, pruning, transplanting and pinching plants**
- **Harvesting, packing and storing crops, using the techniques appropriate for each individual horticultural specialty**

WORK ENVIRONMENT

Physical Environment

Nursery workers work in heated nurseries and greenhouses. Nursery work tends to be very physical and require extensive hard labor, walking, lifting, and bending. Nursery workers are at risk for job-related injuries, including heat stroke, back strain, pesticide exposure, and machine accidents. In facilities where pesticides are used, nursery workers must wear protective gear such as chemical-resistant gloves.

Human Environment

A nursery worker's work environment tends to be somewhat isolated as nurseries and greenhouses can be remotely located. That said nurseries and greenhouses are enclosed spaces where employees work side-by-side towards a shared purpose. Depending on the place of employment, nursery workers may also interact directly with customers.

Relevant Skills and Abilities

Organization & Management Skills
- Making decisions
- Paying attention to and handling details
- Performing duties which change frequently
- Performing routine work

Research & Planning Skills
- Developing evaluation strategies

Technical Skills
- Working with machines, tools or other objects
- Working with your hands

Technological Environment

Nursery workers use machinery and equipment, such as garden bed tools, fertilizing equipment, mulch spreaders, ventilation and heating systems, mowers, pesticide sprayers, trucks, irrigation systems, and hand tools to complete their work. Nursery workers with managerial responsibilities may also be required to use computers, spreadsheets, and Internet communication tools to track plants, growing seasons, and yields as well as communicate with customers.

EDUCATION, TRAINING, AND ADVANCEMENT

High School/Secondary

High school-level study of agricultural science, biology, and business can provide a strong foundation for work as a nursery worker. Due to the diversity of nursery worker responsibilities, high school students interested in this career path may benefit from seeking internships or part-time work with local nurseries, greenhouses, and farms. High school students may be able to secure employment as nursery workers directly following graduation.

Suggested High School Subjects

- Agricultural Education
- Agricultural Mechanization
- English
- Forestry
- Landscaping
- Mathematics
- Ornamental Horticulture
- Science

Famous First

The first greenhouses were erected in ancient Rome, where cucumbers were grown under oilcloth. In the United States, the first glass greenhouse was built by James Beekman in New York City in 1764, although there is evidence that Andrew Faneuil of Boston had a small greenhouse as early as 1737.

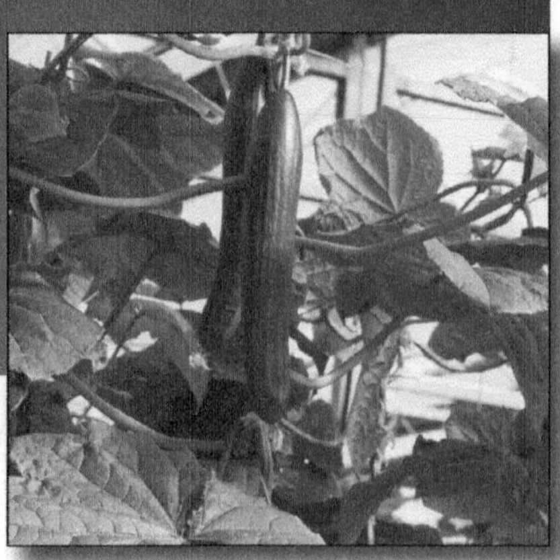

College/Postsecondary

Postsecondary students interested in becoming nursery workers should work towards the associate's degree in agriculture or farm management. Coursework in business and foreign languages may also prove useful in their future work. Postsecondary students can gain work experience and potential advantage in their future job searches by securing internships or part-time employment with local nurseries, greenhouses, and farms. Postsecondary training can lead to managerial positions in the field.

Related College Majors
- Horticulture Science
- Horticulture Services Operations & Management

Adult Job Seekers

Adults seeking employment as nursery workers should have, at a minimum, a high school diploma. Some nursery worker jobs require extensive experience, on-the-job training, and an associate's or bachelor's degree. Adult job seekers should educate themselves about the educational and professional requirements of the organizations where they seek employment.

Adult job seekers may benefit from joining professional agricultural and horticultural associations, such as the New England Small Farm Institute, the American Society for Horticultural Science, United Farm Workers, and the American Farm Bureau Federation. These associations generally offer job-finding workshops and maintain lists and forums of available jobs.

Professional Certification and Licensure

Certification and licensure is not required for nursery workers.

Additional Requirements

Individuals who find satisfaction, success, and job security as nursery workers will be knowledgeable about the profession's requirements, responsibilities, and opportunities. Membership in professional agricultural and horticultural associations is encouraged among all nursery workers as a means of building professional community and ensuring agricultural worker rights.

Fun Fact

The nursery and greenhouse industry is U.S. agriculture's fastest-growing sector.

Source: http://www.agmrc.org/commodities__products/forestry/nursery-trees/

EARNINGS AND ADVANCEMENT

Earnings of nursery workers depend on the individual's ability and technical knowledge and the size and geographic location of the employer. Mean annual earnings of nursery workers were $20,080 in 2013. The lowest ten percent earned less than $17,000, and the highest ten percent earned more than $26,000.

Nursery workers may receive paid vacations, holidays, and sick days; life and health insurance; and retirement benefits. These are usually paid by the employer.

Metropolitan Areas with the Highest Employment Level in This Occupation

Metropolitan area	Employment	Employment per thousand jobs	Hourly mean wage
Bakersfield-Delano, CA	36,590	126.83	$8.87
Salinas, CA	26,700	172.01	$9.27
Fresno, CA	24,870	77.29	$9.07
Visalia-Porterville, CA	18,280	137.36	$9.45
Yuma, AZ	8,530	144.79	$9.01
Santa Barbara-Santa Maria-Goleta, CA	6,860	39.73	$8.97
Madera-Chowchilla, CA	6,180	158.67	$8.81
Stockton, CA	6,170	30.42	$8.72
Modesto, CA	5,860	37.11	$9.41
El Centro, CA	5,680	109.33	$9.21

Source: Bureau of Labor Statistics

EMPLOYMENT AND OUTLOOK

Nationally, there were about 600,000 nursery and agricultural workers employed in 2012. Employment is expected to decline through the year 2022. This is in response to the increasing use of technology in agricultural and horticultural settings. On the other hand, demand for landscaping, groundskeeping, and related services is increasing, and nursery and greenhouse workers may benefit from that growth.

Employment Trend, Projected 2012–22

Total, All Occupations: 11%

Nursery and Agricultural workers: -3%

Farming, Fishing, and Forestry Occupations: -3%

Note: "All Occupations" includes all occupations in the U.S. Economy. Source: U.S. Bureau of Labor Statistics, Employment Projections Program.

Related Occupations

- Farm Worker
- Floral Designer
- Florist
- Forestry Worker
- Gardener and Groundskeeper

Conversation With . . .

BEN SANDERS

Grower, 17 years
Griffith Propagation Nursery, Inc.
Watkinsville, GA

1. What was your individual career path in terms of education/training, entry-level job, or other significant opportunity?

I grew up in a small town in middle Georgia where agriculture, particularly peach production, was the primary industry. My first real job was working in a peach packing shed when I was 11 years old. When I was 13, I started working in the field: helping with the harvest, fertilizing, pruning, and learning what hard work really was.

I was accepted to the University of Georgia's School of Landscape Architecture. In retrospect, I really didn't understand what that was going to involve. I expected to learn about plants and how to use them. Instead, I was taught how to draft and how presentation was the key to selling the customer on your design. At the end of my second quarter, I changed my major to horticulture.

The change was a good one. Plant Materials, Plant Nutrition, Nursery Production, and Environmental Horticulture were all classes that engaged me, and I did well in them. My first job in ornamental horticulture came after a mock interview for my Horticultural Professionalism requirement when one of my professors introduced me to a lady who was looking for workers. She grew perennials, herbs, and other specialty plants along with some bedding plants, none of which I knew anything about. But since her nursery was over half an hour from the university, her main requirement was that you have a way to get to work. I met that requirement, and so I was hired. I learned to water, plant, and listen carefully. I also learned that being conscientious about your work and doing what you are told are far more valuable skills than knowing which fertilizer to use. I worked there until I graduated from college.

My junior year, another professor took me along on a trip to a large container nursery. He cajoled them into offering me a paid summer internship. I learned that who you know is at least as important as what you know. I learned the basics of scouting, spraying, propagation, and weed control. I learned that having a good rapport with your manager and your fellow workers is more important than having a degree or knowing whether an apple is a pome or a berry.

Knowing I was looking at other job opportunities upon graduation, my employer introduced me to the owner of a large, well-respected tree farm in the area. I didn't know anything about ornamental trees, but the farm offered me a job, and I accepted.

I spent the next four-and-a-half years there. During that time I got married to my high school sweetheart, we bought a small piece of land to build on one day, and I learned a few more things. I learned that quality doesn't just happen and can't be taught overnight. It is acquired -- caught, almost like a disease – and starts from the top and trickles down. I learned the importance of clearly communicating with your co-workers and your superiors. I learned that talking about doing something is not the same as doing it.

At the end of those four and a half years, I was offered a job as the production manager of a new nursery. I had very little management experience, but I was hired to run a 500 acre nursery that eventually employed 50 full-time workers. I spent the next eight years there. When the recession hit, the company was forced to downsize, and about half of the employees were let go, including me. During those years my wife and I had three children, and I learned that relationships are more important than business, and that doing a good job isn't always what matters. I learned how hard it is to fire people you care about and how being fired yourself isn't really that big a deal.

Within the week, I had two job offers. One was growing trees, which I had over 12 years of experience doing, while the other was propagating woody ornamentals, with which I had no experience. Since the tree farm required a 200 mile move and the propagation nursery was only six miles from home, I decided to learn to propagate. I have been with my current employer for five years. We have added our fourth (and last) child to the mix. I have learned the importance of communication, the conveyance of approval or disapproval, and what happens when you don't plan ahead. I will turn 40 in a couple of months, and I am thinking of the future. I am starting to feel my age; this industry can be physically tough.

2. What are the most important skills and/or qualities for someone in your profession?

I have a feeling that most people in horticulture actually prefer plants to people, or at least prefer not to interact with people any more than necessary. That is not to say we are all misanthropes, only that we are mostly introverts.

However, owning, operating, managing, or working at a nursery requires working with people, and those skills are the most important ones to develop. Although there are certain technical aspects to producing plants, at the end of the day you have plenty of resources for anything that involves growing.

If you are in any level of management, you have people under you who do most of the work. In my experience, that work is outside in the elements. Nursery workers get hot, cold, wet, chapped, sick, injured, tired, and dirty. If you are a manager, it is your job to minimize all that discomfort, show some empathy, and keep things moving. Your workers understand the work is hard, but you need to understand it, too. Spend some time working with them to experience what they experience. If you find yourself needing a water break every 15 minutes because it is 98 degrees with 95% humidity, they probably do, too. Go to the store and buy a cooler, some ice, and a bunch of 18-ounce Gatorades. You'll be surprised at how well that sort of management works.

If you have people over you, remember that they have concerns that you do not. The owner may be worried about making payroll next week, and if he is not that interested in the fertilizer trial you are doing with his money, you need to get over it. Your manager may be trying to figure out how he or she is going to get all that pruning done with only three people in the next two weeks.

3. **What do you wish you had known going into this profession?**

From a management standpoint, the most important thing I did not do in school was take Spanish classes. I had to teach myself and ended up with a rudimentary ability to understand and speak. Two or three quarters of Spanish in college would have made a big difference in my ability to communicate with the roughly 150 Hispanics I have worked with or managed over the years. If you want to communicate effectively, you literally do have to speak the same language.

On the production side, I wish I had known more about irrigation.

4. **Are there many job opportunities in your profession? In what specific areas?**

There are opportunities out there. Larger nurseries often advertise in industry publications. At UGA there was a job board that advertised both local and regional job opportunities, and there are job boards at most industry gatherings. Once you are in the industry, you discover that a lot of hiring, especially by small- to medium companies looking for managers, is done by word of mouth.

The industry will often hire based less on the job requirement and more on the individual's strength and weaknesses. The advantage for the job-seeker is that nurseries are often looking for intelligent, hard-working individuals, and lack of experience in a particular segment of the industry is not necessarily an issue. People in this industry value hard work and commitment, and those two things will be more valuable than anything else you have to offer.

5. **How do you see your profession changing in the next five years, what role will technology play in those changes, and what skills will be required?**

I don't foresee any profound changes in production horticulture. Plants need sunlight, water, fertilizer, something to grow in, and the rest takes care of itself. Being able to grow a plant will always be the most important skill. Technology, especially in the form of automation, will certainly have its place. Proper implementation will streamline production processes, improve management, conserve resources, and reduce waste.

I believe the greatest change will be in the area of marketing. As a younger generation of workers becomes the next generation of decision makers, I believe there will be more creative and effective uses of technology in general and social media specifically. Knowing what these resources are, what they are capable of, and how to use them will be a skill worth possessing.

6. What do you enjoy most about your job? What do you enjoy least about your job?

While I enjoy many of the things related to horticulture – being outside, working with plants, flexible hours – what I most enjoy is the process of production. Plants are living things, weather is unpredictable, and managing a crop from start to finish requires patience, diligence, attention to detail, knowledge, experience, a certain amount of boldness, and a little bit of luck. I enjoy the challenge of constantly improving the process by speeding up the production cycle, improving the quality, and reducing the inputs required to do those things. This challenge is what keeps the job interesting year after year.

What I find the most difficult are the slow times. Typically the fall is a slow time, since the plants are beginning to shut down. Most nurseries enter into a "clean-up" mode. This is usually when I spend time working with our computer system, trying to smooth out wrinkles that popped up during the busy season.

7. Can you suggest a valuable "try this" for students considering a career in your profession?

The best thing about horticulture for someone considering the field is that it has a pretty low barrier to entry. You don't need a college degree, and you don't need any prior training. All you really need are some seeds or plants, some soil, and access to water. What you do with those three essentials and what you add to them is up to you.

Whatever you do, have a goal in mind, because that is what production is about. Don't just plant some seeds, walk off, and wait for the rain to come. Plant some flowers and tell yourself that, by the end of three months, you will have accomplished a goal, whether that is getting your plants to them to a certain height or producing a certain number of blooms, and then do what you need to do to make it happen. Try to root something and see what happens when you don't keep it moist enough, or if it gets too moist or too hot. Build a $25 greenhouse out of PVC and white plastic from your hardware store and put something in it. Track your goal and learn from your mistakes — how weather and pests go together, how water and fertility interact — and teach yourself to closely monitor the plant. Experience is the best teacher, and fortunately, you can learn a lot of lessons inexpensively in your own backyard.

SELECTED SCHOOLS

Many agricultural, technical, and community colleges offer programs in horticulture. Interested students are advised to consult with their school guidance counselor or to research area postsecondary schools and training programs. For those interested in a career as a nursery manager, it can be useful to hold bachelor's degree from, for example, a state land-grant college.

MORE INFORMATION

American Society of Agronomy
5585 Guilford Road
Madison, WI 53711-5801
608.273.8080
www.agronomy.org

American Nursery & Landscape Association
1200 G Street, NW
Washington, DC 20005
202.789.2900
www.anla.org

American Society for Horticultural Science
1018 Duke Street
Alexandria, VA 22314-2851
703.836.4606
www.ashs.org

Association of Education and Research Greenhouse Curators
PO Box 319
Mahomet, IL 61853
www.aergc.org

New England Small Farm Institute
275 Jackson Street
Belchertown, MA 01007-9818
413.323.4531
www.smallfarm.org

United Farm Workers
P.O. Box 62
29700 Woodford-Tehachapi Road
Keene, CA 93531-0062
661.823.6151
www.ufw.org

Simone Isadora Flynn/Editor

Oceanographer

Snapshot

Career Cluster: Environment & Conservation; Science & Technology
Interests: Marine habitats, natural science, oceanography, geology, ecology
Earnings (Yearly Average): $88,140
Employment & Outlook: Faster Than Average Growth Expected

OVERVIEW

Sphere of Work

Oceanographers are part of an interdisciplinary field that uses chemistry, geology, biology, and physics to study many different aspects of the earth's oceans and seas. They tend to focus on one of four main areas: physical, chemical, geological, and biological oceanography. Oceanographers study water currents and circulation, chemical composition, animal and plant life, and geological formations. Oceanographers often study oceanic weather patterns, environmental issues and pollution, and fossils.

They are also hired to help locate new mineral deposits, deep-sea oil reserves, new fishing locations, and alternative energy sources. Universities, government agencies at all levels, and private businesses and organizations employ oceanographers.

Work Environment

Oceanographers work for federal agencies such as the National Oceanic and Atmospheric Administration (NOAA), as well as colleges and universities, ecological and environmental organizations, and private industry. Some oceanographers conduct the majority of their research aboard offshore research vessels. Others perform office or laboratory work. On land, oceanographers work standard forty-hour weeks, during which they conduct laboratory experiments, examine and record data, and write academic papers. At sea, they may experience extreme weather conditions, rough seas, and cramped living conditions. While conducting research at sea, oceanographers frequently work much longer hours.

Profile

Working Conditions: Work both Indoors and Outdoors
Physical Strength: Light Work
Education Needs: Bachelor's Degree, Master's Degree, Doctoral Degree
Licensure/Certification: Usually Not Required
Physical Abilities Not Required: No Heavy Labor
Opportunities For Experience: Internship
Holland Interest Score*: IRE

* See Appendix A

Occupation Interest

Oceanographers often spend a great deal of time at sea, an aspect of the job that may appeal to those who love nature and enjoy working outdoors. They study firsthand the wide array of animal and plant life, geological formations, weather conditions, and other interesting aspects of the oceans. Oceanographers are respected for their expertise and can influence policymaking related to the environment. Vast stretches of ocean remain unexplored, meaning there is always a possibility of discovering new species or formulating new theories. As an interdisciplinary field, oceanography offers many areas of specialization from which scientists may choose.

A Day in the Life—Duties and Responsibilities

Oceanographers' duties and responsibilities vary based on the subfields in which they work. Physical oceanographers use models and databases to study changes in ocean temperature and salinity, currents, waves, and tidal patterns. Physical oceanographers and meteorologists work together to better understand the relationship between the ocean and climate. Chemical oceanographers take surface water and deepwater samples and use analytical equipment to study the natural and synthetic chemical compounds in those samples. They often seek to understand the impact of pollutants and observe interactions between bodies of water and the atmosphere. Geological oceanographers often use remote-controlled diving equipment to photograph and map deep-sea volcanoes, floor rock configurations, and other solid bodies. These oceanographers track and predict changes in the structure and mineral composition of the sea floor. Meanwhile, biological oceanographers, or marine biologists, locate, trap, tag, and release animal species to track their movement, feeding, mating, and other behavior patterns. Biological oceanographers study aquatic ecosystems and assist in developing techniques for sustainable resource harvesting.

Some of the most important work performed by oceanographers occurs on research vessels at sea. Such research can take place for extended periods, during which oceanographers compile soil and water samples, record temperatures and atmospheric conditions, take photographic images of geological formations and other subjects on the ocean floor, and capture live specimens of plants and wildlife. When they return to the laboratory, oceanographers compile data into databases, build models using computer software, and formulate theories. Using field data, samples, and models, oceanographers draft technical reports and assessments, author scholarly papers and articles, and submit policy recommendations to the government agencies, private businesses, and nonprofit organizations that employ them.

Many oceanographers are also university professors. In this capacity, they lead seminars, lectures, and laboratory sessions, advise students, and work with departmental peers. University-based oceanographers are able to pursue their independent research while teaching courses. They typically draft grant proposals to obtain government funding for their research.

Duties and Responsibilities

- **Planning and conducting field research in marine environments**
- **Collecting and analyzing samples and data**
- **Making maps and charts**
- **Writing reports and research papers**

WORK ENVIRONMENT

Relevant Skills and Abilities

Analytical Skills
- Collecting and analyzing data

Communication Skills
- Speaking and writing effectively

Organization & Management Skills
- Making decisions
- Paying attention to and handling details

Research & Planning Skills
- Identifying a research problem
- Laying out a plan
- Presenting solutions

Technical Skills
- Performing scientific, mathematical and technical work

Work Environment Skills
- Working under different weather conditions

Physical Environment

Oceanographers work at universities, private nonprofit organizations, corporations, and government offices and laboratories. The conditions at each of these venues are clean, bright, and well ventilated. When conducting research, they often travel for extended periods aboard research vessels. At sea, oceanographers are at risk of injury from dangerous weather, sea conditions, heavy lifting, malfunctioning equipment, and/or animal attacks.

Human Environment

Depending on their areas of specialty, oceanographers interact and collaborate with a wide range of scientists and professionals. They may work with marine biologists, laboratory technicians, interns and lab assistants, geologists, engineers, business executives, environmental scientists, ship crews, government officials, and university students and professors.

Technological Environment

Oceanographers use a number of pieces of equipment and technology to take samples and perform research at sea. They may capture animals with nets and snaring equipment, deploy scientific buoys to record measurements, or explore shallow areas with scuba equipment. Oceanographers also use submersible devices (both manned and remote-controlled) to travel to the ocean floor and take samples and photographs. In the laboratory, oceanographers rely on computer modeling, digital mapping, and database technologies to help formulate and validate theories.

EDUCATION, TRAINING, AND ADVANCEMENT

High School/Secondary

High school students should study biology, chemistry, physics, and other natural sciences. Mathematics, including algebra, geometry, and statistics, are important courses as well. Furthermore, high school students should take computer science courses and hone their writing and public speaking skills through English and communications classes.

Suggested High School Subjects

- Algebra
- Applied Math
- Applied Physics
- Biology
- Calculus
- Chemistry
- College Preparatory
- Computer Science
- Earth Science
- English

- Geography
- Geometry
- Mathematics
- Physics
- Science

Famous First

The first high-resolution maps of the ocean floor were published in 1995, when declassified images and data from two satellites, *Geosat* and *ERS-1*, were released by the US Navy. The information provided the first detailed and consistent view of the earth's ocean basins.

College/Postsecondary

Oceanographers must receive a bachelor's degree in a field related to oceanography, such as biology, chemistry, engineering, environmental science, and geology. Most oceanographers have at least a master's degree in one or more related scientific disciplines. Senior researchers and oceanography professors must have earned or be working toward a doctorate in an oceanography-related scientific field. Students can gain experience in the field through internships or research assistantships.

Related College Majors

- Geology
- Geophysics & Seismology
- Oceanography

Adult Job Seekers

Qualified oceanographers may apply directly to government agencies, universities, nonprofit organizations, or corporations with open positions. Many universities have placement programs that can help recent graduates find work. Additionally, oceanographers may join and network through professional and academic associations and societies such as the International Association for Biological Oceanography or the American Society of Limnology and Oceanography.

Professional Certification and Licensure

Oceanographers who also practice as engineers must be certified as professional engineers within the state in which they work.

Additional Requirements

Oceanographers should be able to analyze complex issues and concepts. They must demonstrate exceptional research and writing skills. Knowledge of and capability with mechanical devices greatly helps oceanographers as well. Furthermore, oceanographers should have strong computer skills, particularly with geographic information systems (GIS) and global positioning systems (GPS). Physical fitness and stamina are advantageous for fieldwork.

Fun Fact

Oceanography has four primary, tightly linked disciplines: biological, chemical, geological, and physical. To understand any process or organism in the ocean, you have to consider the whole system. Chemical oceanographers study the linkages between the biology and chemistry of the ocean.

Source: Greg Cutter; Professor, Department of Ocean, Earth, and Atmospheric Sciences; Old Dominion University, Norfolk, VA

EARNINGS AND ADVANCEMENT

Oceanographers with experience may be promoted to teaching or high level research positions as well as administrative or supervisory positions. Graduate study and experience often expand employment opportunities. According to a salary survey by the National Association of Colleges and Employers, graduates with a bachelor's degree in geology and related sciences had average starting salaries of $47,243 in 2012.

Mean annual earnings of geoscientists, of which oceanographers are a part, were $108,420 in 2013. The lowest ten percent earned less than $49,000, and the highest ten percent earned more than $145,000. Oceanographers may receive paid vacations, holidays, and sick days; life and health insurance; and retirement benefits. These are usually paid by the employer.

EMPLOYMENT AND OUTLOOK

Geoscientists, including oceanographers, held about 38,000 jobs nationally in 2012. Many more individuals held geology, geophysics and oceanography faculty positions in colleges and universities. Most oceanographers are employed by the U.S. Geological Survey within the Department of the Interior and for the Department of Defense. Employment is expected to grow faster than the average for all occupations through the year 2022, which means employment is projected to increase 15 percent to 20 percent. Oceanographers, whose work is often research-oriented and dependent on grants from federal agencies, are expected to face strong competition. With more people graduating from oceanography programs than the field can absorb, those with advanced technical and research skills will be most desirable.

Employment Trend, Projected 2012–22

Geoscientists, Including Oceanographers: 16%

Total, All Occupations: 11%

Science Occupations (All): 10%

Note: "All Occupations" includes all occupations in the U.S. Economy. Source: U.S. Bureau of Labor Statistics, Employment Projections Program.

Related Occupations

- Biological Scientist
- Botanist
- Geographer
- Geologist & Geophysicist
- Marine Biologist
- Meteorologist
- Microbiologist

Conversation With . . .
GREG CUTTER

Professor, Ocean, Earth & Atmospheric Sciences
Old Dominion University, Norfollk, VA
Chemical Oceanographer, 38 years

1. What was your individual career path in terms of education/training, entry-level job, or other significant opportunity?

My mother got me Jaques Cousteau books in my youth, and I thought, "This is what I want to do." In college, I started out in biology but switched to chemistry because I didn't like the genetics classes required in biology.

I had work-study grants and worked in the cafeteria making breakfasts. One of my friends suggested I apply for a job at Scripps (Institution of Oceanography), which is part of UC San Diego where I went to college. So I got a job in their data processing and collection group during sophomore year and became an illustrator. All of the famous oceanographers would come and get me to make a map or a graph. Later, another friend -- an English major -- worked as a part-time secretary for a famous chemical oceanographer and suggested I work in his lab. I spoke to him and ended up stopping work as an illustrator and going to work in his lab. It turned out the professor, Dr. Edward Goldberg, is one of several people credited with starting chemical oceanography in this country. His senior technician took me under his wing and taught me to do analytical analyses you wouldn't learn in class.

After graduating, I ran the marine analytical chemistry lab at the University of California, Santa Cruz where I helped people analyze their samples and went on oceanographic expeditions to collect water, plankton, and sediment samples. I went on to get my PhD in chemistry; my PhD research was in chemical oceanography. I then came to Old Dominion University in 1982 as an assistant professor.

In addition to teaching, I run the US Geotraces Trace Element Sampling Facility, which is carefully constructed to allow the cleanest samples possible to be obtained from the ocean. My research has been varied over the years; I will be part of a multi-national research trip to sample the Arctic Ocean next summer and examine the cycling of essential and toxic trace metals in this unique ocean.

2. **What are the most important skills and/or qualities for someone in your profession?**

   You need to be a good chemist, biologist, geologist, or physicist with a solid, traditional science background, but also learn about other disciplines and how you can apply them to your specialty. Be flexible to take advantage of opportunities as they appear. Quantitative skills — math and computer programming — are essential. Finally, you need to be able to write because you have to communicate your results.

3. **What do you wish you had known going into this profession?**

   More math! Modern science is very quantitative, especially oceanography. Advanced math is essential.

4. **Are there many job opportunities in your profession? In what specific areas?**

   If you can understand the ocean, you can understand a lake, a river, or groundwaters. So, if you have the tools, the job market is actually pretty large.

   Chemical oceanography students have job opportunities since there a not a lot of graduates and the chemistry of water is essential to public/environmental health due to pollution and global change, including ocean acidification. With an undergraduate degree you may be a lab technician in an academic or government lab, or at an environmental consulting company. With an MS degree, you can do the same but at a higher level with more local, state, and federal job options such as at a regional water treatment facility or with the National Oceanic and Atmospheric Administration. At the PhD level, everything is available. However, there are not a lot of academic jobs, so you have to be prepared to work in the state and federal governments or perhaps lead an environmental consulting company.

5. **How do you see your profession changing in the next five years, what role will technology play in those changes, and what skills will be required?**

   Technology is changing rapidly, especially in sensitive analytical instruments, so learn the latest methods and instruments. Computer modeling is also changing the way we approach oceanographic problems; modeling and simulation are likely to take on greater importance.

6. **What do you enjoy most about your job? What do you enjoy least about your job?**

   International travel and working with diverse peoples around the world is the best part of my job. Long hours is my least favorite, but after so many years I've adapted so it's not so bad.

7. Can you suggest a valuable "try this" for students considering a career in your profession?

As a science undergraduate, you have to either volunteer to work in a lab that interests you or get a lab assistant job doing whatever -- typically washing glassware. The key is to learn what's going on, meet potential advisors (who will write letters of recommendation for you later), and learn what they do and how graduate students cope with the stresses and demands of graduate education and research. Try to learn new and valuable lab methods. In my lab, undergraduates start off simply washing glassware, but if they are interested and show talent, they start helping the graduate students make reagents, then do analyses, and maybe even go on field trips/expeditions. Be willing to learn new things and stick around, even it if it's past your "shift." This "face time" is crucial to advancing.

Some high schools near universities have summer programs where you can do a project in a research lab. If this is possible, do it, even if it's not exactly in your field of interest. Again, this "face time" will help you get into a university, develop new skills and acquire new knowledge.

SELECTED SCHOOLS

Many agricultural, technical, and community colleges offer programs in horticulture. Interested students are advised to consult with their school guidance counselor or to research area postsecondary schools and training programs. For those interested in a career as a nursery manager, it can be useful to hold bachelor's degree from, for example, a state land-grant college.

Florida State University
Earth, Ocean, and Atmospheric Sciences
PO Box 3064520
Tallahassee, FL 32306
850.644.6205
www.eoas.fsu.edu

Massachusetts Institute of Technology
Earth, Atmospheric, and Planetary Sciences
77 Massachusetts Avenue
Cambridge, MA 02139
617.253.2127
eapsweb.mit.edu

Texas A&M University
Geology and Geophysics, MS 3115
College Station, TX 77843
979.845.2451
geosciences.tamu.edu

University of California, Berkeley
Earth and Planetary Science
307 McCone Hall
Berkeley, CA 94720
510.642.3993
eps.berkeley.edu

University of California, San Diego
Scripps Institute of Oceanography
9500 Gilman Drive
La Jolla, CA 92093
858.534.3624
scripps.ucsd.edu

University of Georgia
Skidaway Institute of Oceanography
10 Ocean Sciences Circle
Savannah, GA 31411
912.5982400
www.skio.uga.edu

University of Miami
Rosenstiel School of Marine and Atmospheric Science
4600 Rickenbacker Causeway
Miami, FL 33149
305.421.4000
www.rsmas.miami.edu

University of North Carolina, Chapel Hill
Department of Marine Sciences
3202 Venable and Murray Halls, CB 3300
Chapel Hill, NC 27599
919.962.1252
marine.unc.edu

University of Wisconsin
Atmospheric and Oceanic Sciences
1225 West Dayton Street
Madison, WI
608.262.2828
www.aos.wisc.edu

University of Washington
School of Oceanography
1503 NE Boat Street
Box 35790
Seattle, WA 98105
206.543.5060
www.ocean.washington.edu

MORE INFORMATION

Association for the Sciences of Limnology and Oceanography
5400 Bosque Blvd., Suite 680
Waco, TX 76710-4446
800.929.2756
www.aslo.org

Consortium for Ocean Leadership
1201 New York Avenue NW
4th Floor
Washington, DC 20005
202.232.3900
www.oceanleadership.org

Satellite and Information Service
National Oceanic and Atmospheric Administration
1335 East-West Highway
SSMC1, 8th Floor
Silver Spring, MD 20910
301.713.3578
www.nesdis.noaa.gov

National Oceanic and Atmospheric Administration (NOAA)
1401 Constitution Avenue NW
Washington, DC 20230
301.713.1203
www.noaa.gov

Ocean Foundation
1320 19th Street NW
5th FLoore
Washington, DC 20036
202.887.8996
www.oceanfdn.org

Oceanography Society
P.O. Box 1931
PO Box 1931
Rockville, MD 20849-1931
301.251.7708
www.tos.org

Woods Hole Oceanographic Institution
266 Woods Hole Road
Woods Hole, MA 02543
508.548.1400
www.whoi.edu

Michael Auerbach/Editor

Range Manager

Snapshot

Career Cluster: Agriculture; Environment & Conservation; Natural Resources Development
Interests: Ecology, land management, conservation science, natural resource management
Earnings (Yearly Average): $63,330
Employment & Outlook: Slower than Average Growth Expected

OVERVIEW

Sphere of Work

Range managers, also called natural resource specialists, wildlife managers, land managers, and habitat coordinators, engage in research, management, and protection of public and private rangeland. Rangeland, which covers approximately one billion acres of the United States and over half of all land on earth, generally refers to unforested land, including prairies, grassland, savannas, deserts, tundra, and shrubland. This land may be used for animal grazing, timbering, or recreation, or may be protected land such as wildlife habitats. In the United States, range managers promote environmentally sustainable forms of development and land use. Range management is a subspecialty of conservation science.

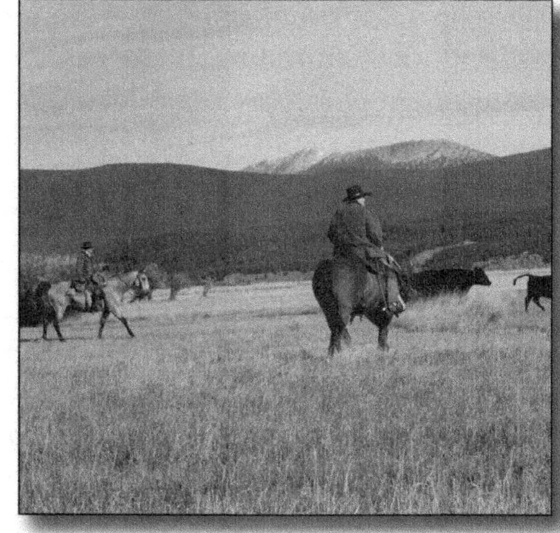

Work Environment

Most range managers work for government agencies, often overseeing field-based research or management efforts in diverse terrain. Others work as consultants or for private companies, and may spend their workdays in an office or a laboratory. Work hours tend to be unpredictable due to the nature of seasonal research and fieldwork. The work of range managers is very physical and may involve hiking in difficult terrain or traveling by truck, motorcycle, helicopter, or horseback.

Profile

Working Conditions: Work both Indoors and Outdoors
Physical Strength: Light Work
Education Needs: Bachelor's Degree
Licensure/Certification: Recommended
Physical Abilities Not Required: N/A
Opportunities For Experience: Internship, Part-Time Work
Holland Interest Score*: IRS

* See Appendix A

Occupation Interest

Individuals drawn to the profession of range manager tend to be people with an interest in the environment and conservation of natural resources. They should be physically fit, have good communication and problem-solving skills, and enjoy working in outdoor settings.

A Day in the Life—Duties and Responsibilities

The daily occupational duties and responsibilities of range managers will be determined by the individual's area of job specialization. Somebody who works with private landowners may help a rancher develop an optimal grazing system or determine the type of animal most suited to the local terrain. An employee of a biological assessment company may document and track the vegetation found on rangeland, prepare environmental impact statements, or study the feasibility and sustainability of land use projects. Government employees may make decisions about hunting and fishing policies, monitor the effects of outdoor recreation activities such as snowmobiling and camping, or meet with land preservation groups to discuss requests for land use or protection. Other possible duties include using fire and herbicides as necessary to control brush, monitoring water composition and volume, meeting with landowners to discuss short- and long-term land management choices and challenges, developing mineral extraction plans, and working to protect rangelands from mineral and energy resource exploitation. Range managers may also be required to aid in times of natural disasters, such as forest fires or mudslides.

Duties and Responsibilities

- Studying range lands to determine the best grazing seasons and the number and kind of animal life for which the land is best suited
- Developing improved practices for range reseeding
- Developing methods to control poisonous plants and to protect the land from fire and rodent damage
- Studying the quality of streams, lakes, ponds and other water resources and recommending needed improvements
- Consulting and working with other experts such as agronomists, foresters, wildlife specialists and outdoor recreation specialists to provide an overall improvement and protection of natural resources
- Planning and directing construction and maintenance of range improvements, such as fencing, corrals, reservoirs and structures for soil-erosion control

WORK ENVIRONMENT

Physical Environment

Range managers may work in offices, laboratories, or the field. Fieldwork tends to be very physical and often requires extensive walking, lifting, and bending. Range managers who work outdoors are at risk for injuries such as twists and fractures, backaches from extended walking with a pack, animal attacks, and extreme heat and cold exposure.

Relevant Skills and Abilities

Communication Skills
- Communication effectively

Organization & Management Skills
- Paying attention to and handling details
- Performing duties that change frequently

Research & Planning Skills
- Developing evaluation strategies

Technical Skills
- Performing technical work

Work Environment Skills
- Working outdoors

Human Environment

Range managers interact with ranchers, farmers, scientists, landowners, land and animal protection groups, and recreational land users. Due to the sometimes heated and divisive nature of land use discussions and decisions, range managers should exhibit tact and patience with land stakeholders.

Technological Environment

Range managers use a wide variety of equipment to complete their work, including computers, calculators, binoculars, cameras, Internet communication tools, land management software, spreadsheets, global positioning systems, soil and water testing kits, and microscopes.

EDUCATION, TRAINING, AND ADVANCEMENT

High School/Secondary

High school classes in agricultural science, biology, and business will provide a strong foundation for work as a range manager or for college-level study in the field. Students interested in this career path will benefit from seeking internships or part-time work with local land management groups, farms, or ranches.

Suggested High School Subjects
- Agricultural Education
- Algebra

- Applied Biology/Chemistry
- Applied Math
- Biology
- Chemistry
- College Preparatory
- English
- Mathematics
- Physics

Famous First

The first animal pounds for stray livestock were required by Connecticut in 1650. The colony decreed that "there shall be one sufficient pound or more made and maintained in every town and village within this jurisdiction, for the impounding of all swine and cattle as shall be found in any cornfield or other inclosure."

College/Postsecondary

Postsecondary students interested in becoming range managers should work toward a bachelor's degree in range management or a related field from a program accredited by either the Society for Range Management or the Society of American Foresters. Coursework in ecology, biology, natural resource management, or environmental sciences may also prove useful in their future work. Those interested in teaching or research positions should pursue a master's degree or doctorate in a relevant subject.

Related College Majors

- Environmental Science/Studies
- Natural Resources Management & Policy
- Wildlife & Wildlands Management

Adult Job Seekers

Adults seeking employment as a range manager should have at least a bachelor's degree. Range managers involved in complex research or graduate-level teaching are generally required to have advanced degrees. Professional land management associations, such as the Society for Range Management or the Soil and Water Conservation Society (SWCS), may offer career workshops or resources for locating available jobs.

Professional Certification and Licensure

Certification is not legally required for range managers, but may be required as a condition of employment, salary increase, or promotion. The Society for Range Management offers the voluntary Certified Professionals in Rangeland Management credential, the requirements for which include college-level coursework, at least five years of experience, an examination, and professional references.

Additional Requirements

Successful range managers should be analytical, observant, persuasive, and good with people. Membership in professional land management associations is encouraged.

Fun Fact

The U.S. officially created grazing districts after decades of homesteading left lands overgrazed due to policies aimed at promoting Western settlement. The Taylor Grazing Act of 1934 led to the creation of grazing districts. The Grazing Service merged with the General Land Office in 1946 to become the Bureau of Land Management.

Source: http://www.blm.gov/wo/st/en/prog/grazing.htmlsoil

EARNINGS AND ADVANCEMENT

Earnings depend on the geographic location of the employer and the employee's education. Range managers employed by government agencies advance to higher pay levels with an increase in responsibility after a certain period of time and after showing leadership abilities.

According to a salary survey by the National Association of Colleges and Employers, graduates with a bachelor's degree in conservation and renewable natural resources received an average starting salary of $40,167 in 2012. Mean annual earnings of range managers were $63,330 in 2013. The lowest ten percent earned less than $37,000, and the highest ten percent earned more than $90,000. Range managers may receive paid vacations, holidays, and sick days; life and health insurance; and retirement benefits. These are usually paid by the employer.

States with the Highest Employment Level in this Occupation

State	Employment[1]	Employment per thousand jobs	Hourly mean wage
Texas	1,740	0.16	$26.59
California	1,440	0.10	$36.33
Washington	1,050	0.37	$27.70
Colorado	1,030	0.45	$30.75
Wisconsin	710	0.26	$30.83

[1] Does not include self-employed. Source: Bureau of Labor Statistics

EMPLOYMENT AND OUTLOOK

There were approximately 23,000 conservation scientists, of which range managers are a part, employed nationally in 2012. Most range managers worked in the U.S. Department of the Interior's Bureau of Land Management, the Natural Resource Conservation Service or the Forest Service. Employment is expected to grow slower than the average for all occupations through the year 2022, which means employment is projected to increase 1 percent to 7 percent. Job growth will be caused by a continuing emphasis on environmental protection and responsible land management.

Employment Trend, Projected 2012–22

Total, All Occupations: 11%

Conservation Scientists and Foresters: 3%

Range Managers: 1%

Note: "All Occupations" includes all occupations in the U.S. Economy. Source: U.S. Bureau of Labor Statistics, Employment Projections Program.

Related Occupations

- Agricultural Scientist
- Botanist
- Farmer/Farm Manager
- Fish and Game Warden
- Fisher/Hunter/Trapper
- Forester and Conservation Scientist
- Soil Scientist

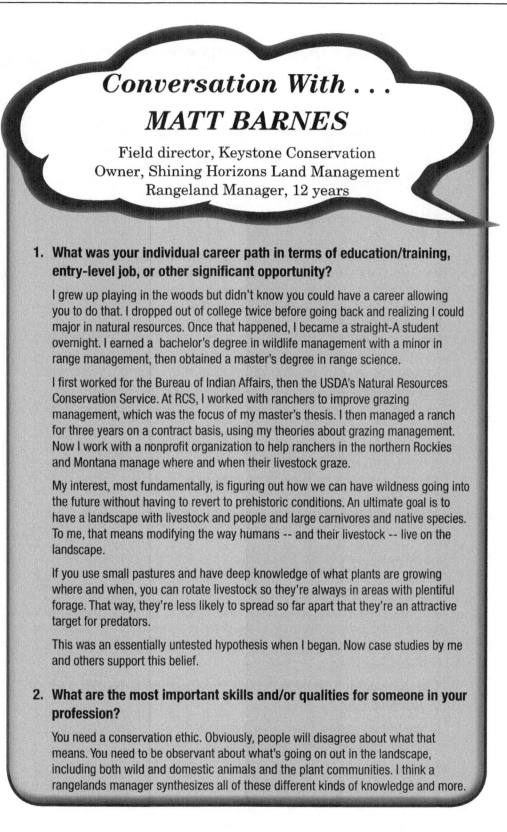

Conversation With . . .
MATT BARNES

Field director, Keystone Conservation
Owner, Shining Horizons Land Management
Rangeland Manager, 12 years

1. What was your individual career path in terms of education/training, entry-level job, or other significant opportunity?

I grew up playing in the woods but didn't know you could have a career allowing you to do that. I dropped out of college twice before going back and realizing I could major in natural resources. Once that happened, I became a straight-A student overnight. I earned a bachelor's degree in wildlife management with a minor in range management, then obtained a master's degree in range science.

I first worked for the Bureau of Indian Affairs, then the USDA's Natural Resources Conservation Service. At RCS, I worked with ranchers to improve grazing management, which was the focus of my master's thesis. I then managed a ranch for three years on a contract basis, using my theories about grazing management. Now I work with a nonprofit organization to help ranchers in the northern Rockies and Montana manage where and when their livestock graze.

My interest, most fundamentally, is figuring out how we can have wildness going into the future without having to revert to prehistoric conditions. An ultimate goal is to have a landscape with livestock and people and large carnivores and native species. To me, that means modifying the way humans -- and their livestock -- live on the landscape.

If you use small pastures and have deep knowledge of what plants are growing where and when, you can rotate livestock so they're always in areas with plentiful forage. That way, they're less likely to spread so far apart that they're an attractive target for predators.

This was an essentially untested hypothesis when I began. Now case studies by me and others support this belief.

2. What are the most important skills and/or qualities for someone in your profession?

You need a conservation ethic. Obviously, people will disagree about what that means. You need to be observant about what's going on out in the landscape, including both wild and domestic animals and the plant communities. I think a rangelands manager synthesizes all of these different kinds of knowledge and more.

You also need to be able to get along with people and to be able to enjoy being by yourself out in the wild for an extended period. You need to know basic outdoor skills.

3. **What do you wish you had known going into this profession?**

   If I had known as a kid that there were careers that involved being in the outdoors besides being a park ranger, I might have discovered this earlier and saved myself four years. But most professions in the world are probably things that an 18-year-old doesn't know exists.

4. **Are there many job opportunities in your profession? In what specific areas?**

   It's a fairly broad field. The government is the primary employer, which is different from most fields. There's competition but less so than for jobs in wildlife biology and conservation. I think it's largely because people don't know what rangeland management is. A typical rangeland manager would work for a government agency managing publicly owned lands, or promote conservation on privately owned rangelands, or manage a ranch. What I'm doing now would not be considered typical.

5. **How do you see your profession changing in the next five years, what role will technology play in those changes, and what skills will be required?**

   It used to be a given that a student graduating in this field grew up on a ranch or handling cattle or hunting and fishing. Those skills are still important but people coming into this field now tend to have much less practical experience than they did in prior decades. They have more of an ecological education.

6. **What do you like most about your job? What do you like least about your job?**

   I get to work in some of the most beautiful places in the world and almost all the people I work with are really fascinating individuals.

   On the other hand, there's more office work than you might imagine, especially if you're imagining a park ranger on horseback in the wild. There are days like that and those are the best days. But there are many days spent working on a computer and talking on the phone and that kind of work is just as essential.

7. **Can you suggest a valuable "try this" for students considering a career in your profession?**

   An internship or a summer job related to this field. For a lot of people, this will be where they learn the practical skills they don't get in college.

SELECTED SCHOOLS

Many colleges and universities have bachelor's degree programs in agriculture, ecology, natural sciences, or similar subjects; some have concentrations in range ecology and management. The student may also gain an initial grounding in the field at an agricultural, technical, or community college. For advanced positions, a master's degree is usually obtained. Below are listed some of the more prominent schools in this field.

Colorado State University
Forest and Rangeland Stewardship
1472 Campus Delivery
Fort Collins, CO 80523
970.491.6911
warner.cnr.colostate.edu

Oregon State University
Department of Animal and Rangeland Sciences
112 Withycombe Hall
Corvallis, OR 97331
541.737.3431
anrs.oregonstate.edu

New Mexico State University
Department of Animal and Range Sciences
PO Box 30003, MSC 3-1
Las Cruces, NM 88003
575.646.2870
aces.nmsu.edu

South Dakota State University
Department of Animal and Range Sciences
Animal Science Complex 103A
Brookings, SD 57007
605.688.5166
catalog.sdstate.edu

Texas A&M University
Ecosystem Science and Management
HFSB 305, 2138 TAMU
College Station, TX 77843
979.845.5033
essm.tamu.edu

Texas Tech University
Natural Resources Management
Goddard Building
Box 42125
Lubbock, TX 79409
806.742.2841
www.rw.ttu.edu

University of Arizona
College of Agricultural and Life Sciences
1330 E South Campus
PO Box 21003
Tucson, AZ 85721
520.621.1384
extension.arizona.edu

University of Idaho
Rangeland Ecology and Management
1875 Perimeter Drive
Moscow, ID 83844
208.885.6163
www.uidaho.edu

University of Wyoming
Ecosystem Science and Management
Agriculture Building 2013
Dept. 3354
1000 E. University Avenue
Laramie, WY 82071
307.766.3114
www.uwyo.edu/esm

Utah State University
Range Science
College of Agriculture and Applied Science
4800 Old Main Hill
Logan, UT 84322
435.797.2282
www.ag.usa.edu

MORE INFORMATION

National Park Service
1849 C Street NW
Washington, DC 20240
www.nps.gov

Nature Conservancy
4245 North Fairfax Drive, Suite 100
Arlington, VA 22203
703.841.5300
www.nature.org

Public Lands Foundation
P.O. Box 7226
Arlington, VA 22207
703.790.1988
www.publicland.org

Society for Range Management
10030 West 27th Avenue
Wheat Ridge, CO 80215-6601
303.986.3309
www.rangelands.org

Society of American Foresters
Career Information Department
5400 Grosvenor Lane
Bethesda, MD 20814-2198
301.897.8720
www.safnet.org

Soil and Water Conservation Society
945 SW Ankeny Road
Ankeny, IA 50021
515.289.2331
www.swcs.org

Simone Isadora Flynn/Editor

Refuse & Recyclable Material Collector

Snapshot

Career Cluster: Environment & Conservation; Natural Resources Development
Interests: Manual labor, debris collection, recycling, driving, working outdoors
Earnings (Yearly Average): $35,280
Employment & Outlook: Faster Than Average Growth Expected

OVERVIEW

Sphere of Work

Refuse and recyclable material collectors collect trash and recyclables and transport them to appropriate facilities for permanent disposal or processing. They differ from other waste-management professionals, such as those in the construction industry, in that they traditionally work without the aid of extensive mechanical equipment. Refuse and recyclable material collectors traditionally work in small groups of two to four people and collect debris manually, with the use of a garbage or recycling truck, from curbside trash receptacles and dumpsters.

Work Environment

Refuse and recyclable material collectors traditionally work specific daily routes in urban and residential communities. Specialized refuse and recyclable material collectors, particularly those working in medical waste or appliance recycling, may work on a client-to-client or as-needed basis. The vast majority of refuse and recycling collection is conducted outdoors, regardless of weather conditions. Many of the tasks inherent to refuse and recycling collection take place in and around potentially dangerous and unsanitary conditions.

Profile

Working Conditions: Work both Indoors and Outdoors
Physical Strength: Light Work
Education Needs: Bachelor's Degree
Licensure/Certification: Recommended
Physical Abilities Not Required: N/A
Opportunities For Experience: Internship, Part-Time Work
Holland Interest Score*: IRS

* See Appendix A

Occupation Interest

Refuse and recycling collection is a predominantly entry-level position that does not require extensive professional experience or academic study. The majority of refuse and recyclable material collectors use the role as a bridge between careers or as a temporary means of employment while considering other professional options, furthering their education, or seeking employment in their desired field.

A Day in the Life—Duties and Responsibilities

Refuse and recyclable material collectors begin their day at a centralized headquarters where garbage and recycling trucks are stored and maintained. They are traditionally employees of municipal outfits such as departments of sanitation or private commercial trash-collection companies.

Garbage and recycling trucks run predetermined routes throughout cities and towns. Refuse and recyclable material collectors alternate between driving the truck and manually loading it with trash from curbside bins and containers. Some contemporary refuse-removal vehicles are automated, meaning that collectors need only ensure that the truck is loading trash properly and returning empty receptacles to their proper positions.

When trucks are full, refuse and recyclable material collectors must travel to municipal recycling centers and dumps to empty them before continuing their collection. Refuse and recyclable material collectors primarily work traditional hours, Monday through Friday, with some exceptions. Electronic- and medical-waste collectors may work on an on-call basis, traveling to different locations and dumping sites depending on client need.

Duties and Responsibilities

- **Picking up trash cans or refuse bags and dumping them into a truck**
- **Operating controls to start compactors to compress the refuse**
- **Cleaning compacting equipment to prevent clogging**
- **Operating lifting devices which raise refuse bins and dump them into the truck body**
- **Driving refuse trucks**
- **Depositing recyclables at the appropriate site at a transfer station**

WORK ENVIRONMENT

Relevant Skills and Abilities

Interpersonal/Social Skills
- Being able to work independently

Organization & Management Skills
- Following instructions
- Performing routine work

Technical Skills
- Working with machines, tools or other objects

Work Environment Skills
- Working outdoors

Physical Environment

Environments vary based on the waste-removal specialty of the employing organization. Sites may range from urban and residential communities to hospitals, schools, chemical laboratories, and public parks. Refuse and recyclable material collectors may also work in recycling facilities and waste dumps. Some trash, especially medical waste, may contain hazardous objects or substances, so refuse and recyclable material collectors must be sure to follow proper safety procedures.

Human Environment

Refuse and recyclable material collectors must work well with others, as they often work in pairs or small groups.

Technological Environment

Technologies used in refuse and recycling collection range from radio-communications technology to trash compactors and waste-collection vehicles.

EDUCATION, TRAINING, AND ADVANCEMENT

High School/Secondary

Most employers prefer but do not require a high school diploma or general equivalency diploma (GED). Training occurs primarily on the job.

Suggested High School Subjects

- Business
- Driver Training
- English

Famous First

The first deposits on bottles were instituted in the early 1800s by drink manufacturers in Great Britain and Ireland. In the United States, the first bottle deposits were instituted in 1934 by the National Recovery Administration, a New Deal agency. The deposits were two cents or five cents, depending on the size of the bottle.

Postsecondary

Postsecondary education is not required.

Adult Job Seekers

Refuse and recycling collection is a popular field among adult job seekers because it does not require experience and has a predictable schedule with a five-day workweek.

Professional Certification and Licensure

Many employers seek candidates with commercial driver's licenses and clean driving records.

Additional Requirements

Aspiring refuse and recyclable material collectors must be able to withstand the physical requirements of the position. They must spend an extensive amount of time on their feet and must often lift many heavy containers and objects.

EARNINGS AND ADVANCEMENT

Earnings of refuse and recyclable material collectors depend on the area of the state in which they work and whether they belong to a union. Earnings tend to be higher for workers in large cities and for union members. Mean annual earnings for refuse and recyclable material collectors were $35,280 in 2013. The lowest ten percent earned less than $19,000, and the highest ten percent earned more than $58,000.

Refuse and recyclable material collectors may receive paid vacations, holidays, and sick days; life and health insurance; and retirement benefits. These are usually paid by the employer. Some employers also provide for work clothes or a work clothes allowance.

EMPLOYMENT AND OUTLOOK

Nationally, there were about 120,000 refuse and recyclable material collectors employed in 2010. Employment is expected to grow faster than the average for all occupations through the year 2022, which means employment is projected to increase 12 percent to 15 percent. An increased awareness of the need to recycle will create the most demand for this occupation. In addition, both population and income growth will continue to increase the need for refuse collection.

Related Occupations

- Freight, Stock & Material Mover

Conversation With . . .
BOB SPENCER

Environmental Planning Consultant
Vernon, VT

1. What was your individual career path in terms of education/training, entry-level job, or other significant opportunity?

I started out as a pre-med student in college because I wanted to be a doctor. By junior year I realized my grades, which were solid Bs, would not get me into med school. I was taking environmental courses and really loved them so I switched to biology. I needed a master's degree to get any real job and it literally changed my life once I got into a program -- in natural resources management -- and networked through alumni. I never intended to be in the solid waste business when I went to college, but I got a graduate school internship with a state environmental agency and that opened doors to a full-time job at a regional planning commission where I managed all of their environmental programs for seven years. The issues surrounding recycling and trash kept coming up and I kept getting asked to deal with solid waste issues. For instance, the county bought machines to cut weeds in a lake, so we harvested the weeds, put them in piles, and kind of left them to rot. The state environmental department read about it in the paper and called and told us we couldn't do that. So I started researching what to do and lo and behold I uncovered composting. Then I got invited to go to Europe to see advanced composing and recycling plants. It was one of those "eureka" moments: I got intrigued and decided to be part of what I saw as the future of waste management. I've been involved with waste management as a consultant for government and private business for many years now, with a specialty in composting. But, I've also done things like environmental impact assessments, land use planning, and teaching at a community college.

2. What are the most important skills and/or qualities for someone in your profession?

You need technical proficiency in science, particularly chemistry and biology. Skills in technical writing and public speaking are essential.

3. What do you wish you had known going into this profession?

That the national economy impacts careers in environmental management. Reductions in federal and state grants mean reductions in staff at both public and private employers.

4. Are there many job opportunities in your profession? In what specific areas?

Almost all counties and cities have a solid waste management program with staff. There's an educational component that involves recycling education with schools and business and communities. There's operations; currently I run a big, 6,000-ton per year recycling processing facility and I've got a staff of 15 people that includes everyone from laborers to the compost facility operator. Also, this is a highly regulated industry with permits at every government level, so there are regulatory jobs. In addition, there are environmental engineering jobs in the solid waste field, as well as state agency jobs. Finally, private industry manages these operations; many towns and cities contract with private companies to run their programs.

5. How do you see your profession changing in the next five years, what role will technology play in those changes, and what skills will be required?

Like many professions, increased use of technology is where most change occurs, including use of laboratory testing equipment, GIS mapping, and computer models for air and water quality projects. The safety and environmental health aspect of this business is very big, as are federal Occupational Health & Safety Administration (OSHA) requirements.

6. What do you like most about your job? What do you like least about your job?

I am contributing to making the planet a better place by recycling organic waste in my current jobs.

My least favorite aspects are constantly looking for funding sources.

7. Can you suggest a valuable "try this" for students considering a career in your profession?

There are many opportunities to volunteer for environmental agencies, and not-for-profit organizations. Internships are an excellent way to learn about a career, and gain entry into the job market.

MORE INFORMATION

American Federation of State, County & Municipal Employees
Attn: Education Department
1625 L Street, NW
Washington, DC 20036-5687
202.429.1000
www.afscme.org

International Map Trade Association
25 Louisiana Avenue, NW
Washington, DC 20001
202.624.6800
www.teamster.org

National Waste & Recycling Association
4301 Connecticut Avenue NW
Suite 300
Washington, DC 20008
202.244.4700
wasterecycling.org

John Pritchard/Editor

Renewable Energy Technician

Snapshot

Career Cluster: Architecture & Construction; Environment & Conservation; Natural Resources Development
Interests: Hydroelectric, solar, and geothermal energy; environmental science; maintenance and repair
Earnings (Yearly Average): $47,741
Employment & Outlook: Faster Than Average Growth Expected

OVERVIEW

Sphere of Work

Renewable energy technicians design, install, manage, and care for the mechanical systems used in the generation of wind, solar, geothermal, biological, and hydroelectric energy. They inspect and maintain solar panels, wind turbines, power generators and other equipment, most often at electric power plants. If these technologies fail, energy technicians may recommend shutting down affected equipment until repairs can be completed. Many renewable

energy technicians work at multiple sites, providing assessment, maintenance, and repair services as requested by the site managers or owners. Some renewable energy technicians design, install, and maintain renewable energy technologies at private residences, educational institutions, or businesses.

Work Environment

Renewable energy technicians work at energy-generating facilities, for example, hydroelectric dams, wind farms, solar farms, geothermal energy plants, and bioenergy installations. Many of these facilities, particularly wind and solar farms and hydroelectric dams, may be located in remote locations, so renewable energy technicians must live close by or be willing to spend a significant amount of time traveling. While on site, much of the work is done outdoors—in varying weather conditions. There are physical risks associated with some job duties, as certain technicians frequently climb to the top of very tall wind turbines or other tall structures to perform their work. Technicians may also be at risk of exposure to extreme heat or electrocution when working close to renewable energy collectors or generators.

Profile

Working Conditions: Work both Indoors and Outdoors
Physical Strength: Medium Work
Education Needs: Junior/Technical/ Community College, Bachelor's Degree
Licensure/Certification: Recommended
Physical Abilities Not Required: N/A
Opportunities For Experience: Apprenticeship, Part-Time Work
Holland Interest Score*: RCI

* See Appendix A

Occupation Interest

Renewable energy technicians provide expertise and services to an exciting new industry that has grown significantly in a relatively short time. The work they do helps to lessen the environmental impact of electric power by reducing society's use of fossil fuels. A young field, renewable energy requires a range of skills, with some technicians dealing directly with electrical systems, others skilled in system installation, and still others participating in system design. Successful renewable energy technicians are well aware of the dynamic nature of the industry and keep abreast, as well as contribute to, the advances in the field. Renewable energy technicians spend much of their time working outdoors, and should be able to climb, kneel, carry tools and equipment, and walk long distances. Working in a relatively new technical field may appeal to individuals interested in being at the forefront of technological development.

A Day in the Life—Duties and Responsibilities

TRenewable energy technicians' daily responsibilities vary according to their particular area of expertise. For example, wind energy technicians work at wind farms, frequently climbing hundreds of feet into the air to work inside a nacelle (the housing at the center of a wind turbine) where they clean and lubricate bearings, shafts, and gears. Geothermal energy technicians also work outdoors, monitoring energy and heat outputs, replacing and installing new piping systems, and testing the efficiency of residential and commercial geothermal heat pumps. Hydroelectric power technicians spend time inside hydroelectric power plants to monitor generators, flow tunnels, and computers that track the efficiency of turbines.

When beginning a project, renewable energy technicians may assess a site to determine the proper systems and methods for the installation of equipment used to collect solar energy, wind power, bioenergy, hydroelectricity, or geothermal energy. After installing the equipment, they prepare it for connection to the electric power grid by priming, flushing, purging, or performing other practices. According to schedule and at the request of the energy company or the facility director, renewable energy technicians also travel periodically to the dam, farm, or other facility to inspect equipment, assess productivity, diagnose any malfunctions, and make repairs. Based on information about the output and efficiency of the facility, technicians will make recommendations for upgrades or modifications.

Duties and Responsibilities

- **Designing, installing, operating and maintaining systems that use renewable energy**
- **Recommending energy efficiency and alternative energy solutions**
- **Researching the latest information concerning renewable energy advances**
- **Consulting with and supervising other technicians and installers**
- **Working with individual clients and government agencies**

OCCUPATION SPECIALTIES

Wind Turbine Service Technicians

Wind Turbine Service Technicians inspect, adjust and maintain wind turbines that harness wind energy.

Solar Energy System Installers & Technicians

Solar Energy System Installers & Technicians build, install and maintain systems on roofs and other structures that harness solar energy. They also install and repair systems that collect, store and circulate solar-heated water.

Hydropower Energy Technicians

Hydropower Energy Technicians maintain hydropower plants that convert water to energy.

Geothermal Energy Technicians

Geothermal Energy Technicians maintain geothermal power plants that convert energy from the earth's core.

Bioenergy Technicians

Bioenergy Technicians maintain bioenergy power plants that convert energy from biomass, such as wood, crops, plants, waste materials and alcohol fuels.

Fuel Cell Technicians

Fuel Cell Technicians research and perform the assembly and testing of fuel cells and also install and maintain existing fuel cells.

WORK ENVIRONMENT

Relevant Skills and Abilities

Communication Skills
- Speaking effectively
- Writing concisely

Interpersonal/Social Skills
- Being able to work independently
- Working as a member of a team

Organization & Management Skills
- Paying attention to and handling details
- Coordinating tasks
- Making decisions
- Performing duties which change frequently

Research & Planning Skills
- Analyzing information
- Developing evaluation strategies
- Using logical reasoning

Technical Skills
- Understanding which technology is appropriate for a task
- Applying the technology to a task
- Maintaining and repairing technology
- Working with your hands
- Working with machines, tools or other objects

Physical Environment

Renewable energy technicians work at renewable energy facilities, such as wind and solar farms, hydroelectric dams, and bioenergy and geothermal energy processing plants. Many of these facilities are located in remote, open areas. Because the facilities process electricity, there may be a risk of electrocution when working on technical equipment. There is also a risk of other physical injuries at different types of electric power plants and wind farms.

Human Environment

Depending on the sub-field in which they work, renewable energy technicians work with a number different people, including environmental engineers, environmental scientists, business executives, construction personnel, utility workers, and energy auditors.

Technological Environment

Nursery workers use machinery and eIn addition to the hand-held tools used to install renewable energy equipment and systems, technicians use and work in close proximity to a wide range of energy-related technologies. Among these devices are portable data input terminals, digital refractometers, temperature gauges, water pressure gauges, nacelles, and photovoltaic cells. Technicians also use computer software, including input/output tracking software, databases, and analytical software.

EDUCATION, TRAINING, AND ADVANCEMENT

High School/Secondary

High school students should study algebra, geometry, and other mathematics courses. Natural sciences such as chemistry, physics, and environmental studies are equally important. Computer science, drafting, and industrial arts courses (such as welding, building trades, carpentry, and electronics) are also useful preparation for this field.

Suggested High School Subjects

- Algebra
- Applied Math
- Blueprint Reading
- Building Trades & Carpentry
- Chemistry
- College Preparatory
- Computer Science
- Drafting
- Electricity & Electronics
- English
- Geometry
- Heating/Air Cond./Refrigeration
- Machining Technology
- Mathematics
- Mechanical Drawing
- Metals Technology
- Physics
- Science
- Shop Math
- Shop Mechanics
- Welding

Famous First

The first hydroelectric power plant to use a storage battery was the Hartford Electric Light Company, Hartford, Conn., in 1896. The storage battery made it possible to supply the company's peak-load requirements from water power that would otherwise have gone to waste during the periods of relatively small demand.

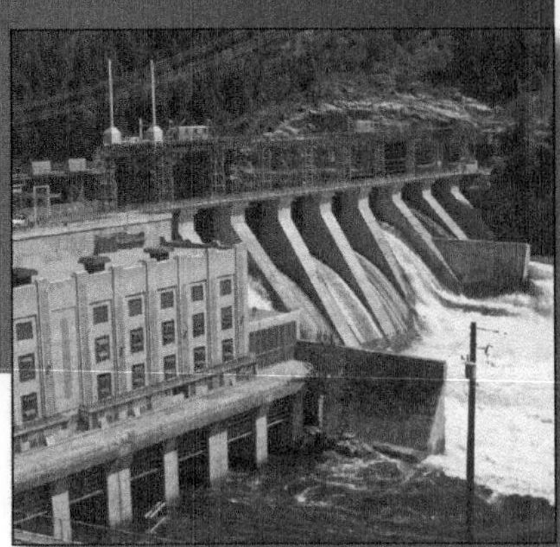

College/Postsecondary

Although employers value practical experience in this occupation, many employers prefer candidates to have an associate's or bachelor's degree. Renewable energy technicians can increase their competitiveness as job candidates by obtaining technical certificates and degrees in related fields, such as hydroelectricity maintenance and wind turbine maintenance. Such programs are increasingly becoming available at two-year community and technical colleges.

Related College Majors

- Electromechanical Technology
- Heating, Air Conditioning & Refrigeration Technology
- Solar Technology

Adult Job Seekers

Some renewable energy technician jobs may be found through technical and community college placement offices. Candidates may also apply directly to companies who advertise in print or online. Individuals with limited experience may join renewable energy firms as interns, or obtain part-time or summer jobs as a means of entry into the field.

Professional Certification and Licensure

There is no required certification for renewable energy technicians. Voluntary certification programs in specialized fields, such as wind turbine maintenance and geothermal energy maintenance, are increasingly available through professional trade associations. Such certification can bolster a candidate's credentials, especially in light of the fact that the renewable energy field is becoming more competitive. As with any voluntary endeavor, candidates should consult credible professional associations within the field and follow professional debate as to the relevancy and value of any certification program.

Additional Requirements

Renewable energy technicians should be detail-oriented and possess the ability to analyze complex systems and problems, as well as excellent mechanical skills. They must be willing to travel, sometimes for long periods of time. Many renewable energy technician positions spend a great deal of time working outdoors and often need to climb tall structures or perform heavy lifting activities. To work effectively with a team of colleagues from different fields, they should have strong communication and people skills.

EARNINGS AND ADVANCEMENT

Median annual earnings of renewable energy technicians were $49,173 in 2012.

Renewable energy technicians may receive paid vacations, holidays, and sick days; life and health insurance and retirement benefits. These are usually paid by the employer.

EMPLOYMENT AND OUTLOOK

Employment of renewable energy technicians is expected to grow much faster than the average for all occupations through the year 2022, which means employment is projected to increase 20 percent or more. Energy and its relationship to sustaining the environment is a rapidly growing field that will continue to create demand for new jobs for many years to come.

Related Occupations

- Energy Auditor
- Energy Conservation & Use Technician
- Energy Engineer
- Heating and Cooling Technician
- Solar Energy System Installer
- Wind Energy Engineer

SELECTED SCHOOLS

Many technical and community colleges offer programs in energy systems installation and repair, often with a concentration in renewable energy. Interested students are advised to consult with their school guidance counselor or to research area postsecondary schools and training programs. For those interested in pursuing a bachelor's degree, a state land-grant college or technical institute is probably the best place to start.

MORE INFORMATION

American Council on Renewable Energy
1600 K Street NW, Suite 700
Washington, DC 20006
202.393.0001
www.acore.org

American Solar Energy Society
4760 Walnut Street, Suite 106
Boulder, CO 80301
303.443.3130
www.ases.org

American Wind Energy Association
1501 M Street, NW, Suite 1000
Washington, DC 20005
202.383.2500
www.awea.org

Biomass Power Association
100 Middle Street
P.O. Box 9729
Portland, ME 04104-9729
703.889.8504
www.usabiomass.org

Energy Efficiency & Renewable Energy Network
Department of Energy
1000 Independence Avenue, SW
Washington, DC 20585
800.342.5363
www.eere.energy.gov

Geothermal Resources Council
P.O. Box 1350
Davis, CA 95617
530.758.2360
www.geothermal.org

National Hydropower Association
25 Massachusetts Avenue, NW
Suite 450
Washington, DC 20001
202.682.1700
www.hydro.org

Renewable Fuels Association
425 Third Street, SW, Suite 1150
Washington, DC 20024
202.289.3835
www.ethanolrfa.org

Solar Energy Industries Association (SEIA)
575 7th Street, NW, Suite 400
Washington, DC 20004
202.682.0556
www.seia.org

Windustry
2105 First Avenue South
Minneapolis, MN 55404
800.946.3640
www.windustry.org

Michael Auerbach/Editor

Soil Scientist

Snapshot

Career Cluster: Agriculture; Environment & Conservation; Science & Technology
Interests: Earth science, topography, vegetation, agriculture, environment
Earnings (Yearly Average): $62,830
Employment & Outlook: Average Growth Expected

OVERVIEW

Sphere of Work

Soil scientists study the formation, classification, and management of soil. Soil scientists generally specialize in either agricultural or environmental soil science. Although each group surveys, analyzes, and monitors soil, agricultural soil scientists work mostly in areas such as crop production, forestry, and ranching, while environmental soil scientists are more interested in the ecology of soil and its effects on natural resources, and in managing soil for construction, recreation, development, and other non-agricultural purposes.

Work Environment

Soil scientists work for county, state, and federal governments; universities and other research organizations; private businesses, including agribusinesses; and engineering, environmental, and land management firms. Some are self-employed as consultants. They typically work a forty-hour week, although occasional overtime may be needed to meet deadlines or when performing fieldwork.

Profile

Working Conditions: Work both Indoors and Outdoors
Physical Strength: Light Work
Education Needs: Bachelor's Degree, Master's Degree
Licensure/Certification: Recommended
Physical Abilities Not Required: No Heavy Labor
Opportunities For Experience: Internship
Holland Interest Score*: IRS

* See Appendix A

Occupation Interest

A career as a soil scientist attracts people who are analytical and research oriented, with a special interest in the environment or agriculture. They are inquisitive, excellent at solving problems, and precise when performing tests and calculations. They should also have strong verbal and written communication skills, be technologically savvy, and be able to easily read and interpret various types of maps.

A Day in the Life—Duties and Responsibilities

TOne of the primary duties of most soil scientists is performing soil surveys, also known as soil mapping. Some scientists work in county and state extension services and test soil samples submitted primarily by homeowners and farmers, but most obtain their samples in the field. Using hand tools or industrial augers or probes, they collect one or more samples of soil from a particular location. They then determine the mineral, organic, chemical, and water content using a variety of gauges and other laboratory equipment. Sometimes they also employ remote sensing technology to gather information, such as aerial photography and light detection and ranging (LIDAR).

Soil scientists also analyze factors that influence the composition and quality of soil, including vegetation, topography, and weather. Using standard taxonomic systems, they classify soil based on these factors, then add the classifications and data to various maps and databases for the benefit of other scientists and the general public. In addition, soil scientists monitor soil for contamination from mining or from hazardous wastes such as pesticides, insecticides, and sewage, and provide advice on prevention and remediation.

Further responsibilities of soil scientists are determined by their area of specialization. Agricultural soil scientists use soil surveys to predict the suitability of soil for growing certain crops, or to give farmers advice on using fertilizers, rotating crops, improving water retention, and other agricultural matters. Environmental soil scientists use soil surveys to determine an area's suitability for development, construction of sewage treatment facilities, or placement of new reservoirs. They also analyze soil for its historical composition and appearance, which is especially useful for archaeological research and study of climate change.

When not in the field or laboratory, soil scientists write plans and reports, which they often deliver at meetings and conferences. Experienced scientists may apply for research grants, plan budgets, direct projects, and sometimes teach at the college level.

Duties and Responsibilities

- **Classifying and mapping soils for farming, engineering, and natural resource development**
- **Developing soil management practices**
- **Predicting soil behavior and potential for crops, grass and trees**
- **Assessing effect on soil of engineering, construction, recreation, community development, forestry, and range management**

WORK ENVIRONMENT

Physical Environment

Soil scientists usually divide their time between the field, laboratory, and office. Fieldwork poses the greatest danger for injuries and environmental risks, and thus often requires the use of hard hats, work boots, heavy gloves, and other protective equipment. Some soil scientists may be at risk for injuries and health problems related to using certain laboratory tools and equipment, though this risk is lessened by the use of proper ventilation and eye protection.

Relevant Skills and Abilities

Analytical Skills
- Collecting and analyzing data

Communication Skills
- Speaking and writing effectively

Interpersonal/Social Skills
- Being able to work independently
- Working as a member of a team

Organization & Management Skills
- Paying attention to and handling details

Work Environment Skills
- Working in a rural or remote setting
- Working outdoors

Human Environment

Soil scientists perform some duties alone in the field or laboratory. They also interact or consult regularly with other members of their research teams, planning commissions, and other professionals, which may include engineers, agronomists, geologists, hydrologists, and environmentalists. They may supervise assistants, technicians, and interns. Unless self-employed, they typically report to a director or manager, although they tend to work independently.

Technological Environment

The work performed by soil scientists tends to be technology-intensive. Desktop and portable computers are used for geographic information systems (GIS) and a variety of analytical, classification, and business applications. Surveying equipment includes global positioning system (GPS) devices, aerial photography cameras, LIDAR, and electrical conductivity (EC) sensors. Analytical tools include electron microscopes, centrifuges, hydrometers, spectrometers, and radiometers. Other commonly used tools and equipment include industrial probes and augers, shovels and other hand tools, digital cameras, cell phones, and walkie-talkies.

EDUCATION, TRAINING, AND ADVANCEMENT

High School/Secondary

The best foundation for a career as a soil scientist is a college preparatory program that emphasizes science and mathematics, with courses in biology, chemistry, physics, earth science, environmental science, algebra, trigonometry, calculus, and statistics. English and communication courses are also important. Vocational programs such as agricultural science or forestry can provide a suitable background if they include the coursework required for most college admissions. Participation in extracurricular science, agricultural, or environmental clubs and activities may also be beneficial.

Suggested High School Subjects

- Agricultural Education
- Applied Biology/Chemistry
- Applied Math
- Biology
- Chemistry
- Earth Science
- English
- Forestry
- Mathematics
- Science

Famous First

The first U.S. county to require its government departments to purchase locally grown organic food was Woodbury County in Iowa. In 2006 the county's Board of Supervisors voted to require county agencies to buy food from a local farmers cooperative, with priority given to organic food. By "local" the board meant within 100 miles of Sioux City, Iowa.

College/Postsecondary

A minimum of a bachelor's degree in soil science or a closely related major is standard for entry-level positions, while an advanced degree is necessary for management positions and for conducting research. Undergraduate programs usually include coursework in chemistry, biology, microbiology, plant physiology, calculus, and statistics, in addition to the principles of soil science, fertility, genesis, mapping, climatology, and other topics. Undergraduates should be prepared to choose between an agricultural and an environmental soil science program. Graduate-level programs allow students to specialize and conduct original research in hydroecology, geomorphology, mapping, mineralogy, agronomy, and other areas. Internships are recommended.

Related College Majors

- Agriculture/Agricultural Sciences
- Agronomy & Crop Science
- Soil Sciences

Adult Job Seekers

Adults with a background in environmental studies, geology, agriculture, or another scientific discipline will have a good foundation for a career in soil science; however, the job market is competitive. Skills and knowledge can be updated by enrolling in a college program or taking continuing education courses offered by scientific organizations, which may also provide valuable resources and networking opportunities.

Professional Certification and Licensure

Licensing of soil scientists is legally required in a small number of states, but there is a growing movement in favor of widespread licensing. As such, soil scientists are advised to research their specific state's requirements. Voluntary certification is offered by the Soil Science Society of America (SSSA) and available, upon satisfactory completion of an examination, to scientists with a minimum of five years experience and at least a bachelor's degree in soil science, or three years experience with a master's or doctoral degree. As with any voluntary certification process, it is beneficial to consult credible professional associations within the field and follow professional debate as to the relevancy and value of any certification program.

Additional Requirements

Soil scientists frequently need a driver's license to get to and from sites. They must also be physically fit and capable of walking, hiking, bending, digging, and kneeling while performing fieldwork.

Fun Fact

Did you know that fifty percent of soil is air and water? The rest is mineral and organic material. In one gram of soil, the number of bacteria ranges from 100,000 to several billion.

Source: http://www.doctordirt.com/soilfact/

EARNINGS AND ADVANCEMENT

A doctoral degree in agricultural science is usually needed for college teaching or advancement to research positions. Mean annual earnings of soil and plant scientists were $62,830 in 2013. The lowest ten percent earned less than $35,000, and the highest ten percent earned more than $95,000.

Soil scientists may receive paid vacations, holidays, and sick days; life and health insurance; and retirement benefits. These are usually paid by the employer.

Metropolitan Areas with the Highest Employment Level in this Occupation

Metropolitan area	Employment[(1)]	Employment per thousand jobs	Hourly mean wage
Des Moines-West Des Moines, IA	1,160	3.51	$35.98
Chicago-Joliet-Naperville, IL	460	0.12	$32.42
Portland-Vancouver-Hillsboro, OR-WA	270	0.26	$27.24
St. Louis, MO-IL	230	0.18	$24.95
Madison, WI	190	0.54	$28.19
Oakland-Fremont-Hayward, CA	180	0.18	$39.18
Washington-Arlington-Alexandria, DC-VA-MD-WV	170	0.07	$44.47
Minneapolis-St. Paul-Bloomington, MN-WI	160	0.09	$30.67
Kansas City, MO-KS	150	0.15	$28.45
San Jose-Sunnyvale-Santa Clara, CA	140	0.15	$27.68

[(1)] Does not include self-employed; includes soil and plant scientists. Source: Bureau of Labor Statistics

EMPLOYMENT AND OUTLOOK

Soil and plant scientists held about 16,000 jobs nationally in 2012. Employment is expected to grow about as fast as the average for all occupations through the year 2022, which means employment is projected to increase 6 percent to 12 percent. Those with advanced degrees will be in better positions for employment. Competition for teaching positions with colleges and universities will be strong.

Employment Trend, Projected 2012–22

Total, All Occupations: 11%

Agricultural and Food Scientists: 9%

Soil and Plant Scientists: 8%

Note: "All Occupations" includes all occupations in the U.S. Economy. Source: U.S. Bureau of Labor Statistics, Employment Projections Program.

Related Occupations

- Agricultural Scientist
- Botanist
- Forester and Conservation Scientist
- Microbiologist
- Range Manager

Conversation With . . .

ROB MICHITSCH

Assistant Professor, 5 years
University of Wisconsin - Stevens Point
Soil scientist, 13 years

1. What was your individual career path in terms of education/training, entry-level job, or other significant opportunity?

I didn't really enjoy high school and even dropped out at one point. But I was a football player, so I went back, played, graduated, and liked the idea of doing an undergraduate degree because I wanted to play more football. I went to the University of Guelph in Ontario, Canada, and majored in environmental science with and emphasis in environmental chemistry and got more and more interested in that topic. (I got into this area because I grew up next to a landfill and my father worked at a wastewater treatment plant...it planted the seed.) After graduation, I sent out 50 applications for jobs and got back two responses: one said no, you're not qualified, the other said yes, you are — but there are 110 people competing. So I decided to get my Master's in soil science and waste management in the Department of Land Resource Science, also at the University of Guelph. As I finished, I had already secured a doctoral spot at Dalhousie University in Nova Scotia. I worked for the Nova Scotia Dept. of Agriculture and Fisheries greenhouse gas mitigation project — I do a lot of work in the waste management field as well as soil science — and it took five years to finish my degree in biological engineering. I was fortunate to get my position as an Assistant Professor at the University of Wisconsin Stevens Point before I finished my PhD.

2. What are the most important skills and/or qualities for someone in your profession?

You need a love for soil. Soil is involved in everything. It grows our food, gives us medicine, is home for trees, and supports our water resources. You need a technical background and communications skills. As a scientist, if you don't have good written and oral communications skills and a sense of logic, you're not going to be successful.

3. What do you wish you had known going into this profession?

I wish I had known more about soils at a younger age. I didn't get into it until I got into my Master's, when I was a teaching assistant. Once I got into teaching I realized what a fun topic it is. Even now, I'm learning new stuff every day.

4. Are there many job opportunities in your profession? In what specific areas?

There are definitely jobs out there. Some of the main areas you can work in are government agencies such as the U.S. Dept. of Agriculture or U.S. Environmental Protection Agency. There are local agencies, non-profits, and conservation agencies, as well as general Cooperative Extension units for universities or government. You can be a land-use planner, soil conservationist, wetlands scientist, soil tester — that involves the construction industry — and on the agronomy side, you can be a consultant or a farmer.

5. How do you see your profession changing in the next five years, what role will technology play in those changes, and what skills will be required?

Global warming and climate change are huge topics as we try to understand the role of soil. One of the main issues from agronomy is maximizing fertilizer use to maximize food production on the soils we have without degrading them. We also have waste management, and dealing with throwing resources back onto the soil. We're making gains in finding microbes in soil from the genetics point of view. There also are all sorts of GIS and GPS applications for handheld technology in the field, which is very important. Anyone in one of the natural resources fields should have some GIS background.

6. What do you like most about your job? What do you like least about your job?

I most enjoy the interaction I have with students. I usually have close to 400-500 students; right now it's summer so I'm at our field camp with 108 students. I also like my flexibility. I love to do research, but I like to teach just as well.

What I like least is that it's as if governments undervalue us and don't understand what we do. We need the research funds that come from government, but money is being cut and obtaining necessary funds is extremely competitive. I also dislike the politics, from within the university on up to the federal level.

7. Can you suggest a valuable "try this" for students considering a career in your profession?

Take a class that has a lab or field component. I also would recommend that students get involved in a professional society; I'm involved in the Soil Science Society of America and they have an undergraduate branch. Also, try to do an internship in a field you're interested in. You get paid, and you get the experience you need to go out and get a job.

SELECTED SCHOOLS

Many agricultural, technical, and community colleges offer programs in agronomy, sometimes with a concentration in soil science. Interested students are advised to consult with their school guidance counselor or to research area postsecondary schools and training programs. For those interested in pursuing a bachelor's or master's degree, a state land-grant college is probably the best place to start.

MORE INFORMATION

National Society of Consulting Soil Scientists
P.O. Box 1219
Sandpoint, ID 83864
800.535.7148
www.nscss.org

Soil and Water Conservation Society
945 SW Ankeny Road
Ankeny, IA 50021
515.289.2331
www.swcs.org

Soil Science Society of America
5585 Guilford Road
Madison, WI 53711
608.273.8080
www.soils.org

US Department of Agriculture
1400 Independence Avenue SW
Washington, DC 20250
202.720.2791
www.usda.gov

Sally Driscoll/Editor

Water & Wastewater Engineer

Snapshot

Career Cluster: Engineering; Environment & Conservation; Natural Resources Development; Science & Technology
Interests: Engineering, civil engineering, mechanical engineering, environmental science, science
Earnings (Yearly Average): $85,520
Employment & Outlook: Faster Than Average Growth Expected

OVERVIEW

Sphere of Work

Water and wastewater engineers design, supervise, and upgrade water-supply and wastewater systems. They also develop and design contemporary wastewater-treatment facilities that minimize pollution and meet the latest environmental protection standards. Water and wastewater engineers are generally considered part of the broader field of environmental engineers.

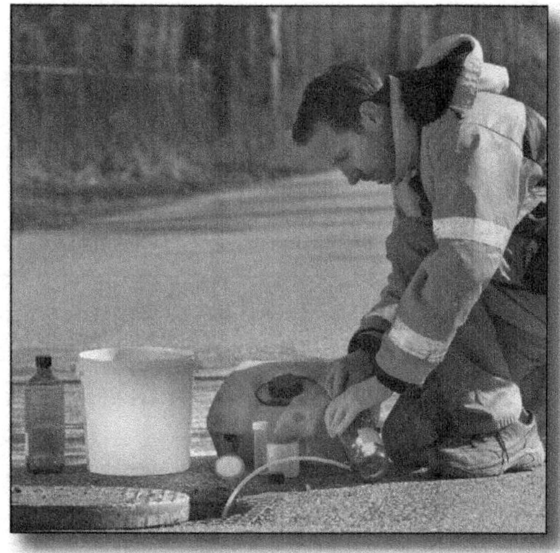

Work Environment

Water and wastewater engineers most commonly work in an office or a laboratory. Some projects may require field trips to the site of particular water- or wastewater-treatment facilities. Teamwork is very common, and water and wastewater engineers work often with other environmental engineers. Many water and wastewater engineers have to liaise with public authorities. They are also expected to present their ideas and findings to non-engineers, including lawyers, businesspeople, and politicians. Good verbal and written communication skills are required, both within a team and when interacting with outsiders such as clients or public agencies.

Profile

Working Conditions: Work both Indoors and Outdoors
Physical Strength: Light Work
Education Needs: Bachelor's Degree, Master's Degree
Licensure/Certification: Required
Physical Abilities Not Required: No Heavy Labor
Opportunities For Experience: Internship
Holland Interest Score*: IRC

* See Appendix A

Occupation Interest

This occupation tends to attract people with strong interests in engineering and science who are drawn to work in the environmental sciences. As the field has very wide range of applications, workers can focus on an area of particular interest. Water and wastewater engineers seek practical solutions to provide and improve upon an essential human service. They often have opportunities to work abroad, particularly in developing countries. This field can also be approached from a more general engineering background, such as civil or mechanical engineering.

A Day in the Life—Duties and Responsibilities

A Day in the Life—Duties and Responsibilities
Since many water and wastewater engineers work in a team, most work regular business hours. This is especially true for those who work in an office and must attend team meetings and meet with clients or third parties during the working day. During peak project times, particularly if working as a consulting engineer, water and wastewater engineers may either begin their day very early or stay at work later in the evening to finish any tasks made urgent by tight project deadlines.

Contemporary engineering work requires a lot of time spent using computers and working in an information-technology-supported environment, and the work of a water and wastewater engineer is no exception. As members of a team, in addition to meeting with the team to coordinate their work with that of their colleagues, water and wastewater engineers pursue their own tasks and put their results into the common project.

Working on a water or wastewater project in a foreign country often includes a heavier daily workload. In domestic positions, most water and wastewater engineers enjoy regular working hours and are requested to work overtime only on a case-by-case basis as necessitated by special projects.

Duties and Responsibilities

- **Designing systems that provide environmentally sound fresh water and waste water solutions**
- **Reworking and troubleshooting systems as environmental standards change or as problems arise**
- **Preparing project plans and specifications**
- **Estimating the costs and requirements of projects**
- **Overseeing project construction and maintenance**
- **Inspecting newly constructed and existing systems**
- **Conducting technical research studies**

WORK ENVIRONMENT

Relevant Skills and Abilities

Analytical Skills
- Collecting and analyzing data

Communication Skills
- Speaking and writing effectively

Interpersonal/Social Skills
- Being able to work independently
- Working as a member of a team
- Having good judgment

Organization & Management Skills
- Initiating new ideas
- Paying attention to and handling details
- Managing time
- Promoting change
- Making decisions
- Meeting goals and deadlines
- Performing duties that may change frequently

Research & Planning Skills
- Creating ideas
- Identifying problems
- Determining alternatives
- Identifying resources
- Solving problems
- Developing evaluation strategies
- Using logical reasoning

Technical Skills
- Performing scientific, mathematical or technical work
- Working with data or numbers

Unclassified Skills
- Using set methods and standards in your work

Physical Environment

Generally, water and wastewater engineers work in an office, with occasional time spent in a laboratory as well. Project sites are often in outdoor settings. Their physical conditions are determined by the specific site, which can be located in a variety of physical environments.

Plant Environment

Water and wastewater plants exist in a variety of settings, ranging from urban locations such as the waterworks of a metropolitan city to remote destinations such as a desalination plant on a desert shore. Office buildings are either permanent, mostly in cities, or temporary at project sites.

Human Environment

Offices and laboratories are generally shared with colleagues working on the same or different projects. Water and wastewater engineers must work well both with members of their own profession within a team and with non-engineers.

Technological Environment

Contemporary water and wastewater engineers rely

heavily on state-of-the art technology, and their work is supported by specialized software applications. Word processing and spreadsheet work is also required to communicate their work.

EDUCATION, TRAINING, AND ADVANCEMENT

High School/Secondary

In high school, students should focus on the sciences, mathematics, and computer literacy, though they should not neglect to acquire good written and oral English and communication skills. Classes in chemistry, biology, physics, and earth science are particularly useful. Mathematics courses should include algebra, calculus, geometry, and trigonometry. Students should also enroll in specialized courses in drafting, electronics, and special physical-science topics if available. Computer-science classes would be beneficial as well.

Students should join science or engineering clubs whenever possible. They should look for offers from professional associations in the field that target high school students. Toward the end of high school, a student should also look into science or technology camps offered by domestic and international colleges and universities.

Suggested High School Subjects

- Algebra
- Applied Biology/Chemistry
- Applied Communication
- Applied Math
- Applied Physics
- Biology
- Blueprint Reading
- Calculus
- Chemistry
- College Preparatory
- Computer Science
- Drafting
- Earth Science

- Electricity & Electronics
- English
- Geometry
- Humanities
- Mathematics
- Physical Science
- Physics
- Science
- Social Studies
- Trigonometry

Famous First

The first water delivery system designed to clean and purify city water was set up in Lawrence, Massachusetts, in 1893. An open filter of 2.75 acres purified water from the Merrimack River by slow sand filtration.

College/Postsecondary

A bachelor's degree in engineering is required for work as water and wastewater engineer. Some universities offer an environmental engineering major, but this specialization is not necessary; a degree in civil engineering, mechanical engineering, or general engineering is typically sufficient. In the last two years of study, courses relating to the field, such as water-treatment-plant design, should be taken. Students should take care to obtain a degree from an engineering program that is accredited by the Accreditation Board of Engineering and Technology (ABET), the prime accrediting institution in the field. They should also seek to obtain an internship or participate in co-op studies before graduating.

A master's degree provides additional professional qualifications. Some universities offer the option to earn both a bachelor's and a master's degree in a combined five-year program. Students interested in research and teaching can also pursue a doctoral degree in engineering.

Related College Majors

- Civil Engineering
- Electrical, Electronics & Communications Engineering
- Engineering
- Environmental & Pollution Control Technology
- Environmental/Environmental Health Engineering
- Mechanical Engineering

Adult Job Seekers

For an adult job seeker, both networking, ideally supported by membership in a professional association, and direct contact with potential employers can be beneficial. State employment offices are an additional resource. Adults transitioning to this field should have some sort of background in engineering or the sciences.

Professional Certification and Licensure

Engineering licenses in the United States are awarded by individual states. A prospective engineer must pass both a Fundamentals of Engineering (FE) exam and a Principles and Practice in Engineering (PE) exam and acquire a certain amount of experience in order to be licensed as a professional engineer in his or her state.

Additional Requirements

A water and wastewater engineer must have a solid background in the sciences, strong engineering skills, and the ability to work in teams and communicate ideas well. Ideally, he or she should also be dedicated to the profession and have a genuine interest in the work.

EARNINGS AND ADVANCEMENT

Mean annual earnings of water and wastewater engineers were $85,520 in 2013. The lowest ten percent earned less than $50,000, and the highest ten percent earned more than $122,000.

Water and wastewater engineers may receive paid vacations, holidays and sick days; life and health insurance; and retirement benefits. These are usually paid by the employer.

Metropolitan Areas with the Highest Employment Level in this Occupation

Metropolitan area	Employment[1]	Employment per thousand jobs	Hourly mean wage
Boston-Cambridge-Quincy, MA	2,030	1.16	$38.98
Washington-Arlington-Alexandria, DC-VA-MD-WV	1,710	0.72	$49.64
Los Angeles-Long Beach-Glendale, CA	1,570	0.39	$50.92
New York-White Plains-Wayne, NY-NJ	1,550	0.30	$45.51
Atlanta-Sandy Springs-Marietta, GA	1,330	0.58	$36.89
Philadelphia, PA	1,230	0.67	$40.11
Sacramento--Arden-Arcade--Roseville, CA	1,200	1.43	$45.33
Houston-Sugar Land-Baytown, TX	1,040	0.38	$52.59
Seattle-Bellevue-Everett, WA	920	0.64	$43.98
Oakland-Fremont-Hayward, CA	850	0.84	$47.03

[1] Does not include self-employed; includes environmental engineers. Source: Bureau of Labor Statistics

EMPLOYMENT AND OUTLOOK

Environmental engineers, of which water and wastewater engineers are a part, held about 53,000 jobs nationally in 2012. Employment is expected to grow faster than the average for all occupations through the year 2022, which means employment is projected to increase 15 percent or more. Demand for water and wastewater engineers will be created by a number of factors, including an increasing emphasis on preventing environmental problems, the need to comply with environmental regulations, and the growth of public health concerns due to the expanding population.

Employment Trend, Projected 2012–22

Water, Wastewater, and Other Environmental Engineers: 15%

Total, All Occupations: 9%

Engineers (All): 8%

Note: "All Occupations" includes all occupations in the U.S. Economy. Source: U.S. Bureau of Labor Statistics, Employment Projections Program.

Related Occupations

- Agricultural Engineer
- Biological Scientist
- Chemical Engineer
- Civil Engineer
- Electrical & Electronics Engineer
- Energy Engineer
- Environmental Engineer
- Environmental Science Technician
- Forester & Conservation Scientist
- Hazardous Waste Manager
- Mechanical Engineer
- Water Treatment Plant Operator
- Wind Energy Engineer

Conversation With . . .
MARK HUDAK, P.E.

Associate, Project Manager, Stantec
Water-Wastewater Engineer, 13 years

1. **What was your individual career path in terms of education/training, entry-level job, or other significant opportunity?**

   I got a degree in mechanical engineering from Ohio State University. I graduated right after the 9/11 attacks and that impacted what field I went into due to ensuing economic problems. I had wanted to go into the automotive industry, but there was a hiring freeze. I ended up getting a job with a small civil and environmental engineering firm and did a lot of site work for developers in private development. I transferred to water/wastewater a few years later when I saw the real estate market starting to crash. Water-wastewater interests me; hydraulics and fluid mechanics are involved. I started as a design-level engineer, then moved up to project engineer, then to project manager, and I'm looking to move up further as a leader.

2. **What are the most important skills and/or qualities for someone in your profession?**

   You need the science and numbers background, but you've got to be able to communicate. I'm a numbers guy, and I am really good at Math and English.

3. **What do you wish you had known going into this profession?**

   Seeing how infrastructure is actually built in the field is a huge advantage. If I had known that early on, I would have spent my first two years on the construction side.

4. **Are there many job opportunities in your profession? In what specific areas?**

   There's a lot of opportunity, with more jobs than a couple of years ago. If you're interested in water-wastewater engineering, you can go into one of three streams working in fields such as product manufacturing or supply; professional consulting engineer; government agency or regulatory; and construction management.

   The three streams are:

- Technical: Start as a design engineer and build expertise in a particular area, such as wastewater treatment or hydraulic modeling.The further up you go, the more specialized you get.

- Sale Engineer: You can transition from a technical role to selling a service or product within the industry. You could be a sales representative for equipment or sell a service such as engineering.
- Management or Operations: People in these positions start out in an entry-level position in a technical field. Typically they are organized and have a skill set as a manager They might manage projects, engineers and field staff, or product lines.

5. How do you see your profession changing in the next five years, what role will technology play in those changes, and what skills will be required?

Technology will increase on many fronts. In water-wastewater, trenchless technology is growing. For old sanitary and waterlines that have reached the end of their useful life and are in need of replacement, trenchless technology is the new normal. The days of open cut excavation or building new trenches and installing new pipes and abandoning or removing the old pipes are dwindling. Trenchless rehabilitation such as cured-in-place pipe; pipe bursting; and micro tunneling allow for increasing the life of the pipe without the social impact of digging up the ground. Others emerging areas are energy reuse and recovery, water reuse; biogas reuse; and nutrients.

6. What do you like most about your job? What do you like least about your job?

I enjoy working with people. It's really satisfying to see something built that you've designed from conception and to see a facility or infrastructure commissioned for the benefit of a community.

What I least enjoy is a necessary evil that comes with any profession, and that's the work-life balance. The higher you move in a company, the more responsibility you take on, the harder you work. There are things you're going to have to do to relax and be outside your career. Your career's important, but it needs to be sustainable.

7. Can you suggest a valuable "try this" for students considering a career in your profession?

See if you can connect with someone in the industry and shadow them, or do an internship or a co-op; keep that relationship. Also, when you start a new job, remember to be humble. There is a tendency to want everything immediately, but if you aren't willing and ready to learn, you put yourself at a disadvantage. There is a team around you, and this business is all about relationships. Nobody is ever done learning– ever.

SELECTED SCHOOLS

Most colleges and universities have bachelor's degree programs in science and engineering, sometimes with a specialization in environmental engineering. The student may also gain an initial grounding in the field at an agricultural, technical, or community college. For advanced positions, a masters or doctoral degree is usually obtained. For a list of selected schools, refer to the chapter "Environmental Engineer" in the present volume.

MORE INFORMATION

Air & Waste Management Association
One Gateway Center, 3rd Floor
420 Fort Duquesne Boulevard
Pittsburgh, PA 15222-1435
800.270.3444
www.awma.org

American Academy of Environmental Engineers &Scientists
130 Holiday Court, Suite 100
Annapolis, MD 21401
410.266.3311
www.aaees.org

American Society for Engineering Education
1818 N Street NW, Suite 600
Washington, DC 20036-2479
202.331.3500
www.asee.org

American Water Works Association
6666 W. Quincy Avenue
Denver, CO 80235
800.926.7337
www.awwa.org

National Society of Professional Engineers
1420 King Street
Alexandria, VA 22314-2794
703.684.2800
memserv@nspe.org
www.nspe.org

Water Environment Federation
601 Wythe Street
Alexandria, VA 22314-1994
800.666.0206
www.wef.org

R. C. Lutz/Editor

Water Treatment Plant Operator

Snapshot

Career Cluster: Environment & Conservation; Natural Resources Development
Interests: Mechanical engineering, chemistry, technology, public works and infrastructure
Earnings (Yearly Average): $45,070
Employment & Outlook: Average Growth Expected

OVERVIEW

Sphere of Work

Water treatment plant operators oversee the provision of fresh water for residential, commercial, and industrial customers. Water arrives at treatment facilities from a variety of sources, including reservoirs and watersheds. Plant operators treat the water with chemicals so it conforms to health regulations and is safe to use and consume. Some water-treatment plants provide specially treated water, such as deionized or demineralized water, to chemical-production facilities.

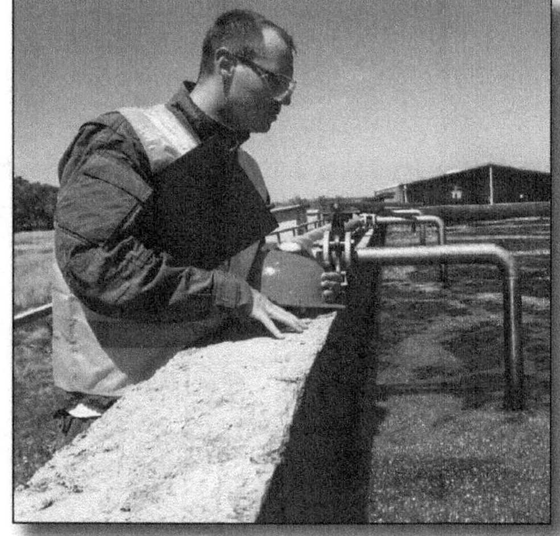

Work Environment

Water-treatment plants exist in all locations where safe, consumable water is needed. They are also often located near chemical and industrial facilities. There are water-treatment facilities in large urban areas and in rural cities and towns. The size of a water-treatment plant varies depending on the number of people and locations it services. At small facilities, a water treatment plant operator might be responsible for a multitude of tasks. At large facilities, tasks are more specialized and apportioned among a larger workforce.

Water treatment plant operators may be required to work in shifts or be on call during nights and the weekends. In the event of an emergency, water treatment plant operators are expected to be available twenty-four hours a day.

Profile

Working Conditions: Work both Indoors and Outdoors
Physical Strength: Medium Work
Education Needs: High School Diploma or G.E.D., Technical/Community College
Licensure/Certification: Required
Physical Abilities Not Required: No Heavy Labor
Opportunities For Experience: Apprenticeship, Military Service, Part-Time Work
Holland Interest Score*: RCE, REI

* See Appendix A

Occupation Interest

Aspiring water treatment plant operators should have an interest in mechanical engineering, chemistry, computer science, and technology. They should also be interested in public works and infrastructure. Operators should be organized, disciplined, and willing to work long, irregular hours.

A Day in the Life—Duties and Responsibilities

Operators are responsible for the orderly function of water-treatment plants. Daily tasks include monitoring, controlling, and adjusting the plant's operation through the system control board and other computer systems. Operators also track data related to the plant.

Routine plant work includes maintenance and emergency preparedness. This involves ensuring that all of the plant's systems, such as pumps, motors, valves, filters, and feeders, are functioning properly and adjusted for performance as necessary. Chemicals are added to treat incoming water. Proper chemical treatment of incoming water supply is the responsibility of the water treatment plant operator. Depending on size and technological capability of the facility, chemicals are dispensed manually or automatically via the plant's computer system.

Operators perform inspections of plant equipment on a daily basis. They also collect water samples and keep records of sample data to ensure that the plant is operating effectively.

Plant equipment requires routine maintenance and can require repair in the event of a malfunction or system failure. Routine maintenance involves the cleaning of tanks and water lines. Operators may do this work themselves or with colleagues, or they may oversee a maintenance staff. Operators are expected to make sure that their plant complies with regulations issued by the Environmental Protection Agency (EPA). Not all water-treatment plants require the presence of an operator at all times. However, operators are expected to be available in the event of an emergency.

Duties and Responsibilities

- **Operating valves, pumps, motors, chemical feeders, agitators and filters to control the flow of water**
- **Adding specified amounts of chemicals needed to disinfect, deodorize and clarify the water**
- **Maintaining a record of the amounts of water processed and chemicals added**
- **Monitoring control panels and adjusting valves and gates to control wastewater flow**
- **Extracting water samples and performing routine laboratory tests**

OCCUPATION SPECIALTIES

Wastewater Treatment Plant Operators

Wastewater Treatment Plant Operators are responsible for sewage treatment, sludge processing and disposal equipment to control the flow and processing of wastes in sewage to treatment plants.

Water Quality Technician

Water Quality Technicians test the biological, chemical and physical properties of water to insure its safety for drinking, for human contact and within the environment.

WORK ENVIRONMENT

Relevant Skills and Abilities

Organization & Management Skills

- Following instructions
- Paying attention to and handling details
- Performing routine work

Research & Planning Skills

- Developing evaluation strategies

Technical Skills

- Performing scientific, mathematical and technical work
- Working with machines, tools or other objects

Physical Environment

Operators work at water-treatment facilities. They often work in offices and laboratory spaces and at computer control boards, but they may also work with outdoor water infrastructure equipment. Potentially hazardous chemicals used to treat and purify water must be handled according to regulations. The job of a treatment plant operator can also involve laboratory work and administrative work.

Human Environment

Operators employed at small water-treatment facilities may work independently or with a small staff. At larger treatment facilities, an operator may supervise a team of colleagues. Less experienced operators often work under the supervision of more senior colleagues. Mechanical and chemical safety hazards are present at all water-treatment facilities.

Technological Environment

Water-treatment plants utilize computer operating systems. They also house water-testing laboratories and an array of mechanical equipment that needs to be maintained and kept in working order.

EDUCATION, TRAINING, AND ADVANCEMENT

High School/Secondary

Most employers require that water treatment plant operators possess a high school diploma or equivalent. Aspiring water treatment plant operators should study algebra, applied mathematics, and geometry. Courses in engineering, chemistry, physics, and computer science are also relevant.

Suggested High School Subjects

- Algebra
- Applied Math
- Blueprint Reading
- Chemistry
- Electricity & Electronics
- English
- Geometry
- Shop Mechanics

Famous First

The first water supply to be fluoridated in order to help reduce tooth decay was in Grand Rapids, Michigan. Starting in January 1945, one part fluoride was added to each million parts of water passing through the water treatment plant.

Postsecondary

Undergraduates interested in work at a water-treatment facility can benefit from a degree in environmental science or chemistry. Many colleges and technical schools offer two-year associate's degree programs in water-quality management.

Related College Majors

- Occupational Safety & Health Technology

Adult Job Seekers

Individuals with no background in a related field should enroll in a college or a technical or vocational school that offers a program in water treatment plant operation. Technical schools are also a great place for job seekers to network. Direct applications to water departments of cities, government agencies, or industrial parks can lead to employment in the field.

Professional Certification and Licensure

Each state requires that water treatment plant operators be licensed. Licensing requirements and procedures vary from state to state. Licensed operators who relocate from one state to another are usually required to take a new licensing exam. A few states accept licenses from some other states.

States typically have four levels of licenses for water treatment plant operators. Each level increases the operator's scope of responsibility.

This four-tiered structure outlines the typical pathway for professional advancement in the field.

Additional Requirements

Aspiring water treatment plant operators should be prepared for extensive on-the-job training. It can take several years before new hires are entrusted with full operator responsibility. In general, operators need good analytical, mathematical, and mechanical skills. They should be detail oriented, possess good leadership skills, and be able to make decisions confidently.

Fun Fact

A generation (or more) of Americans grew up thinking bottled water was healthier than tap water, but now the pendulum is swinging in the other direction–thanks in part to all those empty plastic water bottles. Tap water–and the treatment it receives–is subject to stricter regulation than bottled water

Source: foodandwaterwatch.org and http://water.epa.gov/lawsregs/guidance/sdwa/upload/2009_08_28_sdwa_fs_30ann_treatment_web.pdf

EARNINGS AND ADVANCEMENT

Earnings of water treatment plant operators depend on the type, size and geographic location of the plant and the individual's education, experience, and level of certification. Mean annual earnings of water treatment plant operators were $45,070 in 2013. The lowest ten percent earned less than $27,000, and the highest ten percent earned more than $68,000.

Water treatment plant operators may receive paid vacations, holidays, and sick days; life and health insurance; and retirement benefits. These are usually paid by the employer.

Metropolitan Areas with the Highest Employment Level in this Occupation

Metropolitan area	Employment	Employment per thousand jobs	Hourly mean wage
New York-White Plains-Wayne, NY-NJ	1,720	0.33	$31.43
Los Angeles-Long Beach-Glendale, CA	1,660	0.42	$33.80
Chicago-Joliet-Naperville, IL	1,570	0.42	$28.15
Pittsburgh, PA	1,500	1.32	$23.31
Minneapolis-St. Paul-Bloomington, MN-WI	1,480	0.83	$25.22
Phoenix-Mesa-Glendale, AZ	1,350	0.76	$22.55
Philadelphia, PA	1,250	0.68	$24.36
St. Louis, MO-IL	1,190	0.92	$20.79
Washington-Arlington-Alexandria, DC-VA-MD-WV	1,190	0.50	$25.20
Houston-Sugar Land-Baytown, TX	1,180	0.43	$18.43

Source: Bureau of Labor Statistics

EMPLOYMENT AND OUTLOOK

Nationally, there were approximately 111,000 water treatment plant operators employed in 2012. Employment is expected to grow about as fast as the average for all occupations through the year 2022, which means employment is projected to increase 7 percent to 11 percent. The expanding population and growing suburban geography are expected to increase demand for water and wastewater treatment services.

Employment Trend, Projected 2012–22

Total, All Occupations: 11%

Water and Wastewater Treatment Plant Operators: 8%

Plant and System Operators (All): -1%

Note: "All Occupations" includes all occupations in the U.S. Economy. Source: U.S. Bureau of Labor Statistics, Employment Projections Program.

Related Occupations

- Chemical Equipment Operator
- Power Plant Operator
- Stationary Engineer
- Water & Wastewater Engineer

Related Occupations

- Water & Sewage Treatment Plant Operator

Conversation With . . .
KEVIN DAVIS

Field Supervisor, 14 years
Ramey Water Supply, Mineola, TX

1. What was your individual career path in terms of education/training, entry-level job, or other significant opportunity?

I needed a part-time job to pay for a car so I worked here the last couple of years of high school. I did basic maintenance around the well yards, cleanups, and read meters. I found it really interesting work; a lot of different things go on and I wound up doing something different every day.

Ramey Water Supply is a member-owned coop that serves a rural area between two small cities in Texas. We have 1476 connections, eight wells in operation — we're working on another — and a little more than one million gallons in storage capacity. After high school, the coop's board of directors sent me on to a basic water class through the Texas Extension Service and I got my Class D Waterworks License. Then they hired me full-time as a water treatment plant operator. I was a certified waterworks operator for several years, then took courses in safety and groundwater production to move up to a Class C groundwater treatment operator. I have to have at least ten hours of continuing education every year to maintain this license.

2. What are the most important skills and/or qualities for someone in your profession?

One of the most important is public relations skills. You have to deal with a lot of people, including customers. It helps to keep them informed. That way, you also help out with water conservation.

3. What do you wish you had known going into this profession?

That I would have to work holidays and late nights if we have an emergency. I am on call. It could be a problem with a well; it could be a customer who has a problem with plumbing. If a bad storm knocks the power out, I have to set up a generator.

4. Are there many job opportunities in your profession? In what specific areas?

I think there are going to be a lot of new jobs because there's a lot of new technology. Also, a lot of people in the business are older and starting to retire so jobs will open up.

5. How do you see your profession changing in the next five years, what role will technology play in those changes, and what skills will be required?

One of the new things here in Texas, where there's been a drought, is that a couple of cities are actually recycling treated wastewater. It's going to either come to that, or everybody has to conserve. There's only so much water. Also, we've put in an automated meter reader. I can monitor how much water is used from a laptop in my truck.

6. What do you like most about your job? What do you like least about your job?

I enjoy the diversity of what I do. There's something new every day. For example, last week one of our wells went out and I had to switch that plant to another one. Tomorrow we're going to install new service for a new customer.

I least enjoy working on holidays and during inclement weather.

7. Can you suggest a valuable "try this" for students considering a career in your profession?

The schools around here have a high school work program. I have a student working for me now and I evaluate him and his teacher gives him a grade. It's worth looking into whether your community has a program like that.

SELECTED SCHOOLS

Many agricultural, technical, and community colleges offer programs in engineering, chemistry, and other subjects related to water plant operation. Interested students are advised to consult with their school guidance counselor or to research area postsecondary schools and training programs.

MORE INFORMATION

American Water Works Association
6666 West Quincy Avenue
Denver, CO 80235
800.926.7337
www.awwa.org

National Rural Water Association
2915 S. 13th Street
Duncan, OK 73533
580.252.0629
www.nrwa.org

Water Environment Federation
Public Education Manager-Career Information
601 Wythe Street
Alexandria, VA 22314-1994
800.666.0206
www.wef.org

Work for Water
www.workforwater.org

R. C. Lutz/Editor

Wildlife Biologist

Snapshot

Career Cluster: Environment & Conservation; Science & Technology
Interests: Biology, life sciences, environment, animal behavior
Earnings (Yearly Average): $62,610
Employment & Outlook: Faster Than Average Growth Expected

OVERVIEW

Sphere of Work

Wildlife biologists are scientists who study the origins, physiology, behavior, life cycles, and habitats of animals. Wildlife biologists conduct research on various aspects of animal species, including diseases, nutrition, genetics, and territory. Through their studies, these scientists work to protect animals' natural habitats. As a result, wildlife biologists are also called upon to provide recommendations on the protection of animal habitats.

Work Environment

Wildlife biologists may conduct their research in the field, often in remote locations, but they also have considerable contact with many different people. Environmental companies and consulting groups are increasingly seeking out wildlife biologists in their efforts to comply with government regulations. Other major companies, such as lumber businesses, chemical manufacturers, and ranchers, employ wildlife biologists for similar reasons. Many zoos and nature centers also hire wildlife biologists to provide better information about the species under their care.

Profile

Working Conditions: Work both Indoors and Outdoors
Physical Strength: Light Work
Education Needs: Bachelor's Degree, Master's Degree
Licensure/Certification: Usually Not Required
Physical Abilities Not Required: N/A
Opportunities For Experience: Internship, Volunteer Work
Holland Interest Score*: IRS

* See Appendix A

Occupation Interest

The field of wildlife biology attracts individuals who are interested in studying animals and concerned with their conservation. They enjoy working in remote locations to study their subjects' behavior and then reporting it to their superiors and/or the public at large. However, they also work in the public eye, offering their expertise to businesses, government agencies, and other groups to protect animal habitats from natural and man-made dangers. Wildlife biologists are analytical, attentive to detail, and well-organized.

A Day in the Life—Duties and Responsibilities

OA wildlife biologist spends much of his or her career in the field, studying animal species and their habitats. The biologist surveys the species' numbers, studies their behavior, examines their genetic profiles and life cycles, and observes their relationships with other animals. Wildlife biologists also examine disease outbreaks as well as the impacts of pollution and human activity and development on wildlife and their habitats. Additionally, wildlife biologists may work in a laboratory or other controlled environment, conducting behavioral experiments on live animals. Based on their field and laboratory research, they write research papers and conduct studies to create greater awareness of specific species.

In addition to their scholarly research, wildlife biologists may work as experts for zoos and nature conservancies, for both profit and non-profit businesses and organizations, and for the government. They represent a wide range of industries, from logging to commercial fishing. In this capacity, wildlife biologists use their scholarly expertise and research to provide recommendations to these entities or industries. Such advice can help these organizations understand how the presence of wildlife in a habitat will have an impact on the organization's activities or how the organization's expansion (or human activity in general) into that habitat will affect wildlife and their habitats. The biologists speak to groups on their findings, assist in filing environmental compliance reports, and help organizations or local agencies adjust their policies to protect these habitats if necessary.

Duties and Responsibilities

- **Observing animals in their natural environments**
- **Working in laboratories**
- **Collecting data and writing reports and research papers**
- **Advising officials on public land use regulations**

WORK ENVIRONMENT

Physical Environment

Wildlife biologists often work in the field, studying animals in their natural habitat. Such locations can leave the biologists vulnerable to animal attacks, injuries from traversing remote terrain, or extreme weather conditions. Biologists also conduct their work in animal-oriented parks and institutions, such as wildlife sanctuaries and zoos. Other biologists work in a laboratory and office setting, conducting controlled experiments and writing reports and scholarly articles.

Relevant Skills and Abilities

Analytical Skills
- Collecting and analyzing data

Communication Skills
- Speaking and writing effectively

Interpersonal/Social Skills
- Being able to work independently
- Being patient

Research & Planning Skills
- Identifying a research problem
- Laying out a plan
- Solving problems

Unclassified Skills
- Being curious

Work Environment Skills
- Working in a laboratory setting
- Working outdoors

Human Environment

Although wildlife biologists conduct a great deal of field research, they have considerable contact with other people. As experts in their particular fields, they frequently present their findings and recommendations to their immediate supervisors, employers, and peers and to the general public. Wildlife biologists also often work in teams with fellow biologists and other research scientists as they conduct research and experiments.

Technological Environment

Wildlife biologists employ many kinds of technology during the course of their research, from water samplers, specimen containers, and fishing nets, to satellite-based technology and computer hardware. They should also be proficient with analytical tools such as microscopes. When compiling data, wildlife biologists use computer software to create models and maps, manage databases, and author research papers. Additionally, they may rely on off-road vehicles, boats, and other modes of transportation while working in the field.

EDUCATION, TRAINING, AND ADVANCEMENT

High School/Secondary

High school students who are interested in becoming wildlife biologists are encouraged to study such scientific areas as biology, chemistry, mathematics, geography, and earth science. Additionally, they will benefit from studying computer science, statistics, and even communications, which will help them later compile data and present their findings to others.

Suggested High School Subjects

- Algebra
- Applied Biology/Chemistry
- Biology
- Calculus
- Chemistry
- Computer Science
- Earth Science
- English
- Forestry
- Geography
- Geometry
- Physics
- Science
- Statistics

Famous First

The first wildlife biologist to achieve popular recognition was Jane Goodall, who began studying chimpanzees in Gombe National Park, Tanzania, in 1960. She observed the animals in the wild, and wrote *In the Shadow of Man* (1971). Since then she has written numerous other books and founded a number of organizations focused on conservation and animal welfare.

College/Postsecondary

Wildlife biologists obtain a bachelor's degree in a related field, such as biology, ecology, or environmental science. Most organizations and agencies require that candidates obtain a master's degree and prefer individuals with a doctorate in a related field. Additionally, they expect that candidates have considerable training in specific fields, such as ornithology, animal ecology, population dynamics, or zoology. Students interested in becoming wildlife biologists should consider pursuing volunteer and internship positions at their academic institutions.

Related College Majors

- Botany
- Ecology
- Environmental Health
- Environmental Science/Studies
- Forestry, General
- Human & Animal Physiology
- Marine/Aquatic Biology
- Wildlife & Wildlands Management
- Zoology, General

Adult Job Seekers

One of the most effective ways for adults to obtain a career in wildlife biology is through the school at which they are receiving their master's and doctorate degrees. During the course of their schoolwork they may join research projects and participate in internship programs that can give them exposure to other biologists. Additionally, candidates may find networking opportunities by joining nonprofit organizations such as the Ecological Society of America, National Wildlife Federation, the Nature Conservancy, or the Worldwide Fund for Nature.

Professional Certification and Licensure

Most organizations require completion of a master's and doctorate degrees as a qualification for a wildlife biologist position. Some employers, such as the United States Geological Survey, only hire candidates for certain higher-level positions if they were in the highest third of their graduating class. Wildlife research biologists should have certification or licensure for the vehicles they are using in the field, such as a boating or driver's license.

Professional certification as a Certified Wildlife Biologist (CWB) or Associate Wildlife Biologist (AWB) is optional. Consult credible professional associations within the field and follow professional debate as to the relevancy and value of any certification program.

Additional Requirements

In addition to exceptional training in the natural sciences, a wildlife biologist must demonstrate strong communication skills. These attributes are useful in presenting data and recommendations to the organizations for which they work. Wildlife biologists should also be capable researchers, able to compile and organize a great deal of information and data.

Fun Fact

You may know him as the guy on T.V.'s "Animal Planet," but Jeff Corwin is a wildlife biologist. Another famous wildlife biologist is Jane Goodall, who spent 50 years studying chimpanzees in Tanzania.

Source: www.jobmonkey.com/animaljobs/famous-people.html, www.buzzle.com/articles/wildlife-biologists.html and janegoodall.org

EARNINGS AND ADVANCEMENT

Earnings depend on the type and geographic location of the employer and the employee's education and level of responsibility. Mean annual earnings of wildlife biologists were $62,610 in 2013. The lowest ten percent earned less than $38,000, and the highest ten percent earned more than $95,000.

Wildlife biologists may receive paid vacations, holidays, and sick days; life and health insurance; and retirement benefits. These are usually paid by the employer.

States with the Highest Employment Level in this Occupation

State	Employmen	Employment per thousand jobs	Hourly mean wage
California	2,860	0.19	$34.32
Washington	1,760	0.62	$34.16
Florida	1,350	0.18	$24.36
Oregon	1,150	0.70	$31.70
Alaska	840	2.61	$33.35

Source: Bureau of Labor Statistics

EMPLOYMENT AND OUTLOOK

Wildlife biologists and zoologists held about 20,000 jobs nationally in 2012. Most wildlife biologists are employed by local, state or federal government agencies, such as the United States Fish and Wildlife Service, or by private or non-profit organizations. Employment is expected to grow slower than the average for all occupations through the year 2022, which means employment is projected to increase 3 percent to 9 percent. Budget limitations in these areas will temper the job growth created by the need for wildlife biologists and zoologists to create plans that combat threats such as increased human activity, disease, pollution, climate change and habitat loss.

Employment Trend, Projected 2012–22

Total, All Occupations: 11%

Science Occupations: 10%

Wildlife Biologists and Zoologists: 5%

Note: "All Occupations" includes all occupations in the U.S. Economy. Source: U.S. Bureau of Labor Statistics, Employment Projections Program.

Related Occupations

- Botanist
- Forester and Conservation Scientist
- Marine Biologist
- Microbiologist
- Veterinarian
- Zoologist

Conversation With . . .
ANDY TIMMINS

New Hampshire Fish and Game Department
Bear Biologist for 12 years

1. **What was your individual career path in terms of education/training, entry-level job, or other significant opportunity?**

   Growing up, I had an interest in the outdoors — I did a lot of hunting and fishing — but I didn't for a minute think it would be my career choice. In college, I was exposed to wildlife management and earned a BS in that field. I started working as a wildlife technician for the Fish and Game Department. After a few years, I saw I needed more education to advance in the field. Fortunately, my department paid for me to go to graduate school and earn an MS in wildlife management.

   In grad school, I did my research on wild turkeys and I hoped to became the state's turkey biologist. But the bear position was the only open job when I got out. I had never had any exposure to bears before so it was in some ways an odd step to take. But I love it and wouldn't leave even if the turkey biologist position opened up.

   I do a variety of things. I estimate population sizes, set population objectives and supervise, coordinate and participate in a fair amount of bear research. I'm most focused on nuisance behavior and mitigating bear-human conflict. The latter is a daily task from May through September. I'm the only bear biologist for the state but I have regional biologists that I can call on for assistance and I work with some folks with USDA Wildlife Services.

2. **What are the most important skills and/or qualities for someone in your profession?**

   It's important to be true to your values toward the wildlife, especially in bear management, because I feel the species continues to be persecuted in many ways. It's important to force human responsibility in regards to conflict management, and not cave to pressure to remove bears (by trap or gun). I don't believe you can trap or shoot your way out of a bear problem. You have to educate the public about managing things that attract bears and force them to try to change their behaviors.

   You also need a strong work ethic and a willingness to work long hours. You need a thick skin, especially in summer when you deal with people who are not particularly pleased with the agency or the bear. You have to let them vent and have to let some of that roll off your back. You have to remember you're probably hearing from the vocal minority and that there is a greater public out there that appreciates what you do but you may not hear from them.

3. **What do you wish you had known going into this profession?**

   I wish I'd been a little more prepared for the political side of things and knew that at times science and the best information are not going to drive decision-making. Over the years, I've learned to pick my battles and let the small things roll off my back so I can be more effective with the big issues regarding bear management.

4. **Are there many job opportunities in your profession? In what specific areas?**

   Yes and no. I think most kids in school now have probably heard that it's a competitive profession and there aren't a lot of openings. Actually, I've been amazed at the number of openings that have come along over the years. I'm convinced that if you have a strong work ethic, are dedicated, and are flexible enough to move around, you'll find opportunities.

5. **How do you see your profession changing in the next five years, what role will technology play in those changes, and what skills will be required?**

   There will always be a need for boots on the ground and people in the field but technology will play more of a role. Students should be comfortable with computers and programming and using GIS. That would be a big advantage. A lot of us in the field right now aren't overly computer savvy.

6. **What do you like most about your job? What do you like least about your job?**

   I most like feeling I'm having a positive impact on the state's wildlife resources, particularly bears. I like to think I have encouraged some segment of society to have more appreciation and tolerance for bears. I also appreciate interacting with members of the public, including both hunters and non-hunters, who have an appreciation for wildlife. It feels really good to connect with those types of people rather than the greedy person who always wants more out of the resource or the person who can't tolerate any kind of wildlife on their front lawn.

7. **Can you suggest a valuable "try this" for students considering a career in your profession?**

   Volunteer. Get your name out there. Try to get as involved as you can so you can set yourself apart from the pack. And understand that first impressions mean everything. If you show up but don't pay attention and have no initiative, that's going to stick in people's minds. Work hard, be enthusiastic, and impress people with strong initiative.

SELECTED SCHOOLS

Most colleges and universities have bachelor's degree programs in animal biology, zoology, or other subjects related to wildlife biology. The student may also gain an initial grounding in the field at an agricultural, technical, or community college. For advanced positions, a master's or doctoral degree is usually obtained. Below are listed some of the more prominent schools in this field.

Brigham Young University
Plant & Wildlife Sciences
Life Sciences Building
Provo, UT 84602
801.422.2760
pws.byu.edu

Colorado State University
Fish, Wildlife, and Conservation Biology
109D Wagar Building
1474 Campus Delivery
Fort Collins, CO 80523
970.491.5020
warnercnr.colostate.edu/fwcb-home

Michigan State University
Department of Fisheries and Wildlife
480 Wilson Road, Room 13
East Lansing, MI 48824
517.355.4478
www.fw.msu.edu

Texas A&M University
Department Wildlife and Fisheries Science
TAMU 2258
College Station, TX 77843
979.845.5777
wfsc.tamy.edu

University of Arizona
Natural Resources and the Environment
Biological Sciences East, Room 325
1311 East 4th Street
Tucson, AZ 85721
520.621.7255
snre.arizona.edu

University of Florida
Wildlife Ecology and Conservation
110 Newins-Zeigler Hall
PO Box 110430
Gainseville, FL 32611
352.846.0643
www.wec.ufl.edu

University of Maryland
Wildlife Ecology
Center for Environmental Science
PO Box 775
Cambridge, MD 21613
410.228.9250
www.umces.edu

University of Minnesota
Fisheries, Wildlife, and Conservation Biology
135 Skok Hall
203 Upper Buford Circle
St. Paul, MN 55108
612.625.5299
Fwcb.cfans.umn.edu

University of Missouri
Fisheries and Wildlife Sciences
302 Anheuser-Busch Natural
Sciences Building
Columbia, MO 65211
573.882.3436
www.snr.missouri.edu/fw

University of Tennessee
Forestry, Wildlife, and Fisheries
274 Ellington Plant Science Building
Knoxville, TN 37996
865.974.7987
fwf.ag.utk.edu

MORE INFORMATION

Ecological Society of America
1990 M Street, NW, Suite 700
Washington, DC 20006-3915
202.833.8773
www.esa.org

National Wildlife Federation
11100 Wildlife Center Drive
Reston, VA 20190-5362
800.822.9919
www.nwf.org

Nature Conservancy
4245 North Fairfax Drive, Suite 100
Arlington, VA 22203-1606
800.628.6860
nature.org

The Wildlife Society
5410 Grosvenor Lane, Suite 200
Bethesda, MD 20814-2144
301.897.9770
joomla.wildlife.org

World Wildlife Fund/Worldwide
Fund for Nature
1250 24th Street NW
P.O. Box 97180
Washington, DC 20090-7180
202.293.4800
www.worldwildlife.org

Michael Auerbach/Editor

Wind Energy Engineer

Snapshot

Career Cluster: Agriculture, Food & Natural Resources, Architecture & Construction, Manufacturing, Science, Technology, Engineering & Mathematics
Interests: Mechanical Engineering, Renewable Energy, Environmental Studies, Physics
Earnings (Yearly Average): $90,247
Employment & Outlook: Faster Than Average Growth Expected

OVERVIEW

Sphere of Work

Wind energy engineers design and construct wind farms, wind energy turbines, and related systems and equipment. As part of one of the fastest-growing industries, green energy, wind energy engineers research and study existing wind farms and systems and determine how similar sites may be constructed in new locations. Wind energy engineers are at the center of the growth and evolution of the renewable energy movement, involved in the design, manufacturing,

project development, operations, and maintenance phases of wind farm development.

Work Environment

Wind energy engineers work in office environments as well as laboratories and industrial facilities. While developing these projects, wind energy engineers may travel to remote wind farm sites for extended periods. These engineers must frequently climb to the top of wind turbines, where they experience high winds and other risks to their safety. Back at the laboratory or plant, the wind energy engineer's work is less dangerous yet still very demanding.

Profile

Working Conditions: Work both Indoors and Outdoors
Physical Strength: Light Work
Education Needs: Bachelor's Degree, Master's Degree
Licensure/Certification: Required
Physical Abilities Not Required: No Heavy Labor
Opportunities For Experience: Internship
Holland Interest Score*: RIE

* See Appendix A

Occupation Interest

Wind energy engineers are part of an exciting field that is experiencing strong growth. Wind energy engineers come from a wide range of engineering backgrounds, such as civil engineering and environmental engineering, adding a broad diversity of perspectives to the field. Wind energy engineers are in high demand and frequently travel to foreign countries. They are encouraged to find ways to make turbines, wind farms, and collection equipment more efficient – innovation is an important part of the business. Furthermore, wind energy engineers are part of the worldwide movement to curb greenhouse gases through harnessing renewable energy.

A Day in the Life—Duties and Responsibilities

The duties and responsibilities of wind energy engineers vary based on their individual specialties. For example, civil engineers working in this field design the infrastructure for wind farms, such as roads, turbine foundations, and support buildings. Environmental engineers, meanwhile, analyze the impact of wind turbines on animal species leaving nearby as well as radar and telecommunications systems. Aerospace, electrical, health and safety, industrial, materials, and mechanical engineers may also provide assessments or components for wind farms.

In general, wind energy engineers assist in wind farm design and construction. They conduct research and analyses of the placement, construction, and maintenance of wind farms. Wind energy engineers generate models and schematics for efficient electrical systems and other key turbine components. They also create environmental forecasts, studying wind and weather models as well as geographic surveys of potential farm sites. Once this research is complete, wind energy engineers compile wind farm schematics and design underground and overhead collector systems, generators, blades, and electrical systems for the plant. During construction, wind energy engineers monitor systems integration and component assembly to ensure adherence to specifications and government regulations. Engineers also conduct tests on systems, which may involve climbing to the tops of turbines and entering electrical plants to study structural fatigue, energy collection, and other operational and structural elements. The engineers then write reports and recommend changes and updates to correct any problems.

Duties and Responsibilities

- **Designing wind plants or wind farms that generate electricity**
- **Consulting with utility companies, businesses and community members to determine needs**
- **Preparing project plans and specifications**
- **Estimating the costs and requirements of projects**
- **Overseeing project construction and maintenance**
- **Inspecting newly constructed and existing wind plants or wind farms**
- **Conducting technical research studies**

WORK ENVIRONMENT

Relevant Skills and Abilities

Analytical Skills
- Analyzing data

Communication Skills
- Speaking and writing effectively

Interpersonal/Social Skills
- Being able to work independently
- Working as a member of a team
- Having good judgment

Organization & Management Skills
- Initiating new ideas
- Paying attention to and handling details
- Managing time
- Promoting change
- Making decisions
- Meeting goals and deadlines
- Performing duties which change frequently

Research & Planning Skills
- Creating ideas
- Identifying problems
- Determining alternatives
- Identifying resources
- Solving problems
- Developing evaluation strategies
- Using logical reasoning

Technical Skills
- Performing scientific, mathematical or technical work
- Working with data or numbers

Physical Environment

Wind energy engineers spend most of their time working in offices, where they write reports, compile data, and create schematics and computer models. Some of their time may be spent in manufacturing facilities, where nacelles, blades, and other vital components of a wind turbine are produced. Additionally, wind energy engineers work on wind farm construction sites, which often includes climbing to the top of wind turbines and other physical activities.

Human Environment

Wind energy engineers work with a wide range of technical and construction professionals during the course of wind farm construction. These personnel include government regulatory officials, construction workers, computer scientists, wind energy technicians, environmental scientists, wildlife biologists, and other engineers.

Technological Environment

Wind energy engineers must be skilled at graphic design software, such as computer-aided design

(CAD) and map creation programs, in addition to office and project management systems. Additionally, they use a number of diagnostic and analytical equipment, such as anemometers (which measures wind speed), barometers, temperature sensors, and sonic detection devices.

EDUCATION, TRAINING, AND ADVANCEMENT

High School/Secondary

Interested high school students should take courses in math, such as algebra, geometry, trigonometry, and calculus. They also need scientific training, including physics, earth science, biology, and chemistry. Coursework in drafting, electronics, and computer science is also important for the aspiring wind energy engineer. Interested high school students should also develop their communications skills in English and humanities courses.

Suggested High School Subjects

- Algebra
- Applied Biology/Chemistry
- Applied Communication
- Applied Math
- Applied Physics
- Biology
- Blueprint Reading
- Calculus
- Chemistry
- College Preparatory
- Computer Science
- Drafting
- Earth Science
- Electricity & Electronics
- English
- Geometry
- Humanities
- Mathematics

- Physical Science
- Physics
- Science
- Social Studies
- Trigonometry

Famous First

The first large American wind turbine used to generate electric power was put into service at Grandpa's Knob, Vermont, in the Green Mountains, in 1941. The turbine's "propeller" consisted of two blades, each about 66 feet long, mounted atop a 120-foot steel tower. The unit fed power to the electrical distribution station at Castleton, Vermont. It ran for 1,100 hours, generating up to 800 kilowatts, before a blade broke and was never repaired.

College/Postsecondary

All wind energy engineers must have at least a bachelor's degree in engineering. Many obtain a master's degree or a doctorate in engineering. Wind energy engineering encompasses a wide range of other engineering fields, which means that these engineers may have advanced degrees in civil, environmental, electrical, and mechanical engineering. Some universities, such as Texas Tech University and the University of Massachusetts, offer specialized engineering training in wind energy.

Related College Majors

- Civil Engineering
- Electrical, Electronics & Communications Engineering
- Engineering, General
- Environmental/Environmental Health Engineering
- Mechanical Engineering

Adult Job Seekers

Qualified engineers who seek to become wind energy engineers may apply directly to wind energy companies as postings appear. Many people join the American Wind Energy Association, a large trade association, which maintains a list of open positions in the industry. A number of recruiters specialize in placing professionals in the wind energy and other "green energy" employers. Additionally, many wind energy companies and organizations offer professional workshops and conferences in this field, providing adults with educational resources as well as networking opportunities.

Professional Certification and Licensure

All wind energy engineers are usually licensed as Professional Engineers (PEs). Licensure requirements vary by state. In most states, candidates must hold an engineering degree from an accredited institution, demonstrate a specified amount of work experience, and satisfactorily complete written examinations in fundamental engineering and in their specialty of choice. Many universities and organizations offer specialized certifications in wind energy and turbine technology – although such certifications are not mandatory, they can enhance a wind energy engineer's qualifications. Interested individuals should research the licensure and certification requirements of the home states and prospective employers.

Additional Requirements

Experience with CAD, map-creation, and related software is highly important for a wind energy engineer. Additionally, engineers should be willing to travel for long periods and should be able to work at extreme heights, as they often work at on top of wind turbines. Wind energy engineers should also demonstrate a strong attention to detail and an ability to analyze complex system.

Fun Fact

As of 2014, Spain was the only country in the world that used wind energy as its primary source of electricity. Wind supplied 20.9 percent of Spain's energy in 2013, and nuclear energy supplied 20.8 percent. The United States gets 4.1 percent of its electricity from wind turbines, enough to power the homes in roughly six states.

Source: www.greenbiz.com/blog/2014/01/29/which-country-leads-wind-generation and the American Wind Energy Association

EARNINGS AND ADVANCEMENT

Mean annual earnings of wind energy engineers were $90,247 in 2013.

Wind energy engineers may receive paid vacations, holidays and sick days; life and health insurance; and retirement benefits. These are usually paid by the employer.

EMPLOYMENT AND OUTLOOK

Employment of wind energy engineers is expected to grow faster than the average for all occupations through the year 2022, which means employment is projected to increase 15 percent to 20 percent. Energy and its relationship to sustaining the environment is a rapidly growing field that will continue to create demand for new jobs for many years to come.

Related Occupations

- Agricultural Engineer

- Biological Scientist
- Chemical Engineer
- Civil Engineer
- Electrical and Electronics Engineer
- Energy Auditor
- Energy Conservation and Use Technician
- Energy Engineer
- Environmental Engineer
- Environmental Science Technician
- Forester and Conservation Scientist
- Mechanical Engineer
- Renewable Energy Technician
- Water and Wastewater Engineer

Conversation With . . .
DAN TURNER

Program Analyst and Project Manager
WINDUSTRY, Minneapolis, Minnesota, 4 years

1. What was your individual career path in terms of education/training, entry-level job, or other significant opportunity?

Mine isn't a typical career path. I hold a bachelor's in mathematics and philosophy from Iowa State University, a Ph.D. in philosophy from Ohio State University, and was in academia for a number of years. I taught at various colleges and universities around the country. Philosophy was an area that allowed me to indulge my interest in just about everything, including environmental issues. I was aware of the issues surrounding global warming back around 1980, and taught environmental philosophy.

I later burned out on teaching and started my own computer consulting business. I was in IT for many years, and did things like network design and implementation and project management. A friend, an electrical engineer, got into consulting for utilities in Iowa, and he became a pioneer in helping to understand wind as a way to produce electricity. We met up for lunch when we happened to be in the same city, and I asked him: How would I get into the wind business? Get an engineering degree? He basically took me on as an apprentice at his consulting firm, where I did feasibility studies for organizations that were considering doing a wind project. We ran the financial numbers and came up with feasible business plans. Three years later, I joined Windustry, which is more or less an advocacy organization, but I am a program analyst. I'm kind of the expert on how projects work and how they get put together. I know about small and large-scale wind projects. I don't do much in the way of advocacy except to answer questions about how a policy might affect things because I understand how these systems work.

2. What are the most important skills and/or qualities for someone in your profession?

One needs to have a commitment to the environment, and critical thinking skills. Mathematics is very useful; a lot of people in my profession are engineers. On the advocacy side, there are lawyers. A business background is useful; wind systems are businesses and they have to give a return. Skills in understanding investments are very valuable.

3. What do you wish you had known going into this profession?

I wish my analytical/statistical skills were stronger than they were. Also, the wind industry is very much a boom and bust industry, going back to the modern development of wind energy from about 1995. That's because the federal government is fickle; some years there may be a policy of incentives in place for one or two years, and then they'll discontinue it. These projects take several years to plan and develop.

4. Are there many job opportunities in your profession? In what specific areas?

Turbine technology and the technology that supports wind energy has been improving dramatically so that the cost per unit of electricity delivered to consumers keeps going down. Wind is currently, on the whole, a better bargain than just about anything but hydropower, or natural gas right now. The cost of wind isn't going to increase, and is probably going to be the number one bargain for the future unless some new technology comes up. So, I think that wind energy jobs will be in engineering and research in the sciences related to energy storage, energy conversion and the use of sensors and IT used in controlling turbines to make them more efficient and capable. Also, the bigger you make turbine blades, the more efficient the turbines. So, chemistry, materials science, mechanical and electrical engineering, fluid dynamics, meteorology and climatology...these are areas with the potential for job growth. Wind energy is in a lull right now, but I think it will boom again. It has to. The climate crisis is only getting more severe, and as people wake up to it, they're going to realize we can't keep polluting as if it didn't cost anything.

5. How do you see your profession changing in the next five years, what role will technology play in those changes, and what skills will be required?

I like being part of what I think is really important for the future of civilization. Otherwise, as far as a downside, there's nothing unique to this industry that has any negatives that you don't find in other jobs or industries.

6. What do you like most about your job? What do you like least about your job?

Internship opportunities are available in a variety of organizations. Shadowing is certainly great if you can find someone who will let you do it. There are also instruments that are not too expensive that let you measure the wind. A lot of wind projects are initiated by students in their schools, where they are learning science, math and economics and decide to apply to get a wind turbine for their school. Sometimes, they succeed.

SELECTED SCHOOLS

Most colleges and universities have bachelor's degree programs in engineering, sometimes with a specialization in energy systems engineering. The student may also gain an initial grounding in the field at an agricultural, technical, or community college. For advanced positions, a master's degree is often obtained. For a list of selected schools, refer to the chapter "Energy Engineer" in the present volume.

MORE INFORMATION

American Wind Energy Association
1501 M Street, NW, Suite 1000
Washington, DC 20005
202.383.2500
www.awea.org

Association of Energy Engineers
Alternative and Renewable Energy Development Institute
4025 Pleasantdale Road, Suite 420
Atlanta, GA 30340
770.447.5083
www.aeecenter.org

U.S. Department of Energy
Office of Energy Efficiency and Renewable Energy
1000 Independence Avenue SW
Washington, DC 20585
877.337.3463
www.energy.gov

Michael Auerbach/Editor

What Are Your Career Interests?

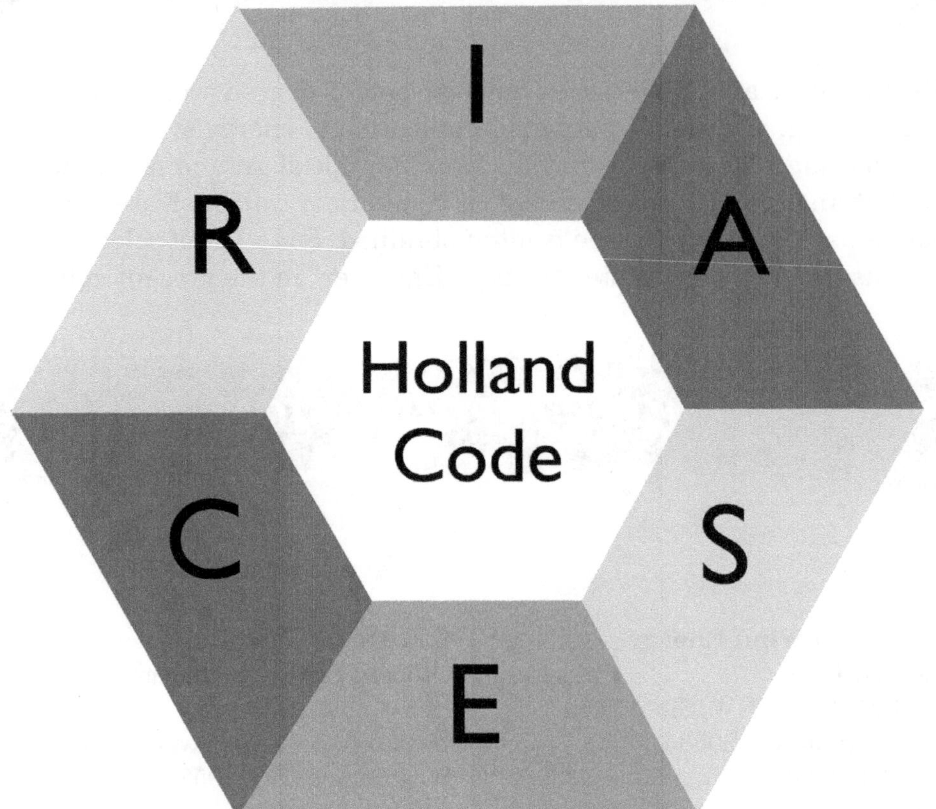

This is based on Dr. John Holland's theory that people and work environments can be loosely classified into six different groups. Each of the letters above corresponds to one of the six groups described in the following pages.

Different people's personalities may find different environments more to their liking. While you may have some interests in and similarities to several of the six groups, you may be attracted primarily to two or three of the areas. These two or three letters are your "Holland Code." For example, with a code of "RES" you would most resemble the Realistic type, somewhat less resemble the Enterprising type, and resemble the Social type even less. The types that are not in your code are the types you resemble least of all.

Most people, and most jobs, are best represented by some combination of two or three of the Holland interest areas. In addition, most people are most satisfied if there is some degree of fit between their personality and their work environment.

The rest of the pages in this booklet further explain each type and provide some examples of career possibilities, areas of study at MU, and co-curricular activities for each code. To take a more in-depth look at your Holland Code, take a self-assessment such as the SDS, Discover, or a card sort at the MU Career Center with a Career Specialist.

Realistic *(Doers)*

People who have athletic ability, prefer to work with objects, machines, tools, plants or animals, or to be outdoors.

Are you?
practical
straightforward/frank
mechanically inclined
stable
concrete
reserved
self-controlled
independent
ambitious
systematic

Can you?
fix electrical things
solve electrical problems
pitch a tent
play a sport
read a blueprint
plant a garden
operate tools and machine

Like to?
tinker with machines/vehicles
work outdoors
be physically active
use your hands
build things
tend/train animals
work on electronic equipment

Career Possibilities (Holland Code):

Air Traffic Controller (SER)
Archaeologist (IRE)
Athletic Trainer (SRE)
Cartographer (IRE)
Commercial Airline Pilot (RIE)
Commercial Drafter (IRE)
Corrections Officer (SER)
Dental Technician (REI)
Farm Manager (ESR)
Fish and Game Warden (RES)
Floral Designer (RAE)
Forester (RIS)
Geodetic Surveyor (IRE)
Industrial Arts Teacher (IER)
Laboratory Technician (RIE)
Landscape Architect (AIR)
Mechanical Engineer (RIS)
Optician (REI)
Petroleum Geologist (RIE)
Police Officer (SER)
Practical Nurse (SER)
Property Manager (ESR)
Recreation Manager (SER)
Service Manager (ERS)
Software Technician (RCI)
Ultrasound Technologist (RSI)
Vocational Rehabilitation Consultant (ESR)

Investigative *(Thinkers)*

People who like to observe, learn, investigate, analyze, evaluate, or solve problems.

Are you?
inquisitive
analytical
scientific
observant/precise
scholarly
cautious
intellectually self-confident
Independent
logical
complex
Curious

Can you?
think abstractly
solve math problems
understand scientific theories
do complex calculations
use a microscope or computer
interpret formulas

Like to?
explore a variety of ideas
work independently
perform lab experiments
deal with abstractions
do research
be challenged

Career Possibilities (Holland Code):

Actuary (ISE)
Agronomist (IRS)
Anesthesiologist (IRS)
Anthropologist (IRE)
Archaeologist (IRE)
Biochemist (IRS)
Biologist (ISR)
Chemical Engineer (IRE)
Chemist (IRE)
Computer Systems Analyst (IER)
Dentist (ISR)
Ecologist (IRE)
Economist (IAS)
Electrical Engineer (IRE)
Geologist (IRE)
Horticulturist (IRS)
Mathematician (IER)
Medical Technologist (ISA)
Meteorologist (IRS)
Nurse Practitioner (ISA)
Pharmacist (IES)
Physician, General Practice (ISE)
Psychologist (IES)
Research Analyst (IRC)
Statistician (IRE)
Surgeon (IRA)
Technical Writer (IRS)
Veterinarian (IRS)

Artistic *(Creators)*

People who have artistic, innovating, or intuitional abilities and like to work in unstructured situations using their imagination and creativity.

Are you?
creative
imaginative
innovative
unconventional
emotional
independent
Expressive
original
introspective
impulsive
sensitive
courageous
complicated
idealistic
nonconforming

Can you?
sketch, draw, paint
play a musical instrument
write stories, poetry, music
sing, act, dance
design fashions or interiors

Like to?
attend concerts, theatre, art exhibits
read fiction, plays, and poetry
work on crafts
take photography
express yourself creatively
deal with ambiguous ideas

Career Possibilities (Holland Code):

Actor (AES)
Advertising Art Director (AES)
Advertising Manager (ASE)
Architect (AIR)
Art Teacher (ASE)
Artist (ASI)
Copy Writer (ASI)
Dance Instructor (AER)
Drama Coach (ASE)
English Teacher (ASE)
Entertainer/Performer (AES)
Fashion Illustrator (ASR)
Interior Designer (AES)
Intelligence Research Specialist (AEI)
Journalist/Reporter (ASE)
Landscape Architect (AIR)
Librarian (SAI)
Medical Illustrator (AIE)
Museum Curator (AES)
Music Teacher (ASI)
Photographer (AES)
Writer (ASI)
Graphic Designer (AES)

Social *(Helpers)*

People who like to work with people to enlighten, inform, help, train, or cure them, or are skilled with words.

Are you?
friendly
helpful
idealistic
insightful
outgoing
understanding
cooperative
generous
responsible
forgiving
patient
kind

Can you?
teach/train others
express yourself clearly
lead a group discussion
mediate disputes
plan and supervise an activity
cooperate well with others

Like to?
work in groups
help people with problems
do volunteer work
work with young people
serve others

Career Possibilities (Holland Code):

City Manager (SEC)
Clinical Dietitian (SIE)
College/University Faculty (SEI)
Community Org. Director (SEA)
Consumer Affairs Director (SER)Counselor/Therapist (SAE)
Historian (SEI)
Hospital Administrator (SER)
Psychologist (SEI)
Insurance Claims Examiner (SIE)
Librarian (SAI)
Medical Assistant (SCR)
Minister/Priest/Rabbi (SAI)
Paralegal (SCE)
Park Naturalist (SEI)
Physical Therapist (SIE)
Police Officer (SER)
Probation and Parole Officer (SEC)
Real Estate Appraiser (SCE)
Recreation Director (SER)
Registered Nurse (SIA)
Teacher (SAE)
Social Worker (SEA)
Speech Pathologist (SAI)
Vocational-Rehab. Counselor (SEC)
Volunteer Services Director (SEC)

Enterprising *(Persuaders)*

People who like to work with people, influencing, persuading, leading or managing for organizational goals or economic gain.

Are you?
self-confident
assertive
persuasive
energetic
adventurous
popular
ambitious
agreeable
talkative
extroverted
spontaneous
optimistic

Can you?
initiate projects
convince people to do things your way
sell things
give talks or speeches
organize activities
lead a group
persuade others

Like to?
make decisions
be elected to office
start your own business
campaign politically
meet important people
have power or status

Career Possibilities (Holland Code):

Advertising Executive (ESA)
Advertising Sales Rep (ESR)
Banker/Financial Planner (ESR)
Branch Manager (ESA)
Business Manager (ESC)
Buyer (ESA)
Chamber of Commerce Exec (ESA)
Credit Analyst (EAS)
Customer Service Manager (ESA)
Education & Training Manager (EIS)
Emergency Medical Technician (ESI)
Entrepreneur (ESA)
Foreign Service Officer (ESA)
Funeral Director (ESR)
Insurance Manager (ESC)
Interpreter (ESA)
Lawyer/Attorney (ESA)
Lobbyist (ESA)
Office Manager (ESR)
Personnel Recruiter (ESR)
Politician (ESA)
Public Relations Rep (EAS)
Retail Store Manager (ESR)
Sales Manager (ESA)
Sales Representative (ERS)
Social Service Director (ESA)
Stockbroker (ESI)
Tax Accountant (ECS)

Conventional *(Organizers)*

People who like to work with data, have clerical or numerical ability, carry out tasks in detail, or follow through on others' instructions.

Are you?
well-organized
accurate
numerically inclined
methodical
conscientious
efficient
conforming
practical
thrifty
systematic
structured
polite
ambitious
obedient
persistent

Can you?
work well within a system
do a lot of paper work in a short time
keep accurate records
use a computer terminal
write effective business letters

Like to?
follow clearly defined procedures
use data processing equipment
work with numbers
type or take shorthand
be responsible for details
collect or organize things

Career Possibilities (Holland Code):

Abstractor (CSI)
Accountant (CSE)
Administrative Assistant (ESC)
Budget Analyst (CER)
Business Manager (ESC)
Business Programmer (CRI)
Business Teacher (CSE)
Catalog Librarian (CSE)
Claims Adjuster (SEC)
Computer Operator (CSR)
Congressional-District Aide (CES)
Cost Accountant (CES)
Court Reporter (CSE)
Credit Manager (ESC)
Customs Inspector (CEI)
Editorial Assistant (CSI)
Elementary School Teacher (SEC)
Financial Analyst (CSI)
Insurance Manager (ESC)
Insurance Underwriter (CSE)
Internal Auditor (ICR)
Kindergarten Teacher (ESC)
Medical Records Technician (CSE)
Museum Registrar (CSE)
Paralegal (SCE)
Safety Inspector (RCS)
Tax Accountant (ECS)
Tax Consultant (CES)
Travel Agent (ECS)

BIBLIOGRAPHY

General

Deitche, Scott M., *Green-Collar Jobs: Environmental Careers for the 21st Century*. Westport, CT: Praeger, 2010.

Goldstein, David G., *Saving Energy, Growing Jobs: How Environmental Protection Promotes Economic Growth, Competition, Profitability, and Innovation*. Richmond, CA: Bay Tree Publishing, 2006.

Greenland, Paul R., and AnnaMarie L. Sheldon, *Career Opportunities in Conservation and the Environment*. New York: Checkmark Books, 2007.

Hess, David J., *Good Green Jobs in a Global Economy: Making and Keeping New Industries in the United States*. Cambridge, MA: MIT Press, 2014.

Llewellyn, Bronwyn, *Green Jobs: A Guide to Eco-Friendly Employment*. Avon, MA: Adams Media, 2008.

Schatt, Stan, and Michele Lobl, *Paint Your Career Green: Get a Green Job Without Starting Over*. Indianapolis, IN: Jist, 2012.

Energy, Construction, and Waste Management

Boyle, Godfrey, *Renewable Energy: Power for a Sustainable Future*, 3d ed. New York: Oxford University Press, 2012.

Fine Homebuilding, *The Energy-Smart House*. Newtown, CT: Taunton Press, 2011.

Grant, Gary, *Ecosystem Services Come to Town: Greening Cities by Working with Nature*. Hoboken, NJ: Wiley-Blackwell, 2012.

Humes, Edward, *Garbology: Our Dirty Love Affair with Trash*. New York: Avery, 2012.

McNamee, Gregory, *Careers in Renewable Energy: Your World, Your Future*, 2d ed. Masonville, OH: PixyJack Press, 2014.

Melander, Paul, *Hazmat Awareness Training Manual*. Boston: Cengage, 2004.

Nemerow, Nelson L, et al., *Environmental Engineering: Water, Wastewater, Soil, and Groundwater Treatment and Remediation*, 6th ed. Hoboken, NJ: Wiley, 2009.

Oles, Thomas, *Go With Me: 50 Steps to Landscape Thinking*. Amsterdam: Academy of Architecture, 2014.

Thompson, Ian, *Landscape Architecture: A Very Short Introduction*. New York: Oxford University Press, 2014.

Thorpe, Dave, *Energy Management in Buildings: The Earthscan Expert Guide*. New York: Routledge, 2014.

Thumann, Albert, Terry Niehus, and William J. Younger, *The Handbook of Energy Audits*, 9th ed. Lilburn, GA: Fairmont Press, 2012.

Environment and Ecology

Ahrens, C. Donald, *Meteorology Today: An Introduction to Weather, Climate, and the Environment*, 10 ed. Boston: Cengage, 2013.

Bolen, Eric G., *Wildlife Ecology and Management*, 5th ed. San Francisco: Benjamin Cummings, 2002.

de Blij, Harm J., Peter O. Muller, and Jan Nijman, *Geography: Realms, Regions, and Concepts*, 15th ed. Hoboken, NJ: Wiley, 2012.

Fishbeck, George, *Dr. George: My Life in Weather*. Albuquerque: University of New Mexico Press, 2013.

Garrison, Tom S., *Oceanography: An Invitation to Marine Science*, 7th ed. Boston: Cengage, 2009

Gould, Peter, and Forrest R. Pitts, *Geographical Voices: Fourteen Autobiographical Essays*. Syracuse, NY: Syracuse University Press, 2002.

Grebner, Donald L., Pete Bettinger, and Jacek P. Siry, *Introduction to Forestry and Natural Resources*. Waltham, MA: Academic Press, 2013.

Hazen, Robert M., *The Story of the Earth: The First 4.5 Billion Years, from Stardust to Living Planet*. New York: Penguin Books, 2013.

Helms, John A., *Dictionary of Forestry*. Bethesda, MD: Society of American Foresters, 1999.

Holenchek, Jerry L., Rex D. Pieper, and Carleton H. Herbel, *Range Management: Principles and Practices*, 6th ed. Upper Saddle River, NJ: Prentice Hall, 2010.

Kareiva, Peter, and Michelle Marvier, *Conservation Science: Balancing the Needs of People and Nature*. Greenwood Village, CO: Roberts and Co., 2011.

Mladenov, Philip V., *Marine Biology: A Very Short Introduction*. New York: Oxford University Press, 2013.

Smith, Zachary, *The Environmental Policy Pardox*, 6th ed. Boston: Pearson, 2013.

Stubbendieck, James, Stephan L. Hatch, Neal M. Bryan, *North American Wildland Plants*: A Field Guide, 2d ed. Lincoln, NE: University of Nebraska Press, 2011.

Farming, Horticulture, and Animals

Echaore-McDavid, Susan, and Richard A. McDavid, *Career Opportunities in Agriculture, Food, and Natural Resources*. New York: Checkmark Books, 2011.

Garner, Jerry, *Careers in Horticulture and Botany*, 2d ed. New York: McGraw-Hill, 2006.

Grandin, Temple, and Catherine Johnson, *Animals Make Us Human: Creating the Best Life for Animals*. Boston: Mariner Books, 2010.

Hodge, Geoff, *Practical Botany for Gardeners: Over 3,000 Botanical Terms Explained and Explored*. Chicago: University of Chicago Press, 2013.

Shepherdson, David J., Jill D. Mellen, and Michael Hutchins, eds., *Second Nature: Environmental Enrichment for Captive Animals*. Washington, DC: Smithsonian Institution Press, 1999.

Walters, Charles, *Eco-Farm: An Acres USA Primer*, rev ed. Austin, TX: Acres USA, 2009.

INDEX

A

B

C

D

E

F

I

J

K

L

M

N

O

P

T

U

V

W

Y

Z